Dedication

To my family and friends for their kindness and support, especially Dave for doing the gardening; to Jerry Wellington and Cheryl Hunt who have extended my learning process; and to Peter Holden who made me well again.

Jennifer Joy-Matthews

To all the developers and others who have touched my life and made a difference. Especially to Vivien, who is a constant source of inspiration, challenge and delight.

David Megginson

For Claire, who has developed me beyond imagination, and Toby, who I'm sure will. To David and Jenny, thank you for your confidence and coaching.

Mark Surtees

THE *MBA MASTERCLASS* SERIES
Series Editor: Philip Sadler

The new *MBA Masterclass* series is designed to meet the needs of MBA students and experienced managers looking for a refresher course in a particular subject. Authoritative but practical, these titles focus on MBA core subjects as well as covering the latest developments in management thinking and practice. Written by international academics, consultants and practitioners, this series is an ideal companion for any busy MBA student or manager.

The Series Editor

Philip Sadler is a Vice President of the Ashridge Business School where he was chief executive for 20 years. He now divides his time between writing, speaking, consultancy and voluntary service. He is a Fellow of the International Academy of Management, a Fellow of the Institute for Personnel and Development, a Fellow of the Institute of Directors, and a Patron of the Centre for Tomorrow's Company.

He has been awarded the honorary degrees of DSc (City University) and DBA (De Montfort University). He holds the Burnham Gold Medal of the Institute of Management and was appointed CBE in 1986.

His recent books include *Managing Change* (1995), *Leadership* (1998), The Seamless Organization (2001) and *Building Tomorrow's Company* (2002).

Titles in the series

Leadership by Philip Sadler
Intercultural Management by Nina Jacob
Strategic Management by Philip Sadler
Human Resource Development by Jennifer Joy-Matthews,
    David Megginson and Mark Surtees

Forthcoming titles

Branding
Finance and Accounting

To obtain further information, please contact the publisher at the address below:

Kogan Page Limited
120 Pentonville Road
London N1 9JN
United Kingdom
Tel: +44 (0) 20 7278 0433
Fax: +44 (0) 20 7837 6348
www.kogan-page.co.uk

Contents

Acknowledgements

We have enjoyed working together and are grateful for the learning opportunity that we have shared: it has been fun. Jenny and David are particularly grateful to Mark for joining us in producing this third edition. We value his commitment, insight and energy.

We would like to thank the following for specific contributions to our thinking or to what is written here:

Mary Anderson of Amethyst; Liz Borredon of EDHEC, France; Ken Boyle, Chair of the Membership and Education Committee of CIPD; Helen Clarke, research participant; David Clutterbuck, for his constant stream of ideas; Ronnie Cope, research participant; Ian Cunningham, Mike Pedler, Andrew Mayo and the rest of the Learning Declaration group; Louise Dorow, research participant; Irene Dovey, Business Development Manager of Nexor. Rich Field, a source of endless inspiration; Jean Floodgate, Chair of the CPD Working Party of CIPD; Susanne Garnett, Executive Director of Village AiD; Bryan Gladstone, IdeaSmith; Polly Grainger of Connexions; James Grant, research participant; Lee Hamilton, research participant; Heather Hirst of Reality; Liz Humphries, research participant; John Hespe, OD Director of GSK; Kate Howsley and Gill Lewis at Kellogg's Europe; Diane Lennan, HR Director of The Barbican; Chris Little, research participant; Glen Robson, research participant; Dean Royles, Head of HR Capacity, Department of Health; Uwe G Seebacher; Amr Shamala and Imane Shoukry of the Europe Arab Business School programme in Egypt; Derek Stockley; Carol Whitaker, HR Director of NEC; Wyn Williams and Dean Fathers at idm group; Dig Woodvine of XCL Ltd; and our colleagues Ruth Garrett-Harris, Bob Garvey, Gareth Morgan, Paul Stokes and Vivien Whitaker.

Last, but by no means least, we would like to thank the team at Kogan Page, who are a delight to work with.

Introduction

The fact that this book has made it to a third edition attests to the importance that management book buyers attach to the subject of human resource development (HRD). We have responded to this interest by carrying out a major rewriting of our second edition. Every chapter has had substantial revision; some chapters have been rewritten completely. The chapter of separate case studies in the second edition has been removed and new cases have been inserted into every chapter, except Chapter 4 where we ask you to supply a case study of your learning, and Chapter 12. These have been selected from the voluntary, public and private sectors, and from large and small organizations. What they have in common is that they illustrate good practice from people who have succeeded in making HRD work. There are more activities included throughout the book.

This text is still for people who want to do things differently, as well as for people who like engaging with current ideas. The ideas are there, and we have illustrated them with examples of current practice. There are also lots of questions. This is because we reckon that managing and developing people is a deep issue. There are no easy, right answers. All our readers are invited to consider the issues in the light of their own situation, their talents and their organization's culture. To help with this process of consideration, we have included a number of questionnaires specifically designed for this book – and some new in this edition. These will enable you to get a fix on your practice and to contemplate possible changes. On occasion, you will be able to use the questionnaires to gain feedback from others.

Chapter 1 establishes the position of HRD in contemporary terms and defines the scope of the subject. The context of HRD is explored in terms of organizational strategy and change, and some compelling evidence is cited for why HRD is a critically important management discipline. Historical and national contexts are also reviewed with brief accounts of some national initiatives. The agenda is set for the rest of the book.

Chapter 2 opens the possibility of there being several ways of doing HRD. It offers a set of leading ideas, and through a questionnaire invites you to examine your own way and to consider changing it. The range of leading ideas has been extended yet again from the second edition, through original research published here for the first time. On this occasion, a long list of 34 candidate leading ideas was offered to respondents, and on the basis of their replies 10 were selected. A questionnaire has been included, designed around these 10.

Chapter 3 recognizes that all managers, whatever their main priority or discipline, encounter workforce development at some point. A number of such associations serve to illustrate the role of HRD when approached from different aspects of general management. By learning to talk the language of these disciplines, HRD specialists can position their services appropriately.

Chapter 4 covers the core issue of learning. As well as giving an introduction to classical learning theories, triggers and problems, we offer a range of contemporary ideas about how learning is situated. We raise the issue of communities of practice and the links from learning to HRD and management. We also invite you to consider how you have become the learner that you are.

Chapter 5 is a new chapter focusing on e-learning and blended learning. This reflects the importance we have come to attach to this topic since we wrote the last edition. We make the case for why e-learning and blended learning are so important, and define some of the key processes involved in creating blended learning packages.

Chapter 6 is another new chapter, focusing upon the revived area of individual development. This has received growing interest recently because of a growth in importance of continuous professional development (CPD), both for members of professional bodies and for organizations. There is a case study of how one big company approaches this area.

Chapter 7 recognizes the pivotal role of groups in organizational strategy and proposes groups as an appropriate focus for development to accomplish organizational change. Some ideas are presented on how to manage change through groups and on some of the dynamics of group interactions. A number of work-based opportunities for group development are identified and the different needs of groups highlighted.

Chapter 8 looks at how to encourage learning throughout the organization. A diagnostic questionnaire is included. The case study used – Nexor

– offers some striking examples of organizational learning in a fast-growing organization in which over half the staff have PhDs and have conducted post-doctoral research in a university before joining the company. We also summarize research that we have carried out on the effect of adopting learning company characteristics on organizational success, and offer a passport to the new frontier of knowledge management.

Chapter 9 introduces the closely related subjects of diagnosis and evaluation as critical aspects of successful HRD. Diagnostic and evaluation processes are described and a case study is offered to illustrate each subject. Models for diagnosis and evaluation are reviewed and ideas for carrying them out are offered. The role of auditing and benchmarking is briefly reviewed.

Chapter 10 covers the deep shift in ideas about management development. It looks at the changes and challenges that need to be dealt with in order to successfully develop managers and offers some suggestions for working with different categories of managers.

Chapter 11 looks at the process of leveraging the HRD function from the general or line manager's perspective. It also offers suggestions for actions a manager needs to take to make the best use of HRD.

Chapter 12 looks at development for the future. This chapter has been newly created with current quotes from a range of learning gurus who contribute their trenchant and perceptive views on how HRD is developing for the future. Our gurus include not just authors and researchers, though there are plenty of these, but also some of the practitioners we most admire. All of them offer challenges to our perspective on the future of development.

We, the authors, are committed to learning, so if you have any points where you want to take issue with us, or where you can give us examples of your own excellent practice, then we would like to hear from you at the following email addresses: joymatthews@supanet.com; d.f.megginson@shu.ac.uk; mark@surteesm.fsnet.co.uk.

1

Positioning human resource development

INTRODUCTION

'Positioning' is a concept drawn from marketing and refers to how something is perceived, in what terms and by whom. Applying the concept of positioning to human resource development (HRD) involves identifying what HRD is, and where and how it fits with general management.

The term 'human resource development' has been in popular use for over two decades although it is a relatively new area of management practice and inquiry. In common with other general management practice, HRD is set against a background of turbulence and change in organizational life, changes in business environments, work processes and organizational cultures, which drive a need for successful change management strategies.

There are a range of concepts and perspectives associated with the development of human resources. There are also different focuses of interest: individual; organizational; present needs; future challenges; different functions and occupations; different stakeholder interests. Increasingly, managers are required to facilitate change and innovation through an expanding repertoire of approaches, which include the development of people.

The scope of HRD is potentially substantial and it is relevant to establish early the 'position' of HRD – that is, its place in the field and why it is important strategically and contextually.

LEARNING OUTCOMES

As a result of reading this chapter and undertaking the activities, you should aim to progress in your ability to:

▌ describe the scope and meaning of HRD;

▌ reflect critically on the relationship between organizational strategy and HRD;

▌ understand HRD in a context of organizational change;

▌ recognize the legacy of the historical context of HRD;

▌ relate strategy, policy and HRD practice;

▌ describe the state of HRD nationally and internationally.

DEFINING THE SCOPE OF HRD

People in organizations – human resources – may 'develop' in terms of head count – that is, getting the right numbers of the right sort of people in place at the right time to function as an organization, or, as one author puts it, 'first get the right people on the bus' (Collins, 2001). However, in this book we discuss how people may develop, either individually or collectively, in terms of their capability.

We acknowledge from the outset that in organizations, people talk about training. As practitioners we often find ourselves adopting this term. However, we believe there is a clear distinction between training and development. In part that distinction lies in the interaction between 'trainer' and 'trainee'. As HRD practitioners our interest is in training, but a trainee's priority is learning. In this book we consider training, development and learning.

Conventional approaches to training resemble a teacher–pupil or instructor–student relationship. However, contemporary trainers know that an understanding of learning and the perspective of the trainee can greatly enhance and enrich the learning experience. As developers we also recognize that work presents many different opportunities to learn, training being only one aspect of a range of opportunities. Thus the scope of human resource development comprises different perspectives including training and learning (see Chapter 4 for further discussion).

There is potential ambiguity in the use of the term 'development'. As Coopey *et al* (1993: 19) point out:

> at a time when we are beginning to acknowledge the political, social and ecological catastrophes perpetrated in the name of development, those of us in management development are compelled to ask ourselves 'development for what?' In particular we need to be mindful of the consequences of development thinking on the lives of less privileged people both in industrialised societies and the Third World.

Defining terms may help to establish shared meanings and common understanding (it also represents conventional academic and quality management practice, ie talking the same language). However, endless exploration of a range of meanings can become tiresome. The context in which development is used here is further illustrated by contrast with other established associated concepts of education, training and learning.

■ *education*: conventionally seen as a highly structured exposure to instruction, the objective of which is to train mentally and morally;

■ *training*: a relatively systematic attempt to bring someone to a desired standard of efficiency by instruction and practice;

■ *learning*: acquiring knowledge of or skill in something by study, experience or being taught – a never-ending process of personal unfolding.

Relevant definitions of development we have encountered may begin to illustrate what can be meant by the term:

■ bringing out what is latent or potential in;

■ bringing to a more advanced or highly organized state;

■ working out the potentialities of;

■ advancing through successive stages to a higher, more complex or more fully grown state.

Human resource development is the term we use to describe *an integrated and holistic, conscious and proactive approach to changing work-related knowledge and behaviour, using a range of learning strategies and techniques.* The strategies and techniques referred to generally are intended to help individuals, groups and organizations realize their full potential for working in a way that allows for individuality and yet enhances effectiveness within particular contexts.

There are many strands to HRD, eg personal development; development for a current job or situation; development in or for new work settings; activities through which individual and organizational goals may be reconciled; and development leading to a better, fuller life for individuals, organizations and wider communities. In a very broad sense HRD may also be seen as 'the capacity to incorporate learning into behaviour' (Coopey *et al* 1993: 24).

HRD includes management training and vocationally oriented education, and so encapsulates all learning that enables individual and organizational growth. HRD is therefore closely allied with organizational strategy and the management of change.

ACTIVITY 1.1 CREATE YOUR OWN DEFINITION OF HRD

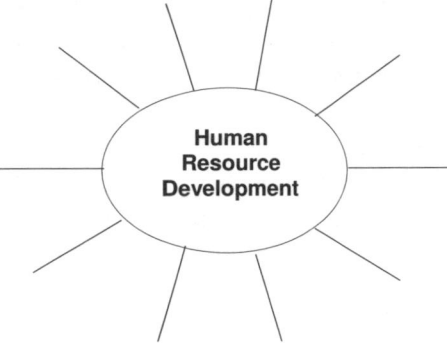

Figure 1.1 *Your definition of HRD*

Take a few moments to think about your own position and scope for HRD by defining what HRD means to you. Start by writing 'Human Resource Development' in the centre of a landscape page, draw 10 radiating lines and attach to each one a key word or short phrase you associate with the words in the centre.

It can be illuminating to compare your own result with that of colleagues. What proportion do you think you will have in common?

HRD AND ORGANIZATIONAL STRATEGY

Worldwide, organizations face competition, turbulence and uncertainty, which can sometimes result in dramatic change. Given that they are faced with such substantial challenges, it would seem sensible that there should be explicit links between business strategy and any management priority, including the development of people. Human resources are finite and need to be managed and valued in the context of organizational strategies and policies. Such integration is necessary to develop strategic capability – that is, achieve alignment of tangible and intangible assets and appropriate resource usage, determine competitive position and maintain stakeholder commitment.

In a general sense it has long been recognized that there is a correlation between how workers are managed on the one hand and sustained organizational performance on the other (Pfeffer, 1994). Recent studies (see the article by S London entitled 'Profit machines that put people first' in the *Financial Times* (London), 27 October 2003) have added to this conviction, citing 'best practices' such as incentives, performance management and extensive training as being as important to competitive advantage as strategy, structure, technology or market share (Pfeffer, 1998). However, the very economic forces that are making so-called human capital more important are also changing the implicit contract between employers and employees. So, as well as organizational best practices, employees nowadays need to take responsibility for their own careers and skills updating (Lawler, 2003).

In the United Kingdom, recent studies (analysis by Guest *et al*, 2000, of 1998 Workplace Employee Relations Survey) have concluded that despite the popular rhetoric, progressive people management practices in areas such as recruitment, training, communication and performance management are still dramatically under-represented. This is despite 'more than 30 studies in the UK and US since the early 1990's that leave no room for doubt that there is a positive and cumulative correlation between people management and business performance' (CIPD, 2001).

Organizational vision and values will assist in the formulation of focused strategy and specific goals. Goals may be set by focusing on business needs and problem-solving or by adopting more comprehensive – eg whole-system – approaches. Whatever the favoured approach conceptually, businesses generally require some framework through which to develop and implement strategy. The appropriate framework will depend on each unique situation. Ultimately, strategic goals need to be translated into plans and objectives at operational level with specific actions and feedback pathways that allow assessment of the contribution of development.

However, strategic capability is complex and is likely to require not only clarity of vision, careful planning and achievable objectives, but also a focus for action. Strategic capability might involve attributes at various organizational levels of management, knowledge and leadership, which HRD may inform and contribute towards. Strategic capabilities, which are likely to require new skills and attributes of managers, may include the following aspects:

■ Where innovation is a goal, there nevertheless needs to be balance between operational and creative activity.

■ Empowerment may mean managers having to adjust their sense of insecurity as they genuinely hand over detailed control of operations.

■ Systems where employment security is reduced may require particularly careful management if strategic value is to be maintained.

These instances begin to identify where HRD can contribute towards strategic capability. However, each particular organization's unique set of needs and circumstances prevent any one universal or prescribed approach. There are no ready-made solutions to the issues of what should and can be done, and what resources will be committed.

Determining strategic perspectives and developing managers is no one-off, quick-fix activity, nor is it optional. Through the actions of management to address the challenges of the present, the conditions are created in which new challenges will eventually arise (Pedler, Burgoyne and Boydell, 1997: 34). Development may happen through experience or by learning from mistakes and successes. This type of *emergent strategy* (Pedler, Burgoyne and Boydell, 1997: 16) is valid; however, all too often the opportunity to learn from experience is not capitalized on. Management influences the lives of people; it is therefore too important a phenomenon to leave to chance (Alvesson and Willmott, 1992: 1). HRD values learning.

By contrast, an organization may recognize a gap between its present state and a desirable future state, and that gap facilitates a *planned strategy*. Realization may emerge as a result of environmental pressures that increase awareness that past 'ways of doing things' do not automatically represent the best choices for the future. HRD values planning.

A strategic assessment of the current situation may be done by asking questions such as:

▍ What changes in skills and competences are required to support improved job performance in specific individuals?

▍ What are the particular deficiencies in performance that need to be addressed?

▍ What organizational changes (eg technology, production processes and culture) are dependent on people learning something new?

▍ What current opportunities are provided to help employees acquire new skills?

▍ What changes in the behaviour of managers and employees would enhance their own and others' job performance?

▍ How can employees be persuaded that continuing development is the norm rather than the exception?

▍ What isn't working? What have we got wrong? What mistakes have been made?

▍ What have we learned from our previous experiences of HRD?

It is one thing to have general organizational goals, eg enhance performance, increase productivity, reduce risk. It is another thing to know how. Questions such as those above take a step towards discovering how. Such questions can be generative but also deeply challenging in their implications for organizational strategy.

ACTIVITY 1.2 CHALLENGING QUESTIONS ABOUT HRD

Consider the above questions in relation to your own organization, or an organization you know well.

What new directions and objectives in HRD need to be established in your chosen organization?

Strategic implications of HRD

Organizational aspirations to improve performance, increase productivity or add value are often at the heart of management strategy. Practices that encourage, empower and reward workers to think and act to improve systems are, it seems, linked to such achievement (Stern and Sommerland, 1999). Development is nowadays firmly established on many corporate agendas, a situation that may have a number of implications:

▌ HRD enhances the attractiveness of the organization to potential employees or other stakeholders.

▌ In the age of flexible working practices, core workforces, through development, expand their capability.

▌ For peripheral or displaced employees, HRD enhances their personal capabilities.

▌ While large firms have traditionally provided the greatest activity, increasingly, smaller firms with necessarily less formal approaches are demonstrating interest in HRD.

Skills required by employers are technical job content and generic including communication, customer handling and team working, which are in short supply now and will be in even greater demand in the future (SSDA, 2003: 8–9). Forces of change and economy are encouraging organizations to realize the fullest possible potential of employees at all levels. However, interest in development is generally limited by managers' and senior managers' abilities to rethink their approaches to sustaining competitive advantage and implement effective strategies.

An illustration of this is provided through the idea of supply chain management. Developing relationships within the supply chain is essential for the smooth running of systems and processes in an organization. Managers form a central element in the supply chain, which can link backwards to suppliers and forwards to customers or consumers, as represented in Figure 1.2.

Depending on where you stand in relation to the 'organization', suppliers and consumers may be internal or external. It is sometimes easier to see the logic of developing them if they are viewed as part of the same system. Table 1.1 summarizes the characteristic ways in which suppliers are treated traditionally and contrasts this with a developmental approach.

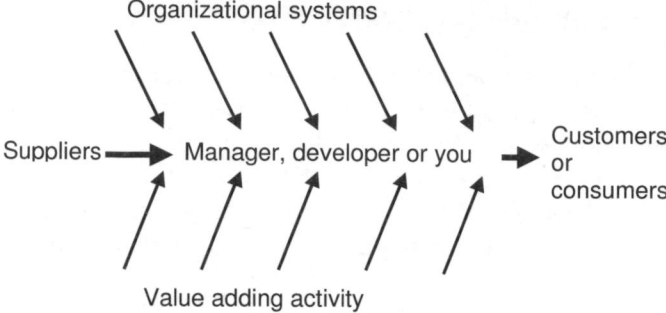

Organizational systems

Suppliers ➡ Manager, developer or you ➡ Customers or consumers

Value adding activity

Figure 1.2   *Supply chain diagram*

Table 1.1   *Traditional versus developmental supplier relationships*

Traditional	Developmental
▌ Pay the minimum amount ▌ Keep them in the dark; always demand best and quickest service ▌ Delay payments as long as possible ▌ Never invest in their learning ▌ Ensure you have multiple sourcing to maximize bargaining power	▌ Offer early involvement in collective activity ▌ Think of things from the suppliers' point of view ▌ Enter all discussions seeking a win–win outcome ▌ Accept that fairness pays off in the end ▌ Develop opportunities for collaboration together

ACTIVITY 1.3 IMPLICATIONS OF HRD

Consider the two lists of characteristic ways of treating suppliers shown in Table 1.1: the traditional and the developmental. Which reflects your normal approach?

Why not check your perception against that of your internal or external suppliers? What do they think of you against these two lists? Can this exploration be used as a starting point for developing the relationship? Can a similar initiative be taken with your consumers?

HRD IN A CONTEXT OF CHANGE

HRD rests in a context that is ever-changing as a result of many pressures, including:

■ the internationalization of business;

■ turbulent political, economic, social and technical (PEST) environments;

■ government interventions and consumer expectations;

■ competition;

■ deregulation;

■ increasing rate of technological change;

■ changing work patterns and relationships;

■ management information systems and increased information volume;

■ complex organizations with wider employee involvement.

Also, the failure, acquisition or merger of organizations is common, particularly in their early years, when the 'mortality rate' is high. Over a third of small businesses close within the first year, owing to poor management (SSDA, 2003). The survivors, on the other hand, are active and full of learning. It is as businesses grow that they lose the capacity to learn. Corporate survivors with ages spanning 100 to 700 years, according to de Geus (1997):

■ are financially conservative;

■ are sensitive to the environment;

■ have a sense of cohesion and company identity among employees;

■ are tolerant of 'activities at the margin';

■ have undergone fundamental transformations or 'historic organizational learning'.

Contemporary organizations such as JVC and EDS are also noted for displaying characteristics of continuous improvement and repeated transformation (Hamel and Prahalad, 1994).

The picture of organizations as entities that can learn and change implies an almost biological metaphor of organizations as 'living organisms' (Morgan, 1986). The image created is one of transformation and flux, of businesses being dynamic and only ever in a state of transition.

The learning that seems necessary to accommodate change is a dynamic field of inquiry and practice. There is, however, a distinction between HRD in organizations as it should be or as HRD enthusiasts would like it to be seen, and, more realistically, how it is. This distinction is the difference between a virtuous learning cycle and the vicious learning sequence (Mumford, 1989) illustrated in Figure 1.3.

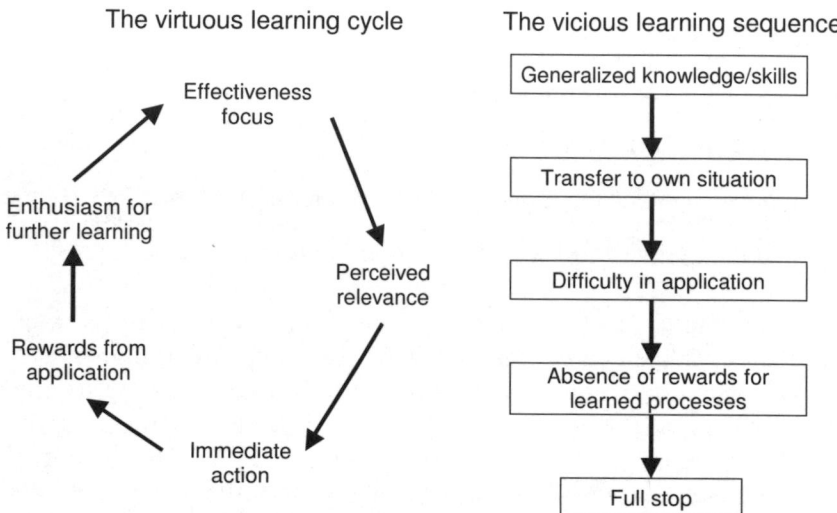

Figure 1.3   *The virtuous learning cycle and the vicious learning sequence*

For a concrete illustration of connection between HRD and organizational strategy, the Ginsters case study at the end of this chapter demonstrates how HRD is taken seriously by senior managers in this fast-moving consumer goods manufacturer.

Critical perceptions of HRD

HRD, and wider human resource strategy, is frequently subject to a number of critical perceptions from managers and employees. For instance:

■ It is too ambiguous: there is too much uncertainty and doubt surrounding its benefits.

■ Occasional training courses are all that are considered necessary but programmes are often badly conceived and their quality, effectiveness and relevance are rarely established.

■ In reality, training is done reactively out of fear of the consequences of not doing it. Managers lack the tools and understanding to implement planned approaches to learning.

■ Long-term effectiveness is difficult to evaluate; assessment is more likely to be linked to short-term training results.

■ Government and labour market exhortations to invest more in training and development are met with scepticism.

Not all these problems are associated solely with the state of HRD, and may indeed be traceable to other managerial deficiencies. The following list identifies some of these sorts of problems that characteristically result from employees doing things wrong or not doing the right things:

■ inability to use technology as quickly and efficiently as possible;

■ low standards of job performance;

■ delays in completing work;

■ costly errors and waste;

■ under-utilized and de-motivated workforce;

■ limited flexibility;

■ absence of a sense of shared responsibility for completing work;

■ lack of clarity in job responsibilities;

■ breakdown in personal relationships;

■ managers developing their own ways of working – or not working!

Organizations large and small, with and without explicit HRD practices, are still prone to such damaging practices. Fundamentally they are expressions of bad management, which HRD alone will not solve in any sustainable way. However, HRD can help by addressing specific ability needs, valuing learning in different ways, being proactive and aligning explicitly with strategy, demonstrating value added, enhancing communications and enabling managers.

> Skills make a real difference to organizational performance, increases in training are associated with increases in productivity, higher skill returns arise when training complements wider human resource practices and investment in skills is linked to innovation and flexibility. (SSDA, 2003: 6)

ACTIVITY 1.4 PERCEPTIONS OF HRD

Consider the above list again; add to it those problems that affect you and your organization, and delete those that are not relevant. Test your views by asking colleagues to go through the same process and compare results.

Are your current training activities achieving results that help to reduce the seriousness of some of these problems? If not, then why not?

The historical context of HRD

Since the late 19th century, new production processes, mass production, different organizational forms and new patterns of working have challenged more traditional processes. Industrialized large modern corporations displaced early patterns of family ownership and management styles in favour of large functional forms and, later, multidivisional forms of organization. These 'modern' forms of organization relied heavily on bureaucracy and principles of scientific management, where officials were no longer family members.

HRD is rooted in a historical context of management practices, which remain recognizable to some degree today. Four main stages in the 20th-century history of HRD are recognizable from the United States and United Kingdom:

1. From the early 20th century to the 1970s, classical management (scientific management), human relations and organizational psychology have left a confusing legacy of ideas about the nature of work.

2. The 1980s witnessed the impact of international competition, subsequent concern for more strategic approaches and the rise of often ambiguously interpreted disciplines such as human resource management.

3. From the 1970s to the 1990s, organizational learning and knowledge management concepts and the search for innovation and transformation have helped to crystallize why human resources or human capital is important.

4. The prevailing organizational paradigm is one of a clear concern for purpose, the lean organization, employability security, the need for integrated policies and the differences between the intended and the realized nature of organizations.

An awareness of industrial history may be vital if we are to understand current organizational conditions, gain wisdom through reflection and develop informed views (Jaques, 1996). Since early in the 20th century, management techniques have come under increasing scrutiny, particularly in the industrialized societies of the United Kingdom and the United States. HRD is set against a background of tension between individual and organizational needs and of differing approaches to achieving harmonious employment relationships in an ever-shifting landscape of work.

Historic differences may have produced the present conditions, but today's managers, around the globe, are the ones expected to avoid the mistakes of the past, learn, and invest in longer-term future development.

ACTIVITY 1.5 HISTORICAL CONTEXT OF HRD

Organizations can have very different purposes, which can change over time. This may in itself be a sign of organizational learning. Those that do not change may need to revisit their purposes from time to time. Check the purpose of your organization by answering the following questions:

- When was your organization founded?

- Why was it founded?

- Is the original purpose still the same today?

- How is purpose renewed and kept fresh in your company?

- Who benefits from the outputs of your organization?

- How can you use a historical perspective?

One of us worked recently with a group of public-sector managers whose organization was relatively young (five years old), but which had been merged from other bodies that had been around for considerably longer. The group plotted their individual journeys through time to get to where they were, citing significant events and historic influences on them and their former employers. This exercise led not only to greater understanding of each other, but to a shared and renewed sense of purpose for the younger organization. In turn these managers were able to produce an approach to development that would be appropriate for the historical diversity represented in their teams.

HRD STRATEGY AND POLICY

The strategic direction and goals of an organization may generate learning needs that can be attended to by linking with HRD. It may also be conceivable that, as suggested by the foregoing sections, HRD can influence organizational strategy. Linking HRD to strategy prioritizes learning that will contribute directly to organizational goals and that may be evaluated in terms of its contribution to achieving the strategy. However, this may mean that learning that is potentially useful but not directly linked to the development vision is neglected. Similarly, it could suppress the critical or lateral thinking needed in organizations if they are to remain adaptable, achieve new competitiveness or be ready to make big changes.

This 'either/or' way of viewing HRD as led by organizational strategy or as contributing to it, or as focused mainly on individuals or the organization, may be less helpful than aspiring towards a position where the extremes are integrated. In discussing organizational policy towards management development, John Burgoyne (1988) has argued that organizations should aspire to mature in their approach along a pathway to towards integration. Generalizing from this, Table 1.2 describes a succession of maturity in organizational approaches to HRD.

Level 6 of the model in Table 1.2 requires the review of the reasoning behind policy and of the very processes by which policy is formed. It requires critical insight and deep searching for motives and meanings; it requires squeezing every drop of learning from experience by asking fundamental questions such as 'Why?' and 'So what?' Thus when HRD is fully incorporated, corporate strategy-making is itself regarded as a learning process.

Table 1.2   *Succession of maturity of HRD in organizations*

Level 1	No systematic HRD	No systematic or deliberate HRD in a structural or developmental sense. Total reliance on 'chance'
Level 2	Isolated, tactical HRD	Isolated or *ad hoc* HRD activities, structural and developmental, but reactive, local and focused on problem-solving
Level 3	Integrated and coordinated structural and developmental tactics	Specific HRD activities, structural and developmental, are integrated and coordinated
Level 4	An HRD strategy to implement corporate policy	HRD strategy supports the implementation of corporate policy and provides a framework for structural and developmental tactics
Level 5	HRD strategy input to corporate policy formation	HRD processes inform corporate decision-making, knowledge management and resource planning
Level 6	Strategic development of the management of corporate policy	HRD processes inform and provide a framework for corporate strategy formation

Source: Adapted from Burgoyne (1988)

Learning organization

One representation of maturity is to focus on company or organization learning, which attempts to overcome the narrowness of individual needs and is embodied in the ideal of the 'learning organization'. This ideal may regard strategy formation and policy making as processes that are best shared as widely as possible. However, some concerns of the learning organization ideal are that:

▌ It is a concept that may be hard to grasp and does not have immediate impact.

▌ It requires a broad view, whereas many people in organizations experience more immediate needs.

▌ It emphasizes learning rather than the more pressing and engaging concerns of managers.

Learning organization concepts and practices have received much critical attention in recent years (discussed further in Chapter 8). Learning organizations require an advanced degree of coordination between HRD activity and organizational policy.

Pedler, Burgoyne and Boydell (1997) identify that HRD activities include structural interventions such as succession planning, career appraisal and careers structuring, and developmental interventions such as courses, open learning materials and mentoring. They conclude that unless these individual tactics contribute to and form part of corporate policy, they will be of limited use. HRD policy, they assert, is concerned with the coordination of the various HRD interventions (structural and developmental) with corporate policy.

ACTIVITY 1.6 HRD STRATEGY AND POLICY

Which of the levels described in Table 1.2 most closely matches the situation in your organization?

Make a list of specific development activities in your organization that would help your organization move through the model.

Compare your thoughts to the leading ideas presented in Chapter 2.

HRD policy and practice

Organizations and individuals alike may experience development as an uncomfortable challenge: 'learning how to develop different behaviours and skills will be a new experience for some employees who will not have engaged in this kind of activity since they were in full time education'

(IRS, 1998: 13). However, encouragement may be drawn from experience distilled from the broader field of human resources.

Many excellent organizations that work within a global context already feature development heavily on their agenda for human resources. Examples include GE, Hewlett Packard, Sears, Baxter Health Care and Amoco (Ulrich, 1998).

Research (Ghoshal and Bartlett, 1998) has indicated that companies that take strategy as important are full of developmental characteristics that link individual and organizational needs and present and future orientations. This credible research into over 20 companies, including notable world players such as GE, 3M, IKEA, Canon, Intel, Kao and McKinsey Consulting, over a sustained period, identifies a number of principal themes, including the following:

▌ Individual initiative is encouraged; skills are developed through training; there is a supportive yet challenging culture with coaching via the line.

▌ The creation and leveraging of knowledge takes place through organizational learning, with new career paths, investment, teamwork on problems, action learning, transparency, and networking to ensure knowledge transfer.

▌ There is continuous renewal through norms of stretch and challenge imposed internally; refinement is balanced with regeneration, and knowledge is used to supplement strategic fit with strategic challenge.

▌ Contracts of control and compliance are replaced with commitment and initiative based on stretch, learning and self-confidence.

▌ Individual competences are developed based on appropriate knowledge, skills and attitudes of front-line, middle and top managers.

▌ Transformation processes, eg rationalization, revitalization and regeneration, are managed by developing new leaders.

Where HRD is strongly represented in corporate policy and practice, there is a risk that individuals will move on from the organization, which has invested in them. However, using this argument to downplay the importance of development is short-sighted. Ghoshal and Bartlett (1998) suggest four ways that employers can address the risk of providing employees with a portable qualification:

■ Begin to invest in individuals' development early, to engender a conviction that the organization is good to work for.

■ Replace the old moral contract of loyalty and obedience with responsibility for the company's and employees' futures resting with empowered employees supported by top management.

■ Make learning part of the organization's core purpose.

■ Support development informally through job-related processes and formally with discrete teaching and learning media.

ACTIVITY 1.7 HRD POLICY AND PRACTICE

Consider how your organization compares and contrasts with the characteristics of companies cited in Ghoshal and Bartlett's research. What are the similarities and differences? In what way(s) can the experiences and practices of these organizations inform the situation in your organization?

An organization actively practising development creates a risk to employers of offering employees a portable qualification or experience. How would you suggest employers address this risk?

HRD IN AN INTERNATIONAL CONTEXT

Different nations have strengths and weaknesses in HRD, but in a general sense, economic success is determined to an extent by how trained, flexible and committed the workforce is. These issues may variously be addressed by recruitment or by managed opportunities to learn or by specific self-directed approaches to learning in individuals and organizations.

Beyond organizations, HRD is situated in the socio-economic context of nations. Within organizations, visions, strategies and policies provide the framework. There are considerable differences between nations in their approaches to vocational education and HRD.

> A range of studies have shown the considerable contribution that skills can make to productivity and economic performance and that differences in the stock of human capital are probably the single most important explanation of differing growth rates across the OECD after trade exposure. (SSDA, 2003)

There are regional perspectives, eg Europe, Asia, the Middle East, North America, Australasia, and cultural perspectives, eg East, West, secular, religious. Labour market characteristics vary across nations, regions and cultures and illustrate the extent to which national policy links general educational systems to economic needs.

Themes in HRD that serve to illustrate some of the key differences between nations include:

■ vocational qualification routes;

■ vocational education and training provision;

■ occupational standards;

■ continuous or adult learning and development;

■ industrial training extent;

■ organizational and national investment in development.

Vocational education arguably has a role to play in establishing and sustaining competitive advantage of nations – that is, providing higher skill levels will add to the options of competing on efficiency and cost. Labour market flexibility may also be an issue related to vocational education. Within Europe, for example, tightly regulated labour market models are present in Germany, France and Belgium. The United Kingdom is rather less regulated. The United States, in contrast, is highly deregulated.

Different political agendas influence the degree to which vocational education is prominent as a strategy in today's global business environment. Also, a country's education system determines its levels of basic education and the workforce's potential to acquire more work-related competence.

HRD has relatively recently developed in the new industrial economies of the Pacific Rim and South-East Asia, where later development of an industrial base has facilitated the simultaneous establishment of HRD. Forms of management and staff development established in the West and in places such as Japan have provided alternatives to guide or inform newer industrial economies. For example, Singapore is an interesting case of deliberately seeking to generate a knowledge-based economy.

For organizations to be effective in international environments, sophisticated competences are required of managers and employees. Such competence can be developed through HRD interventions such as experience with international assignments and training (Trompenaars, 1999).

ACTIVITY 1.8 INTERNATIONAL CONTEXT OF HRD

What are the cultural, regulatory or political influences on HRD in a country you are familiar with other than the United Kingdom, United States or Japan? What responsibilities lie with individual employees, managers, organizations and professional facilitators?

HRD IN A UK NATIONAL CONTEXT

High-performance working is still considered broadly by managers in the United Kingdom to involve getting individuals to work more intensively, whereas evidence suggests that other types of skill are equally important, eg group based, communication and quality skills. UK managers, it seems, consistently underplay the part that management education plays in raising performance (CIPD, 2001: 6–7).

During the 1970s and 1980s, UK management was heavily criticized for its lack of effective development of those responsible for strategic direction in a climate of change and increasing competitiveness (Constable and McCormick, 1987; Handy, 1988). Managers who were uneducated, untrained and undeveloped themselves were unlikely to be committed to education, training and development for others. Apathy towards and ignorance of management development and how to organize learning was widespread. More recently, the Council for Excellence in Management and Leadership (CEML, 2002) has stated that the United Kingdom's shortfall in management and leadership skills is one of the significant factors in low productivity levels compared with those of international competitor nations.

HRD is not an optional extra for managers, who are key to encouraging skills development in members of the workforce. There is ever-growing evidence of the economic case for HRD as a necessary aspect of the management of individual, organizational and national performance (SSDA, 2003). Compared to its international competitors, the United Kingdom has a legacy of under-investment in the quality and quantity of training and development. Today's managers bear the responsibility of not making the same mistakes as their predecessors; they need to invest in their own development and that of other workers.

At a national level, the proportion of the workforce participating in job-related education and training, at 56 per cent, is well above the OECD average of 34 per cent (OECD, 2001). However, the actual amount of time spent training, at two days per year, is the second lowest in the OECD (IER, 2003; DTI, 2002).

Despite considerable recent investment by governments, problems still persist in the achievements of the education system, the standards of vocational training and the level of skill available in the UK workforce (SSDA, 2003). Of course, HRD is not the only variable; however, we assert that a well-trained, flexible and committed workforce is integral to sustained economic success. These attributes are the product of a planned, managed, professional and thoughtful approach to learning.

Buying in knowledge remains an option, but is increasingly difficult and is likely to be more expensive in the long run. Growing your own crop of talent contributes to a culture of development and is affordable. However, in many workplaces this requires a change in attitudes, and it is this that often presents the biggest barrier. Managers need to change how they manage people and the unique resources of knowledge and capability (the *human capital*) they represent. Locally and nationally, senior managers are recognizing the limitations of established practice, and are taking HRD seriously enough to ask the right questions. Unfortunately, very few have the experience in HRD to provide the answers.

The system of National Vocational Qualifications (NVQs) in the United Kingdom enables comparison of the skill level of the general workforce with that of other nations. This reveals a still relatively unskilled workforce in terms of qualifications: 7 million 'functionally illiterate' adults, one in five adults with a reading age below 11 and a rate of participation in adult education among the lowest in the OECD (SSDA, 2003).

Initiatives to increase the number of UK managers with management qualifications have sought to establish relevant competences and formal qualification routes, and to recognize prior experience (eg the Management Charter Initiative (MCI)). There has also been a dramatic rise in the participation in MBA and other postgraduate management qualification courses.

However, it has been argued (Coopey *et al*, 1993: 10) that the focus on qualifications may in itself be too narrow, and managers themselves need to be better informed and more discriminating about the choices available and what is appropriate for particular needs and notions of the future. In reality, the choices often seem limited. One key influence on the choices managers can exercise is the organization in which they work. HRD is also about affecting the perceptions of managers and organizations as consumers of development and also as providers of development for colleagues and subordinates.

The UK Department of Trade and Industry has endeavoured to paint a more encouraging picture, identifying what it describes as 'high-performance organizations' (based on financial and business measures) organizing work around a partnership approach with workers and approaching HRD with seriousness. The sort of details reported include formal training and development policies linked to business plans; formal development of team leaders; training employees to work in teams; and senior management perceptions that training, development and managing people are critical economic success factors.

More recently, then, growth in management development is enabling UK managers to be more likely to link development and strategic business needs. Generally there is greater understanding of what should and can be done before managers commit resources and introduce changes in people's working practices and responsibilities (Hirsch and Carter, 2002). This 'diagnostic' stage is critically important in the development and perception of HRD and its management appropriate to each different situation. The approach must reflect the circumstances of each individual organization; there are no universal, ready-made quick fixes.

ACTIVITY 1.9 FORCES ACTING ON MANAGEMENT ENVIRONMENTS

Changes in the management environment are exerting particular forces on the activities and responsibilities of line managers. What do you think are the top 10 priorities? Are there any other trends relevant to your organization not on this list? If so, note them down. Prioritize your list in terms of importance and in terms of those things that lie within your gift to do something about. If it's important and you can do something about it, what are you waiting for?

UK government initiatives in HRD

UK government departments such as the Department of Trade and Industry (DTI), Department of Work and Pensions (DWP), Department for Education and Skills (DfES) and the Department of Health (DoH) are among those that specifically sponsor national initiatives to provide a context of learning and development in the United Kingdom. These departments also provide benefits and services to individuals of working age in accordance with Acts of Parliament (eg the Learning and Skills Act 2000, the Employment and Training Act 1973) and national strategies. Examples of national strategies include the government's 'welfare to work' strategy for the unemployed or the DTI's 'National Skills Strategy', published in 2003.

Business Link
A DTI agency, the Small Business Service, provides Business Link, a national business advice service. Business Link provides businesses with access to a wide network of business support organizations, information on grants and support schemes, training and development advice on organizations that can help in a particular industry (eg Sector Skills Councils), and information concerning locally available methods and providers.

Sector Skills Councils
Sector Skills Councils (SSCs, established 2002) are publicly funded United Kingdom-wide organizations licensed by the DfES to tackle skills and productivity needs in their sector. They are employer led and involve unions, professional bodies and other stakeholders acting strategically. SSCs and the Sector Skills Development Agency (SSDA) make up the Skills for Business Network.

Learning and Skills Council
The Learning and Skills Council (LSC, established 2001) is responsible for funding and planning education and training for over-16s in England. Through the national LSC and local LSCs (which replaced Training and Enterprise Councils), the aim is to provide a unified approach to improving the quality and provision of learning and skills for people of working age. Modern apprenticeships are managed by the LSC through a network of local providers. The LSC is supported with research and national strategic guidance from the Learning and Skills Development Agency, established by the government in 2000.

University for Industry

The University for Industry (UfI Ltd, established 2000) is a virtual institution established by the government through public–private partnership to address needs of functional literacy and numeracy skills and lack of commitment to lifelong learning among the UK workforce – seen as a major threat to the UK economy.

Learndirect

Learndirect is the trading name of UfI. It brokers courses made available through e-learning media, the Internet and CD ROM. The target audience is regarded as individuals, small and medium-sized enterprises (SMEs) and employees within large organizations.

Investors in People standard

Investors in People (IiP, established 1991) is a national quality standard that sets a level of good practice for improving an organization's performance through training and developing its people. It requires employers to provide evidence of adherence to four principles: commitment, planning, action and evaluation. IiP UK is a public body whose main stakeholder is the DfES.

New Deal

The New Deal (established 1998) is central to the government's 'welfare to work' strategy. Originally for people aged under 25 but now including other groups – 25-plus, 50-plus, disabled people and lone parents – it aims to improve people's long-term employability through options of finding work, full-time education and training, or subsidized employment receiving training and development from an employer.

National Vocational Qualifications

Under the DfES, the government's Qualifications and Curriculum Authority develops National Occupational Standards of performance for individuals in specific occupations based on best practice and demonstrable competence. Competence is assessed and recognized in the form of a National Vocational Qualification (NVQ; SVQ in Scotland). Accreditation of prior learning forms part of the assessment, as well as new knowledge and skill.

Non-governmental initiatives in the United Kingdom

Europass
A European Commission initiative, Europass is administered in the United Kingdom through the British Council and provides a way of recording work-linked training and experience gained through placement in other European countries in a way that can contribute to national vocational training.

European Foundation for Quality Management
The European Foundation for Quality Management (EFQM, established 1989) is a European Commission-backed award scheme designed to recognize excellence in business in accordance with a number of criteria that include significant weighting towards the management, development and involvement of employees.

Chambers of Commerce
Chambers of Commerce are a non-profit-making, company membership-funded network of business affinity groups centred on business communities throughout the United Kingdom and part of a worldwide network. They provide advice, services, management support and resources to members, and campaign on behalf of business at national level.

Chartered Institute of Personnel and Development
The Chartered Institute of Personnel and Development (CIPD) is a professional membership organization specializing in the management and development of people (HRM and HRD) for the United Kingdom and the Republic of Ireland.

Chartered Management Institute
The Chartered Management Institute (CMI) is a membership organization for professional management, promoting management through research, education, training and development, and representation.

Association for Management Education and Development
The Association for Management Education and Development (AMED) is a membership organization based in the United Kingdom with direct involvement in development.

ACTIVITY 1.10 YOUR POSITION ON HRD

What is the policy on HRD in your organization (or one you know well)? What plans or programmes are intended to implement that policy? How does your strategy measure up against that of others in your industry or sector? What national initiatives currently support training in your industry or sector? How can these initiatives be put to better use in your organization?

CASE STUDY 1.1: GINSTERS WORK-BASED LEARNING

Ginsters (part of Samworth Brothers Ltd) manufactures and supplies ready-made savoury foods to the retail market in the United Kingdom. Eight hundred employees produce over 2 million products per week and supply over 9,000 retail customers.

The strategic context of Ginsters is provided by the Samworth Brothers Group of companies, in which training and development, and the quality and well-being of employees, are seen as enabling product quality and businesses profitability, which ensures continued success of the group. All employees are encouraged to fully develop their potential through training, support and by being presented with new opportunities.

Group companies are encouraged to aspire to holding the Investors in People accreditation. Group philosophy includes dignity and respect towards employees, and an annual cultural survey in each business helps to ensure this.

The 'Samworth Academy' is a development designed to promote a learning culture and has four aims:

1. To promote and develop the culture and ethos of the business, People, Quality and Profit, with interventions from senior group management and more local 'Ambassadors'.

2. To develop the skills of senior management within the business and facilitate internal promotions of these teams in the future by providing staff with the necessary training and development on an ongoing basis, which is monitored through annual personal development meetings.

3. To encourage and support site-based training and development of all staff by each business having access to an open learning centre that enables self-development using computer-based training, audio cassettes and reading material. This is available both in and out of work time, for personal or professional use.

4. To develop a learning culture within the group in the longer term.

At Ginsters, work-based learning is considered a strategic development for both employees and the company. Work-based learning opportunities, the company realizes, are increasingly influential in employees' choice of employer. Finding the balance between job-specific vocational training and experiences that develop more rounded individuals is, according to Mark Duddridge, Managing Director of Ginsters (Duddridge, 2003), arguably as important a budgetary decision as the next big research and development push.

The company recognizes that today's commercial environment is changing at a breathtaking pace, influenced by new technologies, new legislation, ever-greater competition and general uncertainty that hampers investment decisions and makes budgets as tight as ever.

Ginsters aims to control budgets but equally to sustain growth by getting the right skills in place now for the business environment to come. Duddridge believes that it would be a false economy for the company to cut investment in staff development during times of uncertainty, because when the market turned in the right direction, it would struggle to take advantage.

The company aims to keep the skills and abilities of its whole workforce up to the pace and challenges of change. This position is recognized as adding value to individuals' experience of employment as well as to the company, as without feeling challenged or learning something new, staff can quickly become de-motivated, which leads to higher staff turnover and increased recruitment costs.

Five key strategic company objectives set the scene for the long-term direction of the company and enable any training and development to be consistent with where the company is aiming to be in the future. While job-specific or vocational training, such as training related to health and safety, production techniques and food craft skills, is normal, as in other organizations, Ginsters, with its large and diverse workforce, has moved beyond the norm.

Employees are offered the opportunity to learn and develop new skills as part of a continuous process of personal growth, seen as allowing each individual to develop to his or her full potential. The range of development opportunities offered by the company includes personal development, life skills and hobbies.

In part, the company takes inspiration from a national initiative known as National Learning at Work Day, coordinated by the Campaign for Learning, whereby employees can participate in a diverse range of learning activity. This initiative aims to promote diversity in work-based learning, encourage people to view learning as a normal part of working life and demonstrate how development benefits staff at work and at home.

Duddridge considers that training and development is integral to the future well-being of Ginsters and proposes that 'it is a brave managing director who will allow any cost-cutting at budget time'.

This case study illustrates the strategic importance with which HRD is viewed by this private-sector company. HRD is linked directly to the culture of the organization, its long-term profitability and success. Policy is expressed through action, and a number of tangible and practical strategies are described. Learning both within and beyond the context of work is valued explicitly for its contribution to real, bottom-line business objectives.

SUMMARY: TENSIONS IN HRD

In this first chapter we have sought to establish the position of HRD in contemporary terms as an essential area of knowledge and practice for individuals, management and organizations. Defining the scope of HRD has set some boundaries; we explore the scope of HRD throughout the book.

We have also reviewed the position of HRD in relation to organizational strategy, citing some compelling evidence for the activity that is going on in the field, although much more needs to be done. This has been set in context by considering the constant state of change faced by organizations and the legacies of previous organizational arrangements. HRD, it transpires, is a critically important element of successful organizational strategy.

National and international contexts play a key role in the position of HRD, and, while this is illustrated with particular reference to the UK, organizations worldwide bear responsibility for their own success. HRD is a powerful catalyst to success.

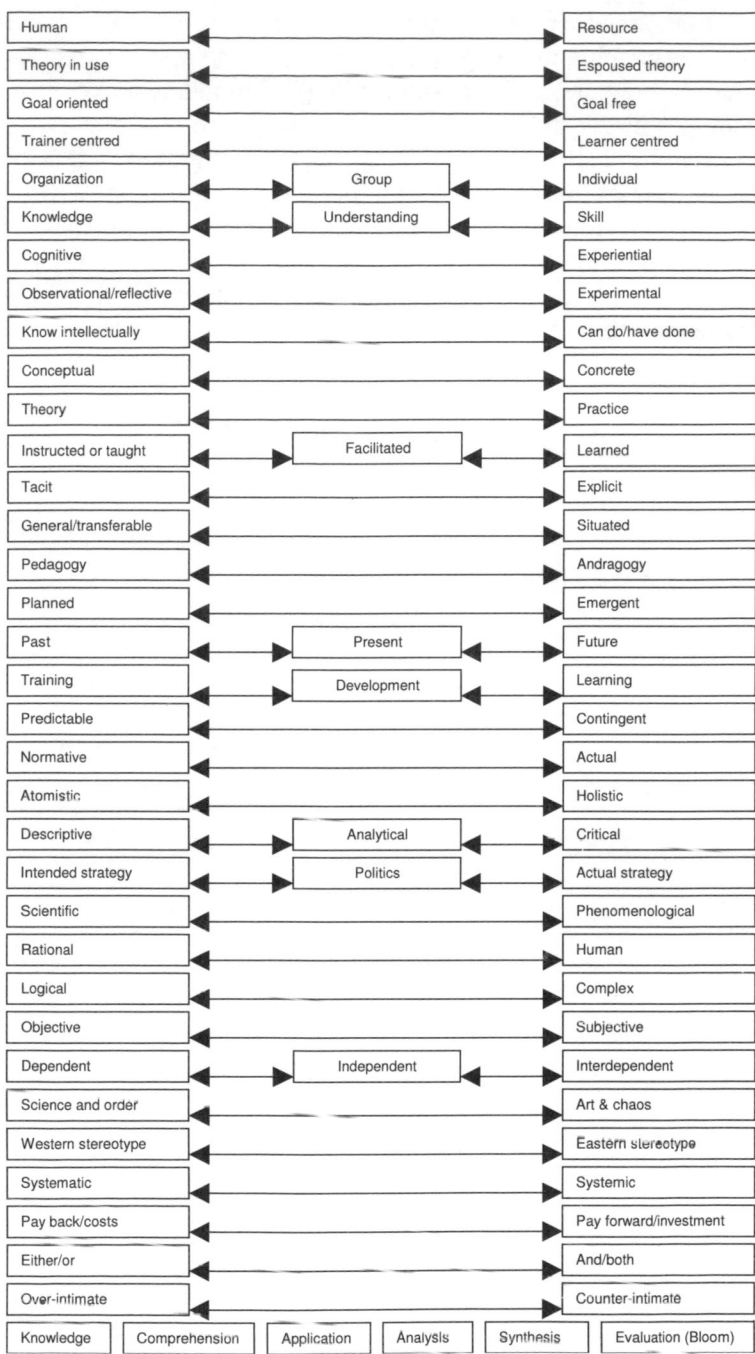

Figure 1.4   *Some tensions in HRD*

As you continue to read through the book, you will (we hope) experience differences in opinion and contradictions between your own experience and our representation. The position of HRD ultimately makes sense in individual contexts and we invite you to make your own sense. There are many tensions in HRD, and we offer you a few in Figure 1.4. Use this to become aware of the tensions you experience. Think about where you would position yourself on each of these dimensions. Remain aware of how the propositions of each chapter affect how you feel in relation to these various tensions, and we will offer you chance to review your experience at the end of the book.

2

Current leading ideas

INTRODUCTION

Leading ideas shape the direction of our use of HRD. They ask the 'Why?' questions behind the 'What?' of the rest of this book. They enable us to answer in a minute – if we have a chance to make our case while travelling between floors in a lift with the Chief Executive – what HRD is for. So it is well to be clear what our leading ideas are. This chapter will enable you to do this. It gives an account of how we came by the current crop of leading ideas, what they are, and the strengths and disadvantages of each. It then gives you an opportunity to test your own ideas and to come up with your one-minute conversation on the purpose of HRD.

LEARNING OUTCOMES

Having read this chapter, completed the questionnaire and reflected upon it, you will be able to:

- outline a range of possible leading ideas;

- identify the advantages and disadvantages of each;

- determine your own leading idea or ideas;

- make a case for their importance.

LEADING IDEAS VERSUS FADS

Leading ideas help us to orient and focus our thinking and action. Fads lead us to make switches from one scheme to another, without following anything through to completion. If people in your organization are saying about HRD policies things like 'It's the flavour of the month' or 'Keep your head down and ignore it, and it'll be dropped in six months' time', then they are in fad mode. If on the other hand they are saying, 'Whatever we do to train people, we can see that it adds value and contributes to the overall direction of the organization', then you are in an organization where development and training is being guided by a leading idea.

In this chapter we trace how leading ideas in training and development have changed over time, and explore the set of ideas that we see as predominant at the moment. We then present a questionnaire to help you to identify your own guiding leading idea, and some thoughts about how to develop it.

THE TIME-BOUNDED NATURE OF LEADING IDEAS

Being guided by a leading idea does not mean that there is no change in the focus of development over time. Rather, it means that the changes that there are reflect a realization that circumstances are different and new needs dominate thinking in the organization.

Since the 1960s there have been some strong leading ideas that have influenced HRD practice in excellent organizations at different periods. Some of the ideas we noticed over this period are as follows:

- 1964–70: Systematic approach to diagnosis of training.

- 1968–75: Standardization of training for job categories by industry. Thorough off-job basic education for skilled occupations.

- 1970–75: Systematic planning of training for all categories of employee.

- 1974–80: Company contribution to training for young people and long-term unemployed to meet national needs.

- 1979–90: Business-oriented training directed at improving organizational effectiveness.

▌ 1988–98: Personal development with individualized plans for which each employee and their boss take responsibility.

▌ 1998 to present: Integration of individual and organizational development strategies and outcomes.

Clearly, these ideas were around for some organizations before the date we suggest as the start, and they continue in other firms long after their heyday. The ideas also emerge in new forms in each era. So, for example, the standardization of training for job categories, which we see as characteristic of the late 1960s, has had a rebirth with the development of the Management Charter Initiative (MCI). This attempted a standardization of management training, and was accompanied more generally with the development of National Vocational Qualifications (NVQs) and competences. Accreditation efforts by those with control of development processes in many professions, government bodies and large organizations continue to this day.

Another, more schematic way of presenting the historical changes that we trace above is given by Megginson and Pedler (1992), who represent the sequence as a series of problems (P1, P2, etc) to which solutions (S1, S2, etc) were found. Each solution in its turn gave rise to the next problem. This schema is developed up to the present day in Figure 2.1.

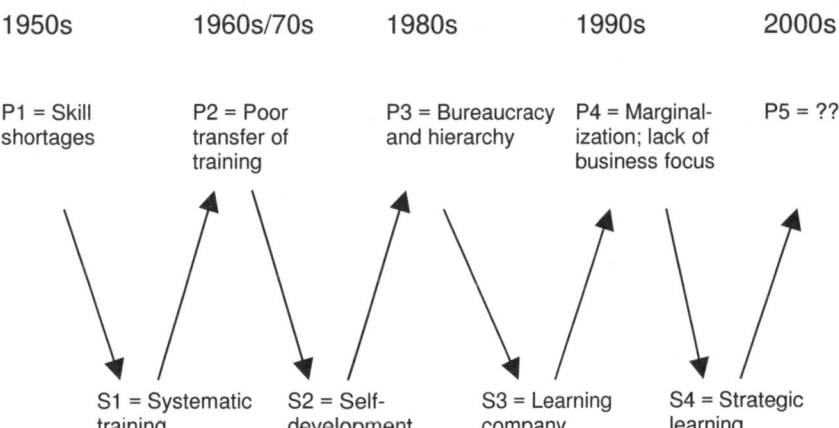

1950s	1960s/70s	1980s	1990s	2000s
P1 = Skill shortages	P2 = Poor transfer of training	P3 = Bureaucracy and hierarchy	P4 = Marginalization; lack of business focus	P5 = ??
	S1 = Systematic training	S2 = Self-development	S3 = Learning company	S4 = Strategic learning

Figure 2.1 *An extended problem-solution map of training and development (extended from Megginson and Pedler, 1992. Reproduced with permission)*

A complex and detailed outline of a huge range of leading ideas and their development over time is spelled out in the report *Developing the Developers* (Boydell *et al*, 1991), based on research funded by the Department for Employment and sponsored by the Association for Management Education and Development.

DEVELOPING THE SET OF LEADING IDEAS

In each edition of this book we have developed a set of leading ideas relevant to the time when it was published. This edition is no exception. We developed a long list of 34 potential leading ideas, and asked experienced developers and others interested in development to tell us which of the ideas represented a desirable future for HRD and which did not. They had the opportunity to vote for up to five positive items and to vote against five negative items.

The list of 34 leading ideas came from the following sources:

- the list of 10 leading ideas selected for the second edition of this book;

- the views of the three authors as to new leading ideas;

- the views of some readers of the second edition, especially the EAMS group (see below);

- the views of several leading HRD theoreticians and practitioners, including Tom Boydell, Chris Blantern, David Clutterbuck, Andrew Mayo and Wyn Williams;

- various contemporary reviews of HRD in professional journals.

One particular group that has worked with the leading ideas in the second edition is senior HRD people working in major organizations in the Middle East. They were attending a programme on development run by the Europe Arab Management School (EAMS). Two of them, Amr Shamala and Imane Shoukry, had particular contributions. Amr suggests that 'Linking learning to the status of your existence' is crucial. He asks, 'What do you want to be? Where do you want to go/stand?'

Imane argues that Mintzberg's (1983) five structures fit with certain leading ideas more than others did. Her suggestions (linked to the 10 leading ideas in the second edition) are:

1. Simple structure fits with *linking learning/work* and *learners responsible for own learning.*

2. Machine bureaucracy fits with *link to strategy, focus on company learning* and *improved communication/briefing.*

3. Divisionalized form fits with the three for the machine bureaucracy, plus *focus on development, empowerment of staff* and *learning between organizations.*

4. Professional bureaucracy fits with the same two as simple structure, namely *linking learning/work* and *learners responsible for own learning.*

5. Adhocracy fits with the same as professional bureaucracy plus *learning between organizations.*

She also relates these to:

▌ individual focus (divisionalized form, professional bureaucracy);

▌ team focus (divisionalized form, adhocracy);

▌ organization focus (simple structure, machine bureaucracy).

This is interesting, as it suggests a new way of using the leading ideas – that their usefulness can be seen as contingent upon certain organizational forms. More work needs to be done to explore these relationships, but they are suggestive.

Reducing the 34 potential items to 10 leading ideas

These ideas were used as a questionnaire to gain responses from experienced HRD practitioners and experts, and a few HRM and line people, about what they saw as items that can lead and impel the HR development process in the next decade. We are grateful to the 40 people who completed the questionnaire, and particularly to the Learning Declaration Group, to John Hespe of GSK, and to Kate Howsley and Gill Lewis from Kellogg's for generating some responses for us. They were asked to put a plus symbol against up to five of those that seem to them to be the most valuable for HRD practitioners and others to follow in future years. Similarly, they were invited to put a minus sign against up to five items that they saw as counter-productive or unhelpful, or representing the past rather than the future of HRD. The results of this survey were tabulated and the difference score was calculated by subtracting the minus ratings from the plus ratings.

The list of potential leading ideas we came up with, ordered by difference score, is shown in Table 2.1. The ten items selected by the process of calculating which had the biggest difference score are presented in Table 2.2. This table shows their positive and negative votes as well as their difference scores.

Table 2.1   *Potential leading ideas in HRD ordered by difference scores*

1.	+12	Talent management and leadership development (as a process)
2.	+11	Linking development to the organization's strategy
3.	+10	Developing a diverse workforce: gender/race/age/orientation
4.	+10	Individual one-to-one development: coaching and mentoring
5.	+9	HRD as business partner
6.	+6	e-Learning and e-HR integration of IT and HR; blended learning
7.	+6	Knowledge management/knowledge productivity/ communities of practice
8.	+6	Visionary and transforming leadership
9.	+5	Improved communication/briefing
10.	+5	Development for all: continuous professional development
11.	+4	Focus on development rather than training
12.	+4	Development around values and principled practice
13.	+4	Building balanced lives
14.	+3	Learning between organizations
15.	+3	Empowerment of staff
16.	+2	Learners responsible for their own development
17.	+2	Involving and participative management, dialogue
18.	+2	Human capital development
19.	+2	High-performance workforce focus
20.	+2	Focus on company or organization learning
21.	+2	Creativity and fun
22.	+1	Organization development as a means to enhance individual learning
23.	+1	Seeking common good between employees and organization
24.	−1	Integrated experiential learning going round the learning cycle
25.	−2	Reflective practice, reflexivity

26. –3   Linking learning to work: learning at and from work
27. –3   Voice to wider range of stakeholders (cf experts)
28. –4   Unit of development not the individual, but individual *and* their context
29. –5   Accreditation and competencies, qualifications
30. –6   Spirit at work as a focus, link learning to the status of your existence
31. –7   Adventure/expeditions/community service as development
32. –7   Managing multiple jobs/learning from portfolio work
33. –8   Reputation management: managing the HRD brand
34. –13 De-layering, re-engineering and downsizing

Table 2.2 *Top 10 leading ideas, showing positive and negative votes and difference scores*

Rank	Leading idea	+ votes	– votes	Difference
1	Talent management and leadership development	13	1	12
2	Linking development to the organization's strategy	12	1	11
3	Developing a diverse workforce: gender/race/age/orientation	13	3	10
4	Individual one-to-one development: coaching and mentoring	11	1	10
5	HRD as business partner	11	3	8
6	e-Learning and integration of IT and HR; blended learning	10	4	6
7	Knowledge management/ communities of practice	7	1	6
8	Visionary and transforming leadership	7	1	6
9	Improved communication and briefing	8	3	5
10	Development for all: continuous professional development	6	1	5

Where items were tied in their difference score, the item with the greater number of positive votes was put first. This also, logically, had more negative votes, so it was popular but contentious – see particularly the sixth item, *e-learning*, which had 10 votes for, but 4 against, compared with *knowledge management* and *visionary leadership*, which had only 7 votes for, but just 1 against. Also, the ninth item, *communication and briefing*, got 8 positive votes but 3 negative, whereas *development for all* received 6 positives and just 1 negative.

Two of the top 10 leading ideas in this edition were also in the top 10 in the second edition in 1999. These were *linking development to strategy* (which came first then, second on this occasion) and *communication and briefing* (third then, ninth in this third edition). So, even though all 10 items from the 1999 edition are included in the potential list this time, only these two appeared in the top 10. This was not necessarily because the leading ideas did not have 'legs', but was – at least in part – because we included a much longer list this time from which to select (the 34 items in Table 2.1, compared with fewer than 20 in 1999).

How does this list compare with other attempts to do a similar analysis? The last chapter of Gibb (2002) offers a similar look forward, though it is not grounded in the sort of empirical research outlined above. He found that 'more and better learning and development at work' relied on 6 items that can be mapped onto some of the 10 we have found. This mapping has been done in Table 2.3.

Table 2.3   *Comparison of ideas from Gibb (2002) with our leading ideas*

Gibb's items	Our equivalent leading ideas
New technologies	6 e-Learning
Long-term economic advantage	2 Link HRD and strategy
HRM strategy	5 HRD as business partner
Social inclusion goals	3 Develop diverse workforce
Knowledge economy	7 KM/knowledge productivity
Stakeholder common interests	10 Development for all
–	1 Talent management and leadership development
–	4 Individual one-to-one development
–	8 Visionary and transforming leadership
–	9 Communication and briefing

THE 10 LEADING IDEAS IN DETAIL

Each of our 10 leading ideas is now discussed, and arguments for and against are outlined.

1. Talent management and leadership development (as a process)

Talent management has become a catchphrase. It replaced the widely discredited 'war for talent', which seemed too militaristic and which also took some knocks in a recent mini-recession. The positive votes for this item were mostly from senior and experienced HR and HRD people in large organizations. Leadership development was proposed in this item, not to emphasize giving a high proportion of the resources for HRD to a small number of senior leaders in organizations, but rather to see leadership as a pervasive process that all could share in. However, whether those who voted for this item saw it in this way is a moot point.

Managing talent and developing leaders is a preoccupation of those at the top of organizations. It is one of the areas of HR that allows senior developers access to the board. Those concerned with HRD need a way of looking at succession and ensuring that each senior post has one or more candidates ready to fill it. This is one way of contributing to the stability of organizations in an uncertain world. Such strategies are more acceptable in the private sector than in the public service, where open advertising of all posts is the norm.

2. Linking development to the organization's strategy

This leading idea received the second most votes from our respondents. It has a persistent place in successive surveys, appearing in the original 1993 edition and being the most voted-for leading idea in the 1999 edition. It confirms the attraction of linking to strategy, which could be seen at its best as a searching for purpose. At its worst, it could be interpreted as sucking up to those in power. If you are attracted to this idea, it may pay to be clear about your motives.

The 'link to strategy' leading idea gives relevance to the HRD process by attending to the needs for learning that emerge from considering the strategic direction and goals of the organization. Some writers, such as Burgoyne (1988), go further, and suggest that development of people can influence strategy too, so that the people we have and their capability determine where we can go as an organization. This is a powerful notion.

The 'link to strategy' idea encourages us to set priorities for learning, giving attention to what will contribute directly to the organization's objectives. It also encourages us to evaluate learning in terms of its contribution to the achievement of the strategy.

This powerful idea has many advantages, including the likelihood of support from those owning the strategy. It has the potential disadvantage that learning that is useful but not part of the big picture may be neglected. Similarly, it could tend to be oppressive, discouraging the lateral thinking that is needed in organizations for them to remain adaptable and be ready to make a big switch. For example, Microsoft's famous move to Web-based products required people to be attending to things that were not a current feature of thinking within the corporation. Companies such as 3M have prospered over many decades by fostering a climate of committed 'thinking outside the box' and principled defiance of the current strategy.

Christensen and Raynor (2003) argue that strategic learning needs both planned strategy (which generates sustaining innovation) and discovery-driven innovation (which generates disruptive innovation). Strategic directors can maximize learning by being aware of the kind of innovation they seek to create. They also need to know the development processes that will help the two kinds of innovation. To generate disruptive development they need to protect the cost structure of new-growth business, use discovery-driven planning and personally intervene in choices as to which strategic process to use (Christensen and Raynor, 2003: 224–25).

The downside of this leading idea occurs where strategy is held in low regard in an organization and is subject to frequent change because there is a lack of constancy of purpose. The benefits of constancy of purpose are shown in the research reported by Collins (2001), who refers to it as the 'hedgehog principle' – hedgehogs being seen as doing one thing famously well.

3. Developing a diverse workforce – gender/race/age/orientation

There is a growing recognition that diverse workforces not only are a requirement of the law but offer a sustainable competitive advantage. Rosinski (2003) suggests that cultural differences should be addressed in an ethnorelative way. This way contrasts with the ethnocentric approach that is adopted in many companies, which ignores differences, or recognizes them but evaluates them negatively or minimizes their importance. The ethnorelative approach, on the contrary:

■ recognizes and accepts differences;

■ adapts to differences;

■ integrates differences;

■ leverages differences (Rosinski, 2003: 30).

Clutterbuck and Ragins (2002) demonstrate how mentoring can be used to further a diversity agenda, with readings from both the United States and Europe on gender, race, disability, sexual orientation and age. Diversity in the context of management development is discussed in detail in Chapter 10.

This leading idea can be reduced to mere political correctness, rather than creating a powerful and positive vision of a diverse and vibrant organization.

4. Individual one-to-one development: coaching and mentoring

The *Developing the Developers* report referred to earlier signalled the growth of mentoring and coaching as a major trend in development as long ago as 1990. At the European Mentoring and Coaching Council's conference each year, leading authorities in Europe and indeed the rest of the world come together to explore what is happening in this fast-moving field. Each year the conference chairs summarize what they see as the main issues emerging in the field. At the time of the publication of this edition, their list read as follows (Megginson and Clutterbuck, 2003):

■ *Value and impact of multiple perspectives and frameworks*. This was important for supervision but also for selecting coaches and for developing coaches.

■ *Intercultural perspectives*, including not only national and continental contrasts but also gender, age, personality and profession.

■ *Who was fit to coach or mentor*. This included both selection and matching of helper and helpee.

■ *Supervision of coaches*. This was becoming a big issue for the emerging coaching profession.

■ *Establishing standards and accreditation*. Does the emerging profession need this kind of safety net? The need in the market is getting more pressing.

▮ *Boundaries*. This included differentiating coaching and mentoring and separating these from counselling on the one hand and bar-room chat on the other.

▮ *Intuition and spirituality* in mentoring and coaching was a matter of increasing interest. Intuition had been raised before but spiritual issues being overtly addressed seemed new.

▮ *e-Mentoring has joined the mainstream*. e-Coaching and (more usually) e-mentoring have been reported at previous conferences but they have tended to be small one-off initiatives. At the most recent conference they seemed to be justifying serious consideration for the first time.

There has been a proliferation of excellent books on coaching in recent years. We will mention just two. Rosinski (2003) has already been discussed under the leading idea of diversity. Lee (2003) offers a strong model of managerial style and helpfully explores their impact on the coach. He talks about authentic, defiant and compliant styles of managing, how coaching can help them, and also the effect on the coach of these styles.

Coaching or mentoring as an isolated intervention is reaching its sell-by date. It is too easy to create dependency on the coach, or to encourage self-interest at the expense of the organization on the part of the coachee. Companies at the leading edge are using coaching and mentoring as part of an integrated strategy of change combined with a range of other interventions (see the Kellogg's case in Chapter 6 and the Nexor case in Chapter 8).

5. HRD as business partner

The Chartered Institute of Personnel and Development (CIPD) uses the phrase 'business partner' as a central plank of its professional development programme. Business partners must add value to the organization and collaborate in supporting the goals and projects of others. The criterion for HRD under this leading idea is that it contributes to the mission of the organization. The language of HRD specialists needs to converge with the language of business leaders. The rationale for action is the same as that of the CEO or the Finance Director.

At its best, this leading idea allows HRD to find its place as a key tool for organization change and renewal. At its worst, HRD efforts are dressed up to pander to the rhetoric of senior management, without anyone having examined whether the rhetoric has any substance behind it. This degraded form of the leading idea offers no prospect of a critical perspective on what will work and what will not, and what the purpose of the organization is and whom it is there to serve.

6. e-Learning and integration of IT and HR; blended learning

e-Learning has been around for a long time, and has, for just as long, significantly over-promised and under-delivered. What is it about e-learning that makes its record so dismal?

The main reason is that in the past, a narrow, tutor-centred model of learning has dominated the medium. As the text has to deliver what is to be learned, there can be no discretion: a right answer must be found, or, if it cannot be found, it must be made up. Most interesting learning in organizations, however, is not about puzzles that have one right answer; it is about problems, which are complex matters of judgement (Revans, 1998).

The good news for the e-learning revolution is that as technology has become more sophisticated, it has become possible to create much more complex learning environments than in the past. There is rich choice for learners in the new e-learning, and alternatives may be considered in depth and worked out fully, rather than being reduced at once to 'one right way'.

There is a current fashion for blended learning, which allows for face-to-face technology to be combined with e-learning, Web enabled or DVD delivered. This has value as an acknowledgement that there are some aspects of learning that are best addressed face to face – including most social skills and especially team working.

On the other hand, pure e-learning has advantages too. In recent studies that we have undertaken, we have found that many respondents only became engaged with learning opportunities because it was offered through an e-mail-only form of delivery (Megginson *et al*, 2003). Other research (Hamilton and Scandura, 2002) has found that e-mentoring relationships that have no face-to-face component are useful in avoiding the dynamics of dominance often found in relationships between the sexes. e-Learning and blended learning are explored more in Chapter 5.

7. Knowledge management/knowledge productivity/ communities of practice

Garvey and Williamson (2002) critique the dominant discourses on expertise, creativity, learning, communication and change. They make three propositions about change that summarize their position clearly:

> Successfully accomplished change requires sensitive leadership and organizational development. . . strategies of change need to be formed as future developmental opportunities for organizations and the people who work in them rather than as threats, fears and anticipated resistance. . . change is sensitively negotiated, owned by those who participate in it and is based on new learning. (Garvey and Williamson, 2002: 179)

Other writers agree. For example, Gladstone (2000: 148) says, 'knowledge management is ultimately about improving the processes of learning, creating and sharing meaning in organizations'.

There is a downside to knowledge management. It can be seen as an information-led, warehousing approach to accumulating know-how, regardless of the needs of the knowledge workers.

Communities of practice and situated learning are major contemporary issues in learning and development and they are addressed at some length in Chapter 4.

8. Visionary and transforming leadership

The appearance of the leading idea *visionary and transforming leadership* again raises some intriguing questions. What is the function of leaders and how can they contribute to a development climate?

Sadler (2003), in this series, argues that leadership has a central position in the development of organizations, and we would agree. For other authorities, such as Gibb (2002), it does not appear on their radar. They seem to feel that general development for each employee is all that is necessary for successful HRD. This perspective neglects the catalytic and enabling effect that leadership can have on everyone around them. Helping to develop this kind of leadership seems an important component of HRD. Jaworski (1996) is influenced by ideas around dialogue and systems theory and discusses how leaders can create 'implicate order' by being in flow (Csikszentmihalyi, 2002). This perspective on leadership is the antithesis of the great leader literature. Rather than seeing things done by the great leader as making the organization great, this perspective suggests that leaders in great organizations enable others to learn to make extraordinary contributions themselves; they are servant-leaders (Greenleaf, 1996). This stance of humility is what differentiates CEOs of companies that make a long-term movement from 'good' to 'great' from heads of comparable companies that did not make a similar improvement (Collins, 2001).

The dark side of visionary and transformative leadership is the big-personality CEO parachuted in from the outside. He (it's nearly always a 'he') shakes up the organization, makes some quick gains and then leaves and writes his autobiography, before things go pear-shaped. There are plenty of examples in the literature from Iacocca (Iacocca, 1985) to Welch. Collins (2001) conducted detailed case studies of companies in a number of major US organizations:

> where a charismatic CEO eventually became a liability for the company. . . Great Western, Warner-Lambert, Scott Paper, Bethlehem Steel, R.J. Reynolds, Addressograph-Multigraph, Eckerd, Bank of America, Burroughs, Chrysler, Rubbermaid and Teledyne. (Collins, 2001: 265)

9. Improved communication and briefing

The idea *improved communication and briefing* just won't go away. We are a little exasperated by this because it seems so limited – focusing on one-way telling people what's happening. What's developmental about that? However, it comes up each time we do a survey. This might be because of the word 'communication'.

One of us discovered the word 'panchestrianism' a long time ago. It refers to a term of such general meaning that it ceases to be of much use in practice. 'Communication' is just such a word, which may account for its popularity in our survey. Nonetheless, improved communication and briefing is an issue. There are a huge number of organizations where 'mushroom management' (keep them in the dark and pour shit on them) is still practised. For these organizations, this leading idea could help. If decision-makers in such organizations doubt this advice, all they would have to do is ask their people. Here lies the rub. Of course, 'asking people' is just what such managers will not do. So the issue is a deep one, related to culture and history, rather than simply to skill.

It is legitimate to consider this idea a development intervention, however. Just giving people the information they need to do their job, or wider information that provides a context for them to make decisions about their work, is a profoundly developmental orientation. Zuboff (1988) tells the story of some mobile maintenance workers who were given two-way radios to aid communication. Two months later the manager responsible for the radios contacted the maintenance workers' boss. He apologized, saying that there had been a mistake and that they had been put on the wrong network so they could hear radio communications between members of management as well as those between themselves and the control room. If the boss would just collect the radios he would have the error corrected. The boss laughed, saying that he had noticed a huge difference in the responsibility and morale of his workers recently, and there was no way he wanted the radios changed.

There is an important conceptual and practical distinction between two sorts of communication. On the one hand there is one-way communication of management strategy, plans and financial information. More radically, there is also two-way conversation and dialogue. Nonetheless, timely and open one-way communication represents a huge step into the light for many organizations.

CASE STUDY 2.1: COMMUNICATING THE VISION

We worked with a small, privately owned plastics company on an agenda of development, running a series of half-day workshops. At the first session we asked the managing director to spell out his vision for the company over the next 10 years. He found it useful to prepare for this, because (although he had the ideas in his head) this was the first time he had articulated them even to himself. Some of the newer managers were dumbfounded. One supervisor said, 'I feel really proud working for a firm that is going to expand into Germany and possibly even America. I thought we were just in a backwater in a northern industrial town.' Through the workshops, the supervisors showed themselves capable of adding to the plans and proposed developments of the firm, now that they had a direction in which to point their efforts.

Some companies, notably the Kao Company of Japan, make all their management information available to all their employees. This is a profound step that has made a huge difference to the company, and one that leads Ghoshal and Bartlett (1998) to number Kao among the leading companies globally in fostering a radically new way of managing.

Some disadvantages of this leading idea are the following:

- It may not be radical enough to capitalize on the deeper benefits of a two-way approach to communication.

- It may be too radical for some management teams – demanding a cultural shift about disclosure and trust that they may not be able to embrace.

- It will need to incorporate other HRD interventions, otherwise the recipients of the news may not have the skills to respond to it adequately.

10. Development for all – continuous professional development

The leading idea *development for all* just gets into our top 10, and it is perhaps having something of a revival recently. It was considered important by Pedler, Burgoyne and Boydell (1991, 1997). They identified 'self-development opportunities for all' as being one of 11 characteristics of a learning company. This was based on earlier work, by companies such as Ford, in introducing employee development schemes (Starkey, 1996: 369). In these schemes, employees were entitled to development, up to a certain cost, at their own discretion, and whether it was relevant to their job or not. This was found to have a profound impact on people's willingness to learn and change in ways that were relevant to the organization.

The idea has gained a new lease of life thanks to a growing interest in *continuous professional development* (CPD) (Megginson and Whitaker, 2003). CPD has become important because a higher proportion of employees today are professional. Professionals have an allegiance to an occupational group that is focused outside the organization. The professional bodies often require members to update their professional knowledge, and though the dinosaurs complain, the pattern of lifetime learning is becoming established for all. Furthermore, professionals are knowledge workers, and their value to their employer is located in what they know and can do. Individuals own this knowledge, and if they leave, they take it with them.

Companies therefore have mustered under the banner of *lifetime learning for all*. Many have separated out their individual development process from their appraisal process, often with benefits to both. For a deeper discussion of this leading idea, see Chapter 6, including the case of Kellogg's Europe.

There are arguments against this approach. It is too generous, not focused enough on strategic intent, and not paying enough attention to team and organization learning. All these are true. And yet, the effects of adopting this approach persuade hard-nosed companies such as Ford and other motor manufacturers that it is worth the investment.

Like all the leading ideas, it needs to be integrated with a congruent set of HRM policies and practices. The next section invites you to consider your own preferences among these leading ideas and whether they make a coherent set of views about the development of HRD within the context of your work.

SURVEY YOUR OWN APPROACH TO HRD

There are a number of HRD surveys available. A very useful one is by Rao and Abraham (1990), which measures the extent to which a developmental HRD climate exists within the organization. The questionnaire that we have developed here is unique in that it concentrates on the role of the line manager, and it is also based on sub-scales that relate to the leading ideas outlined earlier in this chapter. So, it may be useful in highlighting which leading idea or ideas predominate for you, and thus help in planning how you wish to focus your HRD effort in the future. You may also like to consider Imane Shoukry's idea that particular leading ideas may be best suited to different organizational forms. If you are familiar with Mintzberg's (1983) five forms of organization, then you may like to consider which of the current crop of ideas is suited to which form.

ACTIVITY 2.1 ORGANIZATION FORM AND LEADING IDEAS

When you have identified which leading idea or ideas you are keenest on, consider whether they are appropriate to your organization's form. Imane's work was on the leading ideas in the second edition, so we are inviting you to do that same thinking for yourself with the current leading ideas.

Indicate your view of how you are doing on each question by scoring from 0 to 5 in the right-hand column in the questionnaire (Activity 2.2). Remember to score what you actually do currently, rather than what you think ideally should be done. The aim of filling out the questionnaire is not to show how marvellous you are, although if it does this – congratulations! Rather, it is to highlight which leading ideas you tend to emphasize, and thus to give you an opportunity to consider whether you want to reinforce this trend or shift to some other purpose.

The scoring relates to how characteristic the item is of you:

0 not at all;
1 only slightly;
2 somewhat;
3 relatively;
4 highly;
5 totally.

ACTIVITY 2.2 LEADING IDEAS QUESTIONNAIRE

As a manager I:

Score

1. have a process for ensuring that people of talent can grow and progress;

2. start with the goals and strategies of the organization when identifying training needs;

3. ensure that equal opportunities are afforded to all to develop themselves;

4. seek to support and challenge my staff through one-to-one development;

5. focus development on adding value to the organization;

6. use e-learning to maximize the spread of opportunities at minimal cost;

7. identify and share with others my own knowledge and experience;

8. set stretch goals and create a climate where people go for them;

9. communicate with my people whenever I am uncertain of a way forward;

10. enable staff to prepare Personal Development Plans and CPD logs;

11. give priority to developing leaders for the future;

12. determine training priorities in terms of what contributes to the organization's objectives;

13. use diversity as a spur to development, learning from and with difference;

14. provide external one-to-one development for staff from others in the organization or from outsiders;

15. have the same priorities as the people whose development I am supporting;

16. blend e-learning with other development opportunities;

17. notice and reward those who create and share knowledge;

18. redefine the way things are done and engage with others in making change;

19. use technology to ensure that people are informed of decisions that have been made;

20. focus my staff on developing themselves as whole people;

21. ensure that I have at least one person who could take over my role if I move on;

22. review learning and development in terms of its contribution to organization strategy;

23. challenge inequalities whenever they stand in the way of development;

24. seek help for my own development through focused one-to-one help from others;

25. be committed to ensuring that development contributes to the bottom line;

26. integrate Web-based learning with other Web-enabled HR processes;

27. encourage professional and other communities to develop their own practice;

28. provide a clear sense of why it is worth working for my organization;

29. brief staff face to face on the implications of decisions for them;

30. free up time for staff to work alone or with colleagues on developing themselves.

SCORING

Your replies will give a rough indication of which of the leading ideas you follow most ardently. List your scores in Table 2.4. The 10 leading ideas each have three questions relating to them as indicated in Table 2.4.

Interpreting the results

1. Does a clear leading idea emerge from your scores?

2. If so, are you happy that this is the focus of your HRD activity? What can you do to reinforce this idea?

3. If not, what other leading idea(s) do you want to adopt? What steps can you take to institute these ideas?

4. If one leading idea does not score higher than the others, look at the group that was equal highest or nearly so (within one or two points of the highest score). Does one of these represent your current leading idea? If so, return to questions 2 and 3 in this section.

Table 2.4 *Scoring of leading ideas questionnaire*

Leading ideas	Questions	Your score
1. Talent management and leadership development (as a process)	1+11+21	
2. Linking development to the organization's strategy	2+12+22	
3. Developing a diverse workforce: gender/race/age/orientation	3+13+23	
4. Individual one-to-one development: coaching and mentoring	4+14+24	
5. HRD as business partner	5+15+25	
6. e-Learning and integration of IT and HR; blended learning	6+16+26	
7. Knowledge management/knowledge productivity/communities of practice	7+17+27	
8. Visionary and transforming leadership	8+18+28	
9. Improved communication/briefing	9+19+29	
10. Development for all – CPD	10+20+30	

5. If not, are you happy to have more than one leading idea? If so, what can you do to develop and integrate these ideas in your work?

6. If not, which ideas do you think you should give precedence to? What can you do to bring this about?

7. Have a look through Chapter 12. Do the ideas from various thinkers in the field offer other insights into the way forward for HRD in your world?

SUMMARY

Leading ideas help us to organize and integrate our vision for HRD. This chapter offers a thoroughly researched view of leaders in the field who have identified and scored a range of leading ideas that have currency as we are going to press with this third edition. For a more speculative look at the future, turn to Chapter 12, where you will find views of leading authorities in the field as to what the future of HRD might offer.

3

Approaches to human resource development

INTRODUCTION

In this chapter we review a selection of contemporary positions on management and relate them to HRD. The premise is, that whatever your own theory and practice of management, there is a point where you encounter worker development. Here we intend to make these links explicit.

Managers may have different functional backgrounds, which play an extensive role in shaping their perspectives and thus in determining how they manage. Organizational contexts shape the dominant management paradigm – eg quality, customer service, sales – and managers will hold different priorities. Few general managers would disagree that HRD has a role to play, although they might prefer to talk about training or education.

The challenge for managers working from their own perspectives is to be ready to engage with HRD as an aspect of their function as a professional manager. The challenge for HRD specialists meanwhile is to accept the role of HRD as supporting other management priorities and to speak the line manager's language. Throughout this book we discuss a number of general perspectives from which HRD can be approached, eg strategically (Chapter 1), individually (Chapter 6), in terms of groups and change management (Chapter 7), organizationally (Chapter 8) and in terms of business development (Chapter 9). The specific starting points we consider here are:

- human resource management;
- performance management;
- organization development;
- facilitating learning;
- communication;
- quality management;
- project management;
- training;
- creativity.

LEARNING OUTCOMES

As a result of reading this chapter and undertaking the activities, you should aim to progress in your ability to:

- appreciate the relevance of HRD to management in general;
- recognize the crucial role of HRD in achieving a number of specific management disciplines;
- discuss HRD from the perspective of the interests and requirements of others;
- value HRD as a support to different organizational priorities.

HUMAN RESOURCE MANAGEMENT

In a persuasive article published in the *Harvard Business Review*, Professor David Ulrich (1998) set out what the role and agenda for human resources should be. He identifies some generic lessons from the practices of many excellent global companies for the role of HR in organizations, adapted as follows:

- partnership in strategy execution, creating the conditions for constructive dialogue of how to formulate and implement the organization's strategy;

▌ operational expertise through efficiency, effectiveness and economy;

▌ development of employees' contribution and ability to deliver results;

▌ individuals and groups as agents of change.

This analysis reflects much of the current discourse of human resource management, and each lesson implies a need to develop people. How development is managed will be heavily influenced by the size and nature of the organization, its status and history, other strategic concerns, its receptiveness to internal and external stimuli, and its readiness to utilize the resources available. Some organizations manage development effectively within a strategic framework; others are yet to begin.

Managing development as a function is inherently political and involves relative power relations between individuals and functions. In practice, managing development requires a consideration of roles, standards and responsibilities, and organizing, managing and developing capable and appropriately positioned practitioners.

Managing the financial implications of development and marketing the service are similar requirements for any business function. Where investment is required, the function should be accountable and required to feed back the outcomes of implementation so assessment can be made.

Managing HRD can be very involving and distracting. However, activity is not the same as results. Administrative control does not automatically help the organization. HRD should add value and support the business through the timely succession of human capability.

Succession planning

Traditional approaches to succession planning rely heavily on the notion of a coherent business plan and of stability in terms of forecasting needs, structures and career pathways. However, turbulent business environments present considerable challenges to this rational approach and require broader knowledge and understanding from managers than is possible from just considering existing skills and competences.

HRD must link with other human resource systems, eg recruitment, appraisal, diversity, rewards and dispersion, if long-term succession is to be achieved. Increasingly, development (along with other traditionally HR concerns) is being decentralized and devolved to line management to improve efficiency and effectiveness. For many, this means changing their perception of what managing people involves. Three main requirements emerge:

▌ HRD must be owned by learners and line managers; other stake-holders should work in partnership.

▌ HRD itself requires skills in self-development, developing others and cascading development throughout the organization.

▌ HRD simultaneously needs a strategy and to accommodate business and individual strategies.

However, line managers historically have not viewed HRD as part of their responsibility, whether in small organizations where 'training' is seen as a relative luxury, or large organizations with training departments where it is seen as somebody else's responsibility.

ACTIVITY 3.1 HUMAN RESOURCE MANAGEMENT AND HRD

From your experience, how can organizations, large and small, contribute to the creative use of finite human resources while also achieving new sources of supply?

What conditions that affect your organization promote or hinder effective management of the supply of human capability?

PERFORMANCE MANAGEMENT

Performance management lies at the juncture of strategy and actual activity; it involves forming and implementing policy, setting goals and targets, assessing and recognizing performance, developing processes for continuous improvement and establishing links between individuals and organizations. Performance management requires an appreciation of the learning needs of individuals and job-specific needs; an understanding of learning processes and theories; knowledge and experience of different approaches to (and types of) learning; and how individual job performance might be considered and developed.

HRD provides ways of releasing potential in performance, removing blockages to improved performance and promoting effort and energy from individuals. Individual performance rests within, and informs, wider contexts, ie group, unit, organization, sector and the environment (IRS, 1998: 23).

In general, the organizational context exerts the most profound influence acting on the work environment, the work and finally the individual worker (Rothwell, 1996: 33) and therefore is the higher priority strategic context (Figure 3.1). However, individuals within an organization are at the hub, so solutions that are relevant to individual contexts may be more meaningful.

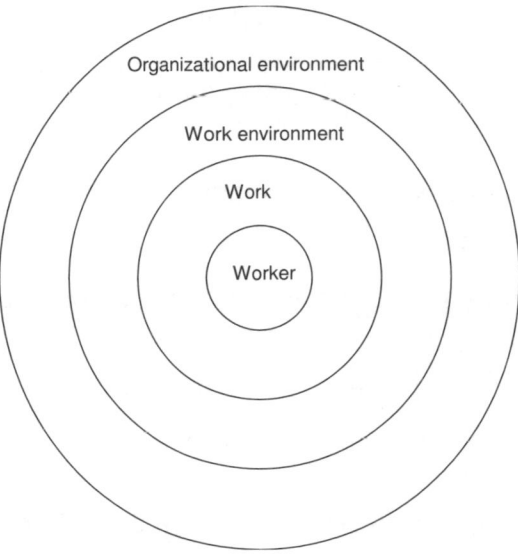

Figure 3.1 *The environment of human performance (after Rothwell, 1996)*

HRD is not alone in influencing performance: particular contexts, culture, existing practices and prevailing attitudes influence how HRD might contribute to enhanced performance, and any one factor may be difficult to isolate. Models of performance management can provide guidance to managers hard pressed by time and other commitments, but it is likely that the apparent objectivity and simplicity of such approaches will need to be reviewed in the light of experience (Harrison, 1997). Typical job performance models emphasize activities rather than outcomes, what is done rather than what is delivered, and tend to overlook the crucial issue of sustainability, ie maintaining staff; encouraging the use of existing abilities; eliciting a want to use those abilities; rewarding; and implementing corrective action.

There may be any number of variables affecting individual human performance. Egan (1995) lists several: key objectives, work programmes, initial training, compensation and reward, monitoring, appraisal, feedback, facilitation, delegation, development and individual performance plans. These all represent inputs. As well as all these inputs, any view of performance must also sensibly consider outputs and results, and the sustainability of these over time (Ulrich, 1998). Thus development is part of the performance spectrum, interdependent with other performance variables, which requires appreciation of the whole organizational system.

A gap in performance may be represented not only by the difference between what is required and what is available in an individual case, but also by the difference between what is required and what an individual is capable of. Relevant principles important to the enhancement of human performance noted by Rothwell (1996) include:

1. Human performance, viewed in terms of results, is different from human behaviour, which produces the results.

2. Human performance gives rise to organizational performance.

3. Costs of improving performance equate to and should be regarded as investments.

4. Performance is defined by a combination of organizational goals and individual goals.

5. Human performance enhancement is contributed to by the management function, the development function and the system.

6. How performance is improved is as important as why.

7. Human performance enhancement requires a critical understanding of the present and imaginative planning for the future.

8. Examples of performance provide the clearest images of standards.

9. Problems can arise in both the person and the environment.

10. Problem identification and solution are contingent and so performance enhancement strategies need to be comprehensive or holistic.

If enhanced performance is the purpose of HRD, then development needs have to be related to business aims and objectives. Development therefore requires integration with business outcomes and benefits. A framework for achieving such integration (Boydell and Leary, 1996) considers performance (whether of people, systems, processes, teams, groups or the organization as a whole) at three different, additive levels. Each of these three levels of performance is further characterized by different modes of learning as described in Table 3.1.

Table 3.1 *Levels of performance*

	Type of learning	Mode
Level 1	Doing things well: implementing	Adhering Adapting Relating
Level 2	Doing things better: improving	Experiencing Experimenting
Level 3	Doing new and better things: innovating	Connecting Dedicating

Source: Pedler, Burgoyne and Boydell (1997: 200–11)

These levels of performance may be further illustrated with reference to the areas of benefit to the business, or organization, at each of the three levels (see Table 3.2). Also, when considered against the perspectives of organizations, groups or individuals, these levels of performance create a framework for recognizing performance enhancement opportunities.

ACTIVITY 3.2 PERFORMANCE AT THREE LEVELS

Imagine a performance discussion with a specific member of your staff or a colleague. Use the levels described in Table 3.1 to establish performance criteria for this person – that is, what is it that he or she is required to do in terms of implementing, improving or innovating? Now put yourself in that person's position. Where does that person see him- or herself as having

Table 3.2   *Levels of performance and individual, group and organizational perspectives*

	Level 1	Level 2	Level 3
Individual needs	Competent as required	Continuous improvement skills	Working creatively
Group needs	Working together to standards	Continuous improvement teams	Working across boundaries
Organizational needs	Meeting current objectives	Reaching for higher objectives	Changing objectives
Systems benefits	Successful implementation	Improvement	Better choice
Marketing benefits	Matching competitors, satisfying customers	Beating competitors, delighting customers	Growing the market, engaging customers
Legislation benefits	Meeting requirements	Improving on requirements	Creating the requirements
Technology benefits	Effective introduction	Efficient use	Developing own
National benefits	Meeting standards	Exceeding standards	Setting new standards
Relationships	Businesslike	Collaborative	Creative
Individual possibilities	Meeting minimum career requirements	Following a career path	Creating your own career

Source: Adapted from Boydell and Leary (1996: 18, 24)

opportunity to innovate? What systems does that person think can be improved? How is he or she judging the quality of the implementation?

What needs or opportunities arise out of this discussion and what can you do about them? Compare your thoughts with those of a group of staff who were asked the same question about performance development activities:

- Talking things over with my boss; getting constructive feedback (adhering);

- sharing problems with my colleagues; thinking about my career (adapting);

- understanding myself better; working in a team (relating);

- working out a plan or strategy; learning and applying new skills; thinking about critical incidents that happen at work; having project responsibility (experiencing);

- experimenting with new ideas; trial and error (experimenting);

- being consulted over possible performance improvements; developing closer relationships with my 'customers and suppliers' (connecting);

- having opportunity to make justified choices about courses of action; thinking about my job in a broader sense (dedicating).

ORGANIZATION DEVELOPMENT

Ideally, HRD policies fit into an overall strategy for the development of the organization as a whole and complement 'organization development'. Organization development (OD) is an established concept and field of practice concerned with enhancing the capabilities of the organization as a whole. Since the 1960s, OD has been used to describe the need for organizations to change and become more adaptable and flexible in response to external influences of accelerating technological, commercial, social and environmental changes. When part of a wider strategy, it can enable the accomplishment of change through its traditional focus on strategies, structures and processes and on interpersonal and inter-group issues (Cummings and Worley, 1993: 2).

> Organization Development is a top management supported, long range effort to improve an organization's problem solving and renewal process, particularly through a more effective diagnosis and management of organizational culture. . . with the assistance of a consultant–facilitator and the use of theory and technology of applied behavioural science, including action research. (French and Bell, 1990: 17)

Internal influences also provide opportunities for organization development that address the tensions created as organizations grow or require employees to adopt different views on the corporate situation as well as their own, interdepartmental communication, customer service, etc.

OD uses simplified themes to tackle complex situations and 'is the field of the chief executive and team, the personnel director and employee development executive, and the external OD or process consultant' (Moorby, 1991: 45). OD helps participants gain better understanding by standing outside the politics and power situations, and provides a broader perspective typically focusing on three strategic questions:

1. Where is the organization now?

2. Where does it want to get to?

3. How does it get there?

OD represents a somewhat conventional view of change. However, OD practice typically involves interventions that are based on people learning in some way; for example:

- developing corporate missions and visions;

- developing collaborative effectiveness and relations within work teams;

- working to improve effectiveness between teams and departments;

- emphasizing process rather than content;

- reviewing and reshaping the values and beliefs within the organization – that is, its culture;

- designing organization structures that support primary goals and operations.

ACTIVITY 3.3 USING METAPHOR IN ORGANIZATIONAL CHANGE

With a group of colleagues, use a metaphor to develop an impression of how the organization is, where it needs to be and how it will get there. Powerful metaphors we have seen used in the past include animals, containers, vehicles, buildings and maps.

For example, a group of managers from a food manufacturing company chose a racing car metaphor. Their car representing the present had wheels hanging off, the wrong fuel being put in and no driver. The car of the future was a Formula 1 grand prix winner with a dedicated pit team joining in the champagne celebration. This was revealing not only of how these managers felt about their situation but also about the potential they felt the company had to be world class.

FACILITATING LEARNING

An increasing number of organizations explicitly value the learning of their workforces in ways both directly and indirectly concerned with work. National contexts also can support learning (see Chapter 1). In Chapter 4 we look at the concept of learning in detail; however, here we focus on organizational moves that facilitate learning in employees of all levels.

Creating a learning environment

Generic methods that help make use of the workplace as a context for development include *networking*, being *creative*, being *proactive* and through *critical reflection*.

Networking can involve widespread, remote and relatively infrequent contacts; more local, available and frequent contacts; formal and informal relationships inside and outside the organization at different levels; and creating, contributing to and benefiting from a community of interest.

Creativity involves enabling learning to come from experiences in the normal course of work. It requires imagination, effort and experimentation on the part of both individual and organization. Individual contexts are unique; managers need to be creative in how learning can meaningfully be extracted and applied.

Proactivity in self-development – continuing to take the initiative and to seize opportunities for learning – adds up to assuming ultimate responsibility for one's own development. No one else can learn for the individual person, individual group or individual organization. Thus the individual must be ready to take the initiative, willing to experiment and able to take responsibility.

Critical reflection. Readiness to learn is one dimension; reviewing experience to extract useful lessons, in a process of critical reflection, is another. For example, examine the meanings you attached to HRD in Activity 1.1 (page 7). Asking why those meanings are ascribed begins to surface and open up for examination the attitudes, beliefs and values that influence our ability to learn in different ways (Reynolds, 1998). Reflection involves taking time out to recall and review experiences and to become more aware of how we form our mental models so that we may take action to perform or learn more effectively in future. Managers often talk about the benefit of learning from experience. Reflective practice in management enables more thorough learning from experience in the sense both of past history and of the day-to-day unfolding of events.

Many of the activities in this book can be completed by groups as well as individuals, thus creating opportunities for these four methods.

Explaining development

In a sense, development involves learning about adding to the existing range of choices about how to engage with and interact with the world around us. Through development, existing choices are not removed, but are added to.

Learning and development are related. Research in the United Kingdom by AMED (Boydell *et al*, 1991) suggests a number of characteristics for the nature of development and its principles:

▌ It is both continuous and discontinuous, continual though with characteristic phases.

▌ It is transformational, integrating older and newer perspectives.

▌ It is irreversible.

▌ It leads to confusion at a higher level.

I   It requires readiness in terms of ability, conditions and motivation.

I   It is not easy or inevitable. Behaviours become habitual and it requires effort to move on.

Boydell *et al* (1991) draw an analogy with the developmental stages of an infant learning to increase its mobility. Initially static, the infant begins by rolling around. Gradually, it learns to crawl, walk and eventually run. Each stage is quantitatively different from its predecessors, while encompassing them completely. That is, existing choices are not removed, but added to.

In assimilating these ideas, the idea of a development spiral proposes a model that is cyclical; brings a new plane with each cycle; provides new perspectives with each new plane; and enables wider perspectives.

As our choices expand, so the learning implied by the cycle may be thought of as an expanding spiral, accompanied by a notion of moving forwards or upwards, or advancing. Several ideal stages in the repeating, advancing spiral may be identified: orientation; diagnosis; strategy formation; design; method selection; implementation; review and evaluation.

Developers, managers and learners: a learning community

Most management situations involve a community of individuals or interest with some degree of shared ownership, mutual objectives, common experiences, common levers for change and common causes of problems. Individuals can be developers as well as learners, whatever their formal role, although interacting with others in one's own development involves advantages and disadvantages, logistical problems and benefits, risks and opportunities.

Managers can develop their own skills in facilitating and enabling entities (individuals, groups, systems, etc) to change faster; develop others; work with fewer resources and layers of management; be more flexible; have broader responses; and be more responsive to organizational community needs.

The manager is increasingly being characterized as the provider of the service of management to consumers or customers, who include staff and subordinates. Thus in addition to normal managerial responsibilities, there is a need to attend to the immediate and future development needs of different people.

Managers with a developmental orientation exhibit hard skills such as specifying goals, challenging lack of clarity, handling anger and being honest about their own convictions, but also other, 'softer' skills such as:

▌ listening to others' comments, recording what is said, acknowledging feelings and seeking contributions;

▌ identifying priorities and helping individuals to make choices;

▌ introducing new ideas and generating synergy;

▌ practising self-development;

▌ living strongly held values including autonomy, risk-taking and learning;

▌ learning from success and adversity;

▌ being optimistic for the future.

Development has at its centre the needs of the individual, or organization, with a history of development and with a future potential. Development ideas and processes can be applied to individuals, groups, organizations and communities. Development refers to a process of qualitative change towards enhanced, more complex successive stages. The skills associated with development are facilitating and enabling.

HRD recognizes that the individual person, group, organization or community owns both the motivation to learn and the results of learning. Any combination of listening, questioning, supporting, challenging, offering resources, reflecting back and providing counsel at the right time facilitates change. Compared to training, HRD reflects different purposes, assumptions, concerns, skills and processes and a wider community of interest.

ACTIVITY 3.4 HOW WELL DOES YOUR ORGANIZATIONAL ENVIRONMENT SUPPORT LEARNING?

Use the following questionnaire (adapted from Pedler *et al*, 1997: 155–56) to analyse your organizational learning environment. For each consideration suggested, rate it as good, adequate or poor in your case:

▌ the physical environment: space, time, light, privacy, noise levels, temperature, ventilation;

▌ learning resources: training staff, packages, books, equipment, IT facilities;

▌ encouragement: interest in new ideas, taking risks, experimenting;

▌ communications: easy and open expression, secrecy;

▌ rewards: recognition for good work, blame and punishment for mistakes;

▌ conformity: rules, norms, regulations, policies, free thought;

▌ practical help: colleagues' knowledge, skills and willingness to help;

▌ warmth and support: friendly, good place to work;

▌ standards: quality, challenging standards or minimum?

Would the results be the same in other parts of the organization? What would be the explanation for this?

COMMUNICATION

Communication is a common yet ambiguous and often confusing organizational theme. Employees have differing expectations of communication, expectations that vary with time and circumstances. Communication can be considered at various levels: organizationally, managerially, between people and individuals. The scope of communication is large, involving everything from interpersonal communication to corporate information systems and public relations agendas.

However, in many ways communication is almost synonymous with HRD. This is because at the heart of HRD is learning. In communication, people learn about the perspectives or intentions of others. Communication is a two-way process: the message intended is not necessarily what is received. Thus in sending communication, we are well advised to think about how and what the receiver or audience will learn from the message we intend. In receiving communication we will be wise to consider our own learning preferences in order to better understand the situation. Thus the quality of communication can be greatly enhanced with an understanding of learning.

In organizations, formal communication happens in different ways: one-to-one conversation, briefings, meetings, negotiations, presentations, reports, correspondence, notices, promotions, etc. Informal communication is also a very real aspect of organizational life: the overheard conversation, rumour, etc.

With all these facets of communication there is much that can be learned to enhance the quality with which communication takes place. For example, interpersonal communication, ie that which takes place directly between people, can be greatly improved with understanding of individual learning preferences and styles. There are many tools available to help with this. For example, the field of neuro-psychology known as Neuro Linguistic Programming (NLP) has become a popular vehicle for enhancing the understanding of communication in recent years.

Presentation skills training courses are available in abundance and can improve individuals' capabilities, whether they are presenting to one or two people or to a whole audience. Negotiation too involves skills that can be learned; again, numerous courses and books exist on this topic. A more recent manifestation of the interest in how people communicate involves the concept of dialogue, and how through dialogue and interaction we construct our own sense of the world around us.

An organization's approach to internal communication may be explicitly articulated through a communication strategy. One way to approach communication strategy is to consider what is needed from organizational members (Quirk, 1996), or what are the objectives of communication. A succession of different communications objectives are illustrated in Figure 3.2, from awareness to commitment, and defined in terms of, degree of change and degree of involvement.

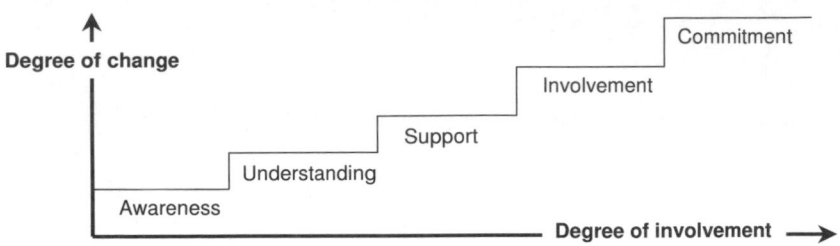

Figure 3.2 *Succession of communications objectives (from Quirk, 1996)*

Communication influences, and is influenced by, the speed and urgency of change. Developing a strategy for communication therefore needs to take account of objectives, information, relationships and resources, specifically resources of time, energy, knowledge and ability to learn.

All communication objectives have associated training and development needs. Table 3.3 provides a framework through which these needs can be assessed. This framework can be used to raise awareness of the scope of communication issues and be used to evaluate what you already do.

ACTIVITY 3.5 DEVELOP A COMMUNICATION STRATEGY

Use Table 3.3 to critically review your current approach to communication. Are your communication objectives clearly linked to degrees of change and involvement? How does your organization currently communicate with employees? What training and development are needed to enable the success of your communication objectives?

QUALITY MANAGEMENT

Quality is a core concern for most organizations, whether product or service quality. The quality movement has become a powerful arena of practice and wisdom for public-sector, private-sector and not-for-profit

Table 3.3 *General communications strategy*

Communication objective	Expected impact on code of behaviour or objectives	Means of creating communication	How it will be developed	Test for effectiveness of communication	Who?	Led by?	Training and development needs
Awareness	Provide information about key strategic objectives, acknowledge reality of constraints, eg time	Corporate identity, bulletin boards, campaigns, memos, annual reports, e-mail	Newsletters, e-mail, notice boards, video. Designed for general audience	Check if information received and understood, surveys	All stakeholders	Director, executive, board, chairs	Education skills, imaginative design expertise, accessible writing, efficient distribution
Understanding	Share management thinking, clarify responsibilities and personal objectives, acknowledge common interests, demonstrate fairness in decisions.	Greater feedback, more interactive and tailored towards more defined groups	Face to face, manage by walking about (MBWA), conferences, briefings, meetings, AGMs – present rationale and get feedback	Get feedback and check understanding	Stakeholders directly affected	Business unit director, divisional heads, team leaders, chairs	Briefing and presentation, questioning and answering
Support	Clear sense of purpose, value personal contact, consult, listen, willingness to challenge and be challenged, elicit acceptance of objectives and rationale	Interactive, focus on education, involve input from outside, face to face	Seminars, training events, sharing experience, guest speakers, continuous discussion, MBWA	Surveys to establish perceptions, degree of support and safety to challenge direction	Essential groups	Team leaders, line managers, portfolio heads, executive group, chairs	Interpersonal skills, effective listening, educational skills, management skills

Involvement	Share thinking, assess implications, explore alternatives, review implementation, share concerns, raise objections, personal contact, feedback, enabling, accept pluses and minuses of collaboration, develop via reflection	Aim of dialogue, pooling expertise, cross-functional discussions	Team meetings with responsibility for action, project teams, feedback forums, safe areas, interactive conferencing	Monitor meeting outcomes, perceptions of involvement and levels of participation	Small targeted groups needed by the objective	Executive group, chairs, portfolio heads, project managers	Team leadership and chairing skills, group dynamics, facilitation
Commitment	Pride and identity, reflection, realizing full potential of individuals, sense of purpose and ownership	Participation in strategy generation, talk, reviewing, scenarios, flexibility	Retreats, away-days, informal feedback sessions, cross-functional updates	Survey of ownership and commitment	Specialist groups, task forces, critical to the objectives	Executive team, chairs, project managers	Relationship building, trust, maintenance

Source: Adapted from Quirk (1996)

organizations, large and small. The movement, although not new, continues to go through its own evolution reflected in the common discourse of quality. Total Quality Management (TQM) recognized the opportunities beyond simple compliance and checking, to get things 'right first time' (the *kaizen* of Japanese manufacturing practices, which so thoroughly embraced the principles of 'gurus' such as Demming and Juran). TQM gave rise to the principle of Continuous Improvement. Best practice, benchmarking and the use of standards are quality practices that have widened their popularity. Contemporary manifestations of the quality movement include Business Excellence, performance management and, to an extent, the Learning Organization. Writing in Peter Senge's *Fifth Discipline Fieldbook*, Charlotte Roberts and Suzanne Thompson conclude:

> The quality movement is unique in its transformational potential, even today. It inherently focuses people on the whole system, on both hard and soft issues, on collective learning and action, and on their own desires for improvement. The failures have come, in a nutshell, because organizations have expected too much from the 'quality programme', and too little from themselves. An organization cannot be a quality organization without the pursuit of collective learning. (Senge *et al*, 1994: 453)

Conventionally, the outward expressions of quality management include business plans and strategies, policies and procedures, systems and standards. However, quality, continuous improvement and excellence all involve communication, change, teams or groups, planning and implementation, education and training as well as management styles and structures. In an ever-changing world there is always a demand to learn more about these areas, both individually and collectively. HRD supports this learning that is at the heart of quality management.

Contemporary models of quality management have made this link to HRD very explicit. The European Foundation for Quality Management Business Excellence model (Chapter 1) includes people management as a fundamental concept in sustainable business excellence. People management specifically means people development and involvement, continuous learning, innovation and improvement. The model identifies these factors not only as enablers to excellence but also as results that in themselves define excellence.

The Investors in People standard in the United Kingdom (Chapter 1) is a quality standard that is intended to set minimum levels of best practice in how workers are managed in pursuit of quality and performance. Similarly, there are quality standards published by the British Standards

Institution that refer to systems of management, known generally as ISO 9000:2000.

ACTIVITY 3.6 ATTITUDES TOWARDS QUALITY

Use the following questions to explore your attitudes towards quality.

The organization:

- Does your organization have a mission or purpose statement?
- Does it have supporting principles and values?
- Are these known by everyone in the company?
- Does everyone know what consequent behaviour changes are required of them?

Consumers:

- How do you believe your customers view your quality?
- How do suppliers view you?
- How do employees see the organization?
- How does the competition view your organization?
- What are the consequent areas for improvement?

Employees:

- How effective is teamwork in your organization?
- How effective is communication within your organization?
- How serious is your organization about quality?
- How committed is the organization to employee and management development?

If you emerge from these questions with a glowing report, you may have a distorted sense of reality; time to check out your perceptions against those of others. If your report was unflattering, then take heart: you have already achieved the most challenging step, that of recognizing the need to change. Sharing this questioning with others will begin the process of changing attitudes and developing quality among your colleagues.

PROJECT MANAGEMENT

There is an accumulated body of knowledge and management techniques concerned with improving performance or productivity and efficiency while minimizing risk, which has grown over a number of decades into the theory and practice of project management.

Project management is based on the effective implementation of a rational, linear problem-solving model requiring skills of project managers and teams in planning and control to ensure that the results the project brings about are as predicted. Certain fundamental principles of project management have proven, through repeated validation in practice, to be durable and robust in just about any circumstances where they are appropriately applied. These principles include the following:

- By definition, a project involves some elements of uniqueness.

- Projects bring about change in people's lives.

- Project success is judged subjectively by different stakeholders.

- The biggest variables in any project are people.

- Project management must balance the benefits of a rational systematic approach with the reality of changing contexts and organizational politics.

Project management has learning at its core. The 'project' must learn:

- about what it is meant to achieve – that is, the goals of the project must be defined;

- about the differing expectations of stakeholders and customers, and how to manage them;

- from the existing body of knowledge and its own unique position, how best to plan and implement its work;

- how to communicate effectively;

- when to recognize that its work is done or when it has changed beyond the tolerance of its original scope.

Mantel *et al* (2001: 93) conclude, 'the effects of learning, even in "one time" projects, should not be ignored'.

The tools and techniques of project management achieve nothing on their own. The people who use them achieve everything that the project accomplishes. Those people, by virtue of their involvement with the project, are engaged in learning. At one level, they are learning to use the tools and techniques of convention skilfully and appropriately. Also, owing to the characteristic uniqueness of a project, project managers, teams and stakeholders are engaged in learning how to achieve the aims of any one project, together.

Managing risk and continually improving project management approaches involve learning from feedback and reviewing successes and mistakes. Some of this learning can be embedded in the system, but only if someone has learned it first. So, the learning that people achieve underpins the key principles of project management.

HRD can support the learning involved in project management:

- Organizations can learn to become better at project management by capturing and learning from experience.

- The skilled project manager recognizes that he or she does not know all the answers, but coaching members of the team will mean that solutions to problems will be discovered by the team.

- Teams work better in an atmosphere of trust and confidence; working effectively as teams involves skills and knowledge that can be learned.

- Controlling projects and managing risk is greatly facilitated by regular communication and review. Skills in reviewing with project teams and stakeholders are important factors in success.

ACTIVITY 3.7 PROBLEM DEFINITION USING THE TEAM

Think about an example of a past project that went wrong, or a current project that is in difficulty, or just a problem that it might be possible to turn into a project. Define this problem in detail by writing all its individual component parts on cards or sticky notes. Continue to brainstorm in this way until you run out of ideas. If working on a current problem, get the team to do this same exercise individually, then pool your ideas, allowing any further ideas that are prompted. Arrange the notes into 'like' clusters.

Breaking the problem down in this way will identify more manageable chunks against which action can be taken – the first step of a project plan. Involving the team in problem definition will create greater understanding and ownership of the plan.

TRAINING

Contemporary, enlightened training practice takes a substantially more developmental approach than the provisions of the classic systematic training cycle. Learners are at the heart of such practice rather than administrative efficiency. Trainers have a responsibility to develop knowledge, behaviour and attitudes in people. The role of training in positively intervening in this relationship may be debatable, but knowledge, behaviours and attitudes can be learned and HRD is arguably a more appropriate frame of mind to adopt.

Training is viewed classically as a systematic process with an inherent and generally acceptable logic that begins with identifying needs, designing an intervention, implementing it and then evaluating. This logic is often represented in the form of a 'training cycle'. Managerial and administrative effectiveness are equally part of the conventions of this training cycle.

Development is distinct from training (see the section 'Explaining development' on page 68). In summary:

■   Development is learner centred rather than expert or trainer dependent.

■   People learn in a variety of ways, not just by being taught or trained.

- Work presents a range of opportunities for learning, not just attending training courses.

- There is a difference between what people are told and what they remember.

- Training represents one approach in the repertoire of development.

Contemporary approaches to training recognize the importance of the trainee or learner. Alison Hardingham (1997), for instance, offers 10 fundamental design principles and 5 key concepts to consider (see Table 3.4).

Table 3.4 *Design principles and key concepts in training*

Design principles	Key concepts
Maximize action and interaction	Credibility
Signpost, signpost and then signpost again	Commitment
Vary pace and rhythm	Risk
Map the participants' world	Attention
Give participants choices	Manoeuvrability
Surface objections	
Balance theory and practice	
Design in feedback	
Design for closure	
Chunk content	

Source: Hardingham (1997)

A memorable and developmental way of approaching training is to consider content, process and environment ('CPE'): the content to be learned, the process by which the content is communicated, and the environment in which the communication occurs, encompassing organizational context, physical space and the people involved. 'CPE' is powerful in its relevance to diagnosis, design, intervention and evaluation.

Our CPE model also acts as a useful reminder that these three things are not fixed constants, but have facets and can vary. Process, for instance, includes contemporary methods such as self-development, mentoring, action learning and reflective practice and more traditional practices such as courses, reading, electronically mediated information (so called e-learning) and on- and off-the-job techniques.

ACTIVITY 3.8 SHARING RESPONSIBILITY IN TRAINING

It is easy to think that the responsibility for getting the content, process and environment right lies with the trainer. However, think of the last time you were a delegate on a course. What did you do to contribute to the C, P and E?

Here are some thoughts about what you could do next time:

▮   *content*: prepare, research; set yourself some realistic learning objectives; make offers;

▮   *process*: try it out: if it feels uncomfortable, go with it; try something new; ask questions; assist others; avoid distractions;

▮   *environment*: accept the things that are beyond the trainer's control; be awake and attentive; share insights; offer constructive feedback.

CREATIVITY

Creativity is a widespread phenomenon. We are all creative in different ways. Consider how we deal with unique customer complaints; improve the quality of our work; play a favourite team game; carry out home maintenance tasks; bring up our children; offer our services voluntarily to some charity. Pressures that impel the development of creativity in organizations include:

▮   problem-solving; applying different minds to problems; generating insights;

▮   continuous improvement; originality; ingenuity; competition;

▮   communication; emerging stakeholders with no previous precedent; inspiration;

▮   innovation and invention; doing different things and doing things differently;

▮   change, imposed and self-determined; imagination and intuition;

▮   learning, individual and organizational illumination.

Simultaneously, there are pressures that retard creativity in organizations: management control, short-termism, over-analysis of ideas, pressure to do more with less, drives for efficiency, risk-averse attitudes, politics and perceived stability. The challenge, it seems, is to develop creativity, originality and innovation while keeping the benefits of a rational, systematic approach at personal and organizational levels.

In organizations, HRD can support the useful application of creative thinking by removing personal and organizational barriers, developing supportive management approaches, creating the right environment, spreading understanding of the process and enabling individuals to learn to think differently.

Theoretically, notions of left and right brain characteristics, mind and body connection, comfort and learning or stretch zones and the role of fun all have some mileage that can help managers and practitioners facilitate creativity in organizations. At a more practical level there are various tools and techniques aimed at activating creative thought and practice, including mental exercises, analytical exercises, relaxation techniques, changing environments and experiences that disrupt us. Teams are often perceived as being a source for creative thought – the 'two heads are better than one' or brainstorming approach.

ACTIVITY 3.9 ACTIVATE YOUR CREATIVE SELF

A marketing team based in Germany was experiencing a creative block in its weekly meetings. These meetings took place at the same time in the same room on the same day every week. Everyone even sat in the same places. With a bit of help, the team decided to explore its environment a little more. The team members visited museums and galleries, went to the cinema, used their city's transport system, visited buildings of special architectural worth, went to the fair and enjoyed some of the public open space available to them. In each of these different environments they sought inspiration and opportunity. Weekly meetings were never quite the same again.

What can you do to activate your creative self? What inspiration is available to you, just outside your door?

CASE STUDY 3.1: TETRA PAK – CONTINUOUS IMPROVEMENT

Tetra Pak (established 1952) develops, manufactures and markets systems for the processing, packaging and distribution of food and liquid food. The company provides machinery, card and ongoing engineering support globally.

Tetra Pak currently has 77 market companies around the world, 63 packaging material plants and 14 packaging machine assembly factories. The company has 20,900 employees and in 2002 reached net sales of 7.5 billion euros. Tetra Pak products are sold in over 165 markets.

The global agenda for Tetra Pak is articulated through the company's statements of vision and mission, together with the company motto and core values.

Company vision
We commit to making food safe and available, everywhere.

Company mission
We work for and with our customers to provide preferred processing and packaging solutions for food.

We apply our commitment to innovation, our understanding of consumer needs and our relationships with suppliers to deliver these solutions, wherever and whenever food is consumed.

We believe in responsible industry leadership, creating profitable growth in harmony with environmental sustainability and good corporate citizenship.

Company motto
The company motto, 'Protect what's good', refers not only to how packaging protects the good qualities of the food it contains, but to the whole value chain: suppliers, employees, customers, retailers, consumers and society.

Tetra Pak core values
The Tetra Pak core values are:

▌ freedom with accountability;

▌ partnership with customers, suppliers and colleagues;

▌ long-term perspective;

▌ innovation and creativity;

▌ commitment and fun.

How this global agenda is translated on a more local level is illustrated by the continuous improvement agenda adopted by the UK Technical Division and given impetus in this quotation from President and CEO Gunnar Brock: 'Our customers will always get what they want, either from us or from our competitors.' This particular division devised a mission that reflects the global mission as it applies locally, and is summed up in the statement:

> Mission: For Technical Division to become a team committed to innovation, creativity and continual improvement, delivering value to all of our customers.

In pursuit of this mission, the UK Technical Division employs Continuous Improvement Technicians and Team Leaders in small, self-managed teams providing on-site support and driving continuous improvement at customers' premises and finding workable solutions to problems. The teams work full time on customer sites carrying out mechanical repairs and responding to emergencies, but also empowering customers to change their behaviour to perform diagnostics themselves – extending the 'team' to include the customer in order to facilitate the continuous improvement process.

The starting point and main driver for Tetra Pak UK Technical Division is continuous improvement. However, this agenda requires the support of HRD practices in succession planning, team learning and subsequent facilitation.

Initially, recruitment plays a substantial role, with certain specified entry-level skills and competences being required, such as customer handling, people handling, motivating, sensitivity, planning, coordinating, communication, problem-solving, computer literacy, flexibility, product knowledge, company knowledge and time management. Recruitment is followed by a defined succession plan based on sets of technical skills and professional competence. This identifies a clear route to succession for individuals within the teams, from field service engineer to global consultant. Development objectives for each step of the way are therefore established via this human resource management approach.

Teams working on customer sites are empowered with autonomy and authority. They are also charged with similarly empowering customers. The UK Technical Division realizes that these are responsible and challenging roles, and may represent unfamiliar ways of working for individuals. So, teams are supported with a number of HRD strategies.

Identifying learning needs is one of the responsibilities of teams. Team members and leaders are encouraged to understand their preferred styles and other styles of working within teams and extended teams. As an aspect of their interaction with each other and with customers on-site, teams are encouraged to explore coaching skills and their application to the continuous improvement process.

This development is facilitated through training courses, benchmarking, continuous improvement groups, regular team meetings and reviews, representing a broad scope of human resource development practice.

This case illustrates how, although the priority for this division is continuous improvement (or quality), understanding development is key to the role of the continuous improvement teams. Guidance is provided by a solid foundation of clearly articulated purpose and values and a provision for 'protecting what's good' about the workforce.

SUMMARY

In this chapter we have reviewed a number of different management disciplines from which managers and organizations inevitably approach learning and development. All these approaches share a concern with organizational success, however defined. Thus the full scope of HRD is of relevance to any manager, whatever his or her main focus. This realization also acts as a reminder that HRD is not necessarily a department or specific individual's responsibility but a discipline of general management.

The same is true of learning: whether as an individual, a group or as an organization, it is not someone else's responsibility, it is everyone's. We have considered in this chapter the role of learning in achieving various management objectives as well as valuing the learning process itself explicitly. In Chapter 4 we explore the subject of learning in greater depth.

Finally, knowing the contribution to organizational success of any initiative or discipline seems sensible. In HRD it is essential, and we return to the subject of evaluation in Chapter 9.

4

Learning

INTRODUCTION

In this chapter we concentrate on the theory and mechanics of learning, and in this edition we value the importance that blended learning and e-learning have assumed, so much so that the next chapter is devoted to them. In the first edition of this book we concentrated mainly on planned learning as delivered by formal training and development events. While we knew, when preparing the second edition, that this planned learning was still essential, we recognized the increasing importance of emergent learning (Megginson, 1994). We feel that this demonstrates the trend away from formal training courses to more individual forms of learning within organizations.

Learning is at the heart of training and development. Whether organizations adopt a formal and systematic approach, or are committed to the ongoing and long-term process of individual and organizational growth and development via a systemic approach, learning is the essential precondition for any change in performance at work.

In the 1980s, Garratt (1987) said, 'Learning has become the key developable and tradable commodity of an organization.' This is probably even truer today, when knowledge management is seen as an important issue for many companies, and intellectual property is equally important for individuals and for organizations.

LEARNING OUTCOMES

By reading this chapter, undertaking the suggested activities and reflecting on the content and your own prior knowledge, you will achieve the following learning outcomes:

▋ knowledge of the theories of learning both classical and newer ones;

▋ an understanding of how learning happens;

▋ some ideas about where learning takes place;

▋ knowledge of learning cycles and learning styles.

DEFINITIONS

The *Oxford English Dictionary* suggests that the purpose of learning is to gain knowledge or skill in a particular field. This definition emphasizes the results of learning rather than the process itself. The US writer Peter Senge (1990) is critical of the view that equates learning with the taking in of information, an act that he believes is only distantly related to real learning. In his opinion, real learning is closely related to what it means to be human. In an almost metaphysical way he believes that 'Through learning we re-create ourselves. Through learning we become able to do something we were never able to do. Through learning we extend our capacity to create, to be part of the generative process of life.'

The situation in which certain authorities equate learning with the acquisition of factual information while others, like Senge, give it a somewhat mystical identity makes it impossible to offer a simple, consistent and shared definition of what learning means. Moreover, it makes little sense to search for a meaning that is acceptable to all.

Nevertheless, some basic conceptual grasp of what learning can mean is necessary: it would be difficult, particularly for trainers, developers and educationalists to be effective in their roles unless they were clear about what learning involved; about what they were trying to achieve. The same applies to managers and learners. Imagine the problem they would face in trying to answer questions from their own staff about the learning process if they themselves were uncertain and confused!

Learning can perhaps be best understood as a change in an individual's range and repertoire of behaviour. It is the process by which behaviour is modified, either by the addition of new and different capabilities, or by the extension and enhancement of those that an individual already possesses.

It is important for managers and learners to understanding the significance of these theoretical distinctions. The arguments put forward in Chapter 1 imply that increasing numbers of managers who previously have had little responsibility for improving the performance of their staff are now expected to do precisely that. To make this contribution, they need to enhance their own knowledge of key concepts and processes.

The pressure to change, to improve, to be more flexible and adaptive in each case assumes the need to learn, because these objectives are not going to be realized by wishful thinking or by edict. If people do not learn, then their capabilities will not change. Without this change, it will be impossible to achieve the levels of performance increasingly required for organizations to perform effectively.

The message contained in the following phrase highlights the issues of learning and change – or rather, lack of change!

'If you do what you always did, you get what you always got.'

ACTIVITY 4.1 DEFINITION:

We have chosen to define learning as:

'the never-ending process of becoming different from what we were.'

Do you agree with this definition? Do you want to change it in any way?

THE COMPONENTS OF LEARNING

In coming to terms with learning, it is helpful to distinguish between outcomes and processes.

Outcomes

Knowing what a person is supposed to learn, and ensuring that this is known and understood, is quite simply a vital part of any planned learning activity. In almost all examples of learning at or for work, the required behavioural change which learning is supposed to facilitate should be clearly established. If it is not, people will not know what is expected of them and are unlikely, except by chance, to acquire the desired capabilities, ie to learn.

These intended outcomes can be categorized in terms of:

▌ Learning to do things well. This is sometimes described as vertical learning (Boydell and Leary, 1996).

▌ Learning how to do what a person can already do, better, differently or to higher standards. This is also described as vertical learning, because people would be increasing their capability in an area in which a certain level of competence already exists (Boydell and Leary, 1996).

▌ Learning how to do something new that is different from a person's existing capabilities. This can be understood as horizontal learning, because the person would be extending his or her capabilities into new areas (Boydell and Leary, 1996).

Both horizontal and vertical learning are expressions of outcomes. In reality, learning that supports job performance is often a combination of both. It is important to establish the relative emphasis on one or the other because this has implications for the design and content of learning activities.

Processes

The processes by which people learn relate to the way learning takes place rather than its outcomes. Some writers and trainers prefer to use expressions such as 'approaches to learning' or 'methods of learning' to indicate the existence of options as to how a person might be stimulated to learn, but these do not have exactly the same meaning as the word 'process', which in the context of learning is something internal to the person.

The simple truth is, we just do not yet know enough about the way in which the mind works to be sure about the internal processes affecting changes in memory, perception, creativity and the analytical powers that lead to learning, although people such as Susan Greenfield (1997) and William Calvin (1996) are engaged in researching this fascinating area.

Most managers and development practitioners cannot realistically be expected to operate at the forefront of developments in our knowledge of the mind. For them, the fundamental process that leads to a person learning is experience and making sense of that experience. The more vivid and extensive it is, the greater likelihood there will be of some kind of learning taking place. Differences in methods and approaches relate to differences in the nature of these experiences, which in turn impact on the extent and nature of the learning that takes place.

IMPLICATIONS FOR DEVELOPMENT AND TRAINING

If learning is based on and follows from experience, then it seems clear that learning will be influenced by a person's exposure to different situations. Learning outcomes leading to increased capabilities will, therefore, reflect the nature, variability and intensity of what people are required to do and the opportunities that they have to experience new and different situations.

Whatever managers and trainers do or do not do, learning will continue to occur, because people are human and learning is one of the defining characteristics of what it means to be human. Learning *at* work is often seen as learning *for* work, and there is a strong expectation that part of what people learn will be related to and support current and future work requirements. For many, the higher the proportion of learning that is work related, the more a person's capability at work is increased. We believe that learning outside of work can also enhance work performance. So, learning – both inside and outside work, both relevant to narrow work agendas and serving a wider agenda – must be seen as the fundamental objective of any organization's training and development policy.

Achieving learning implies getting a great many things right. It does not necessarily mean that a newly acquired capability is translated into performance. It is a basic misconception to believe that learning will result in better performance. How to motivate someone who has successfully learned something of value is also important, as is creating the organizational circumstances in which they are able to perform and use their new learning.

There is, unfortunately, no consistency in the definitions of training and development. 'Training' can still be used to describe learning that takes many years to complete, and development can include learning experiences that have a powerful effect but are over relatively quickly. The simple rule is, know what you mean, explain to others what you mean and agree on an acceptable compromise where differences in terminology and understanding exist!

It might be useful for those who are searching for a helpful distinction to consider the following:

▌ Training involves preparing someone to do a job.

▌ Development involves preparing someone to be something.

ACTIVITY 4.2

Make your own sense of the two definitions above. Ask your colleagues for their opinion. What does 'being something' mean? Can you give examples of behaviours associated with doing a job that differ from other types of behaviours related to being a particular kind of person?

It is generally accepted that the central process in training is learning. It has been suggested that the experience of training 'will' modify the behaviour of participating employees. This position represents what might be described as the prevailing orthodoxy about the relationship between learning and training.

Unfortunately, it is wrong on two counts:

▌ Learning is the intended outcome of training, but by no stretch of the imagination could it be said that learning always occurs in the development process. Boredom and frustration are often as much a part of the experience of training as learning something new. A simple explanation for this is that very often a training programme involves participants who are there for the wrong reasons. They either already possess the capabilities that are the intended outcomes of the programme, or find the whole 'learning experience' (or parts of it) a major turn-off, and switch their thinking to neutral.

▌ The false assumption that training will inevitably result in performance improvement or behavioural change is faced with a further challenge: when learning does take place, it may not result in behavioural change. The experience of many people is that job performance does not change as a consequence of the job-holder attending a training course. Even where learning has taken place, there are several reasons why evidence for it is absent. It is possible that the person does not know how to apply any acquired learning to his or her specific job, or the new learning may not relate to that person's current job, or it may be that the job environment is hostile to 'new ways of doing things', or the person may simply not want to use his or her new capabilities.

There is a wealth of experience about training and development, which could and should be used to reconstruct the body of theory that is so important to successful learning. What managers of the learning process have to do is to capture the accumulated experiences for themselves and begin to share this learning about learning, which is very important for an organization's HRD strategy. Argyris (1991) talked about the difference between what people 'espoused' and what they actually did. He gives an example of consultants reviewing their interactions with clients and their inability to learn from either the consultancy or the reflection process.

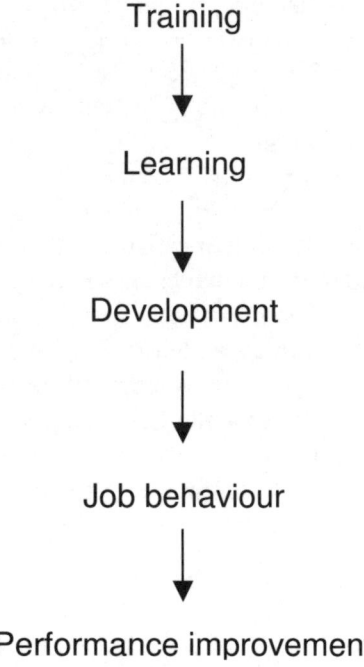

Figure 4.1   *The process of improving performance*

ACTIVITY 4.3 LINKING LEARNING, DEVELOPMENT AND TRAINING

Consider the following:

■ Is learning an inevitable outcome of any training experience? If not, why not? What are your experiences?

■ If learning does occur as a result of training, to what extent is what is learned consistent with the intended and the planned learning outcomes? If the outcomes are not consistent with those intended, what might explain the discrepancy?

■ How can learning be measured? If it is possible, how can it be done? If it is not subject to measurement in conventional ways, how else might this be achieved?

■ Is there a difference between your 'espoused' theory about developing staff and your theories in use? How could you find out? (See Activity 7.2, page 157.)

■ Can learning occur despite rather than because of training? If so, what accounts for learning that is not linked to training?

Bass and Vaughan (1966) defined training as 'the management of learning', and in so doing highlighted the relevance of how learning is managed to the choice of approaches or methods, and to the outcomes of planned learning.

At one level, this conceptualization of training suggests that its success – that is, training that results in the intended outcomes being largely achieved – is a function of the quality of its management. Poorly managed training is unlikely to have the desired learning outcomes because certain key requirements will have either not been identified or not been built into the training/development process. Conversely, where training opportunities are professionally managed and reflect 'good practice', there is a greater likelihood that learning will take place.

MANAGING LEARNING

The key to understanding the difference between learning that occurs naturally and spontaneously, and that which has a particular rationale and intent, is whether the process is managed, be this by specialists, line managers or individuals.

Before we consider in more detail the different ways people can learn and the psychological processes that underpin these, it is worth emphasizing that many examples of training have been, and continue to be, based upon an inadequate and partial understanding of the learning process and its management.

If this is the case, and managers continue to feel uneasy about the value of training, it is little wonder that despite recent initiatives and schemes to promote training and development at work, there is still considerable concern and doubt expressed about the long-term impact such measures will have on employee competences and capabilities.

People can learn in different ways:

- They can be taught: a narrow range of stimuli under the control of the teacher.

- They can be instructed: this is used for physical rather than cognitive skills, and often involves demonstration with supporting explanations.

- They can have an experience. This is often seen as necessary to provide fresh stimulation for continuing learning. The experience can be planned or random.

- People learn from the well-known process of trial and error, and trial and success: through experimentation with various responses, the person learns the one(s) that seem to be most appropriate to the situation.

- Learning can be based on observation and perception; it involves the process of making sense of the world we live in, through 'seeing' it and giving meanings to what is 'seen'.

- Learning can be an individual activity or can involve dialogue and participation with others.

- Learning can follow thinking and reflecting: this involves using cognitive powers, such as reasoning and analysing, to make sense of things that we do or are required to do.

As learning can be neither observed nor measured, it is difficult to relate specific examples of learning to particular methods. In other words, we cannot isolate the contribution one method of learning makes to a discrete 'element of behaviour'. It is reasonable to assume that learning job-related capabilities involves several different methods, in combination or sequence, that have a complementary and cumulative effect. Eitington (2001) lists over 200 different training and learning methods, so the choice is virtually endless!

Other factors that influence the choice and mix of learning methods include:

■ the experience and skills of the developer/trainer/instructor;

■ learner preferences;

■ facilities and resources, including time, location of learning, existing capabilities and familiarity with learning process, technology;

■ the nature of what is to be learned: whether this is simple or complex, abstract or applied, and so on.

Different methods and approaches have their distinctive characteristics and limitations, in addition to adherents and supporters. In deciding which to use, the question to consider is not which is the 'best' in any absolute sense, but which one(s) are appropriate and relevant to any given situation (Mumford, 1997; Eitington, 2001).

ACTIVITY 4.4 CHECKING YOUR OWN LEARNING EXPERIENCES

In order to explore the different ways people can learn, try this simple exercise:

1. Identify six different competences you have learned in the past five years, eg learning to drive, using a computer, working in teams, making decisions, or any others of the same order.

2. For each competence acquired, write down on a separate sheet the part played by:

- being taught;
- being instructed;
- experience;
- trial and error/success;
- observation and perception;
- thinking/reflecting.

3. Compare what you have written on each of the six sheets. Look for any pattern in the use of different learning methods. If one or more appears, try to establish what this might mean about how you have learned. Are there any general statements about your learning that you would feel justified in making?

4. Ask your staff or colleagues to participate in the same exercise. Compare the results and discuss their implications for how work-related learning might be improved.

PROBLEMS WITH LEARNING

Learning is sometimes perceived as a successful and rewarding experience. However, it is often frustrating. People can spend time 'learning' but frequently feel that they have learned nothing. What explains these quite different reactions? Rarely are the reasons for success and failure in learning made explicit. Yet without the ability to distinguish the circumstances that result in relative success or failure, trying to improve the learning process becomes very much a hit-and-miss affair. Establishing the reasons for people failing to learn, despite the political and personal implications of this, is a necessary part of any learning activity. This is integral to learning how to learn. The following represent some of the more frequently experienced problems with learning:

▋ Learners are uncertain about what new behaviours they are supposed to be learning. This can sometimes be compounded by confusion and contradiction over intended outcomes. There is also the problem of who decides on the intended outcome: the learner or the trainer/developer?

■   A lack of performance may be confused with a lack of ability and therefore a need for learning. Very often the behaviours are not totally absent; indeed, they may exist in well-developed forms. The problem in such cases is the reluctance or refusal to use what has already been learned. In these circumstances, a quite different learning requirement exists: learning to use existing capabilities (or being allowed or encouraged to use them). This results in people being assumed to have a learning deficiency, and being sent on a training programme, the objective of which is to give them the chance to learn something they already have or know. This is a familiar and major diagnostic error.

The last point is related to an interesting characteristic of learning: it can't be seen or observed to be taking place. Often, an individual might not even be aware that he or she has learned. Even in a laboratory, learning can only be inferred from observations of an individual's behaviour in relation to specific activities or contexts. This means that learning may have taken place, in the sense that new behaviours have been acquired, but until they are used and tested, certain assumptions – not always proven valid – have to be made about learning having occurred.

■   Learning presupposes relatively permanent changes in behaviour, or the capacity to behave in certain ways. Over time, these behaviours can become reinforced and sharpened by use and practice, or they can become diluted and, in extreme cases, effectively lost to the person. In a work context, few of the behaviours are instinctive or naturally recurring, and if they are used infrequently, and are inherently difficult, the chances are that over time, a person will lose the capacity to perform to required standards.

■   'Learners' sometimes do not want to learn. There are many reasons for this, and without the desire or motivation to learn, failure is predictable. Having positive reasons to learn something is essential for successful learning. The existence of motivators cannot be taken for granted.

■   Learners become disillusioned with the apparent lack of progress and give up. The ability to persevere with learning in the face of frustration, fatigue and self-doubt is a very important requirement. Without it, people simply stop actively participating in the learning process because they fail to recognize that successful learning does take time. Successful learning often depends on people solving problems that inhibit progress. These are features of learning that are often forgotten or not fully understood.

ACTIVITY 4.5 SOLVING LEARNING PROBLEMS

Determined learners and skilful facilitators find ways of overcoming the difficulties and problems outlined above. The need to develop strategies that minimize the effect of these on the learning process cannot be stressed enough. This short exercise is designed to help with the task.

1. Identify any learning problems that you have experienced.

2. In relation to a particular learning experience – you may want to select a different one for each problem on the list, if this is helpful – try to remember how the problem arose. Were there any obvious causes or circumstances that could explain it?

3. Was any action taken at the time to try to solve the problems? If so, by whom? How effective were the solutions?

4. Knowing what you now know about learning, how would you tackle the same problems if they arose again?

To make the exercise even more useful, you may want to discuss these questions with colleagues.

TRIGGERS FOR LEARNING

One of the most important influences on the relative success or failure of any learning is the motivational state of the learner. A person's internal physical and psychological state at any given time influences their motivation, which, consequently, is not a static issue: it changes in relation to time of day and external stimuli, etc. Learning depends for its success on the person involved being ready or motivated to learn and maintaining that motivation during any learning event.

The following represent some of the better-known influences on a person's motivation to learn:

▋ *The innate capacity to learn* varies between people and is affected by, among other things, age and personal circumstances. Successful learning often presupposes an existing standard or level upon which further and often more demanding learning is based. The capacity to learn is therefore a function of innate abilities and existing capabilities. Learning objectives become meaningful only if they reflect people's capacity to learn. People are motivated to learn only if there is some feeling that they *can* learn.

▋ *The fear of failing* is often associated with psychologically damaging experiences. Few of us have avoided experiences that have left lasting memories of frustration, anger, failure and, in extreme cases, humiliation. The fear of failing to learn leads people to avoid any learning opportunities that are perceived to be potentially threatening. Those for whom learning is associated with liberating, stimulating and rewarding experiences are, quite naturally, likely to have a positive and committed attitude to further opportunities to learn. However, failing can be a useful learning opportunity if handled positively (Argyris, 1991). As Confucius said, 'Our greatest glory is not in never failing, but in rising every time we fall' (Confucius, 2003: 58).

▋ *The anticipated outcomes of learning.* Successful learning of new skills and competences, leading to enhanced job satisfaction, more opportunities to do different work, and/or increased pay or promotion, will obviously create a different motivational state from that which results in perceived negative and threatening outcomes.

▋ *The behaviour of the people structuring and delivering the learning process.* Learning in the context of education, training and development is often associated with a teacher, a trainer or mentor. The skills, approaches and general behaviour of these people have an important effect on the individual's psychological predisposition to learn, in addition to the degree of continuing commitment to the learning process. Given that learning often occurs over a period of time, during which misunderstandings, apparent failures to learn and uncertainties over both process and outcomes can be experienced, the ability of the developer to create a supportive and psychologically safe learning environment is critical.

THE SCIENCE OF LEARNING

Early scientific attempts to understand the learning process in terms of its cognitive and behavioural dimensions are linked to two, quite distinct, theoretical positions:

Classical conditioning

In Pavlov's (1927) experiments with dogs, he used a bell to elicit salivation, initially in conjunction with an unconditioned stimulus – food – and then on its own. The learning was based on the dogs' ability to link the sound of a bell with food, which stimulated an unconditioned or natural response, ie salivation.

What is not learned in classical conditioning is the behavioural response, which can be demonstrated. The emphasis is on the ability to stimulate such responses by focusing on the learning of non-natural stimuli, represented by the *stimulus → response* model of learning.

Instrumental or operant conditioning

Skinner (1953) viewed learning as a much more active process than implied in classical conditioning. Instrumental conditioning is more relevant as an explanatory model of human learning because it emphasizes the learning of behaviours that are not instinctive and automatic, but socially and environmentally based. This model attaches considerable importance to the consequences of behaviour rather than antecedents – that is, whether certain kinds of behaviour result in other things happening. It recognizes the active and instrumental role of the learner in learning behaviours that relate to his or her existence in a particular environment. Behaviour cannot be seen simply to follow the existence or application of stimuli. Rather, it reflects the individual's own complex motivational structure, and the efforts of any external influence on the person's perception of his or her world. Instrumental conditioning can be represented as a process of learning based on a *stimulus → response → reinforcement* relationship, where behaviour is shaped and maintained by its consequences.

If human learning is based on the instrumental conditioning model, then much of its success or failure can be related to the way in which reinforcements are used to condition behaviour. Skinner identified three broad categories of reinforcement:

1. *Positive reinforcers*. These strengthen behaviours that lead to their use or application – for example, giving rewards, either symbolic (praise) or material (more pay, better work).

2. *Negative reinforcers*. These strengthen behaviours that result in their removal or avoidance. For example, the removal of threats or the fear of failure can help to create a situation in which learners are prepared to take risks and make mistakes to facilitate their own learning.

3. *Punishers*. These weaken behaviour that results from their use. For example, the threat or application of punitive sanctions can have the effect of inhibiting or suppressing certain kinds of behaviour that are seen as interfering with the learning process.

Skinner's work indicated that it was much more effective to reinforce desired behaviour than to punish undesired behaviour. There seem to be two reasons for this:

▋ Human beings react emotionally to punishment, and this often freezes the capacity for subsequent learning.

▋ Punishment specifies what not to do, but is necessarily unspecific about what is the desired behaviour.

The practical implications of this are that if you want to train using instrumental conditioning, then focus on rewarding desired behaviours.

Emphasizing the consequences of behaviour and the use of appropriate reinforcement mechanisms in shaping the process and effectiveness of human learning provides managers and developers with a theoretical and practical framework for organizing and structuring the learning process. That such a framework is necessary cannot be in doubt, and it may well be the case that many training programmes are conceived, implemented and evaluated in the absence of any significant understanding of the scientific basis of learning. If this is so, then it represents a particularly worrying feature of planned learning.

While these classical theories of motivation and learning are important, some more recent theory on learning has been emerging. Much work has been undertaken on the situated nature of learning (Lave and Wenger, 1991; Joy-Matthews, 2003). David Stein, discussing the concept of situated learning and adults, says:

A situated learning experience has four major premises guiding the development of classroom activities (Anderson, Reder, and Simon 1996; Wilson, 1993): (1) learning is grounded in the actions of everyday situations; (2) knowledge is acquired situationally and transfers only to similar situations; (3) learning is the result of a social process encompassing ways of thinking, perceiving, problem solving, and interacting in addition to declarative and procedural knowledge; and (4) learning is not separated from the world of action but exists in robust, complex, social environments made up of actors, actions, and situation. (Stein, 1998: 1)

Stein (1998: 1) continues by suggesting that these 'four premises differentiate situated learning from other experiential forms of acquiring knowledge. In situated learning, students learn content through activities rather than acquiring information in discrete packages, organized by instructors.' The four main premises are content, context, community of practice, and participation.

This has considerable implications for course design and the whole process of training and development. Building on their work on situated learning (Lave and Wenger, 1991), these authors went on to identify the concept of 'legitimate peripheral participation' (LPP). Atherton (2000: 1) proposes:

It is *legitimate* because all parties accept the position of 'unqualified' people as potential members of the 'community of practice'.

Peripheral because they hang around on the edge of the important stuff, do the peripheral jobs, and gradually get entrusted with the more important ones.

Participation because it is through *doing* knowledge that they acquire it. Knowledge is *situated* within the practices of the community of practice, rather than something which exists 'out there' in books.

Another key area that Lave and Wenger (1991) discuss is that of the 'community of practice' (COP), which they define as follows:

It [COP] does imply participation in an activity system about which participants share understandings concerning what they are doing and what that means in their lives and for their communities. . . A community of practice is a set of relations among persons, activity, and world, over time and in relation with other tangential and overlapping communities of practice. (Lave and Wenger, 1991: 98)

This implies that the COP is continually changing as members become more established and new members join, and as the area of their concerns grows or changes. This change in position and role has significance for learners in the community.

While it is easy to write about 'the COP' in an abstract sense, in reality it is a somewhat ephemeral entity. The community will be composed of different people at different times, the interests of the COP will change over time and the degree of peripherality of its members will also change.

It has been suggested that it is not necessary for the members of the community to be co-present, clearly defined or identifiable or that there should be obvious boundaries to the group, but Lave and Wenger (1991) say that community implies 'participation in an activity system about which participants share understandings concerning what they are doing and what that means in their lives and for their communities'. For them, the concept of community that underpins LPP and 'hence "knowledge" and its "location" in the lived-in world, is both crucial and subtle' (Lave and Wenger, 1991: 98). Building on his earlier work with Jean Lave, Wenger (1998: 3) gives a description of community of practice as 'a social construct that places learning in the context of our lived experience of participation in the world'.

The unequal power relationships within a COP need to be given some consideration. This links with Roth's (2000) comments on more senior members of a university department giving encouragement to junior members and students to engage in the process of research rather than merely using them for the tasks no one else wants to do.

It seems clear to us that the COP has a collective responsibility towards the learning of all its members and potential members. Heaney (1995: 2) says, 'Learning is an individual's ongoing negotiation with communities of practice which ultimately gives definition to both self and that practice. In this framework, all learning is apprenticeship.' Heaney suggests that there is 'conflict across borders, especially where communities of practice lay claim to the same land as, for example, in the intersection of training and adult education'. He also suggests that there is 'conflict within communities of practice as various constituencies compete on an unequal field for power' (Heaney, 1995: 3). So, while the concept of community is useful, it is also problematic.

Hildreth (2000: 2) provides an interesting summary of COPs. Using the literature, he 'extracted some key points' and 'some other characteristics which would be present to a greater or lesser degree' in COPs:

▊ Common language: the group has some sort of language of its own, eg jargon.

▊ Shared background: the members have some sort of shared background or knowledge.

▊ Common purpose: the group has some sort of common purpose that gives it an internal impetus.

▊ Creation of new knowledge: through the work of the group and the interaction of the members, some new knowledge will be created for those members.

▊ Dynamism: this relates to the social distribution of the knowledge in the group.

▊ Evolution: there is some sort of development in the group.

▊ There is more than simply interaction.

▊ Unofficial nature: in many cases a community of practice is not set up, but evolves.

▊ Voluntary nature: it can often be found that membership is voluntary.

▊ Narration: swapping war (*sic*) stories is seen by many as a key way in which members share domain knowledge.

▊ Legitimate peripheral participation (LPP).

▊ Informal nature: the group is often informal, ie there is no hierarchy.

▊ Fluidity: newcomers arrive and old-timers leave.

▊ Similar jobs: in an organization there will be individuals doing similar jobs.

A key point is that you cannot set up a community of practice. Some groups will function as one and others won't; it depends on the members (Hildreth, 2000: 2).

In a recent piece of research, HRM and HRD students were asked, 'How have you become the learner you are today?' (Joy-Matthews, 2003). The analysis of the research produced five key categories for defining their learning:

▊ *The mechanics of learning*: practical examples, illustrations; factual and clear subject matter; case studies and examples; novelty; reality;

repetition; reflections; project work; discussions and debates; watching, observing and reflecting back; relating academic and practical issues were all seen as important in the learning process.

▋ *People*: having inspirational teachers, coaches and mentors was highlighted as particularly important. Support, or lack of it, from partners, parents, friends and colleagues also played a major part in people's learning.

▋ *Motivation*: both intrinsic and extrinsic motivation was highlighted, although by far the most influential category was 'the student's own responsibility'.

▋ *Participation*: being actively engaged in the learning process and having a community within which to learn were highlighted as critical to the learning process.

▋ *Fun*: all the students mentioned that having fun while learning was important and that when the learning process was boring, they tended to switch off.

Each of the categories could be viewed as having both positive and negative facets. It all depended on who the learner was. This poses a challenge for trainers and developers: How do we include items and methods that will have maximum appeal?

ACTIVITY 4.6 HOW HAVE YOU BECOME THE LEARNER YOU ARE TODAY?

Think about what has shaped you as a learner. Record your thoughts: you could use a mind map, a tape recorder or a sheet of paper or. . .

Then reflect on your thoughts. Are there any key categories that jump out at you? What has helped or hindered your learning?

Can you make improvements to your learning process for the future?

In what ways does this affect the way you work as a trainer, developer or manager?

THE LEARNING CYCLE

The idea that learning is a circular process with a distinctive number of stages and activities is attributed to Kolb (1984). His work has been particularly influential with contemporary trainers and academics, who either implicitly or explicitly incorporate his ideas in their own activities and writings (Honey, 1990).

The concept of a learning cycle is based on the belief that there are four critical behaviours that learners themselves need to engage in, behaviours that are not the intended outcome of any particular learning event or activity. In other words, for learning to take place – or, more precisely, for the learning process to be more effective – certain activities must be built into the learning process. These represent examples of what Argyris and Schön (1978) call deutero-learning, or learning how to learn.

Kolb's work provides a persuasive and influential answer to a question that many people have asked at one time or another: 'What does the act of learning involve me, as the learner, in doing?' It also provides the developer, manager or other persons involved in managing other people's learning with a methodology that can be used to support learning covering a wide variety of situations and participants.

Figure 4.2 represents a simplified version of the Kolb learning cycle.

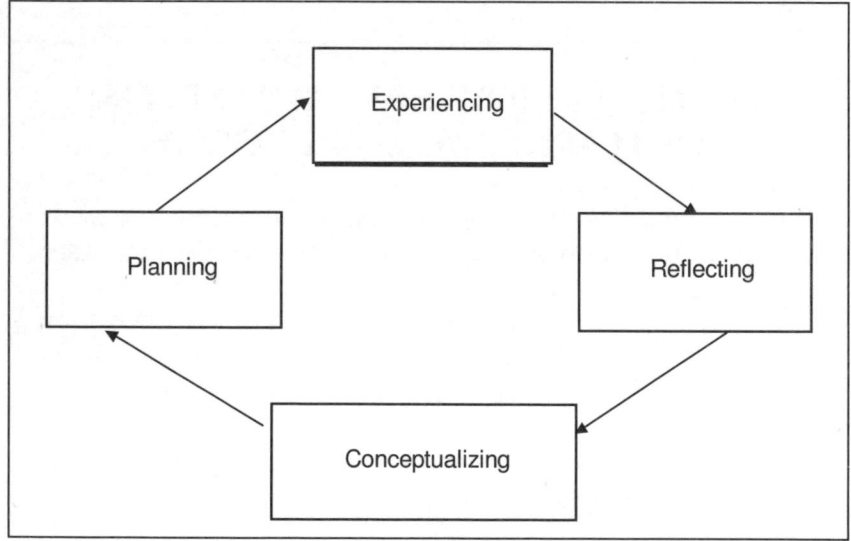

Figure 4.2   *The learning cycle (after Kolb, Rubin and MacIntyre, 1984)*

Using the Kolb learning cycle

Each stage requires the learner to engage actively in a particular type of behaviour that relates to the cycle's four stages. Knowing of them and of their significance is not in itself sufficient: the learner must carry out the activities specified.

It is the learner (not the developer/trainer) who needs to engage in these four activities, which can be summarized as:

▊ experiencing;

▊ reflecting;

▊ conceptualizing;

▊ planning and testing out.

The role of the developer/trainer should be to help the learner learn how to carry out these activities so that they become part of the individual's internalized, learned behaviours, available for use in any future learning situation.

The learning cycle usually takes as its starting point the existence of some activity or experience that is relevant to a person's work or non-work life and that provides the material and opportunity to reflect, conceptualize, plan and test out. Accordingly, it sees learning as being founded on some initial experience or activity, which can then be subject to certain cognitive processes to help make sense of the experience. The cycle requires people to consider what they intend to do the same, differently or better, or perhaps not do, the next time they are required to undertake certain tasks. It reinforces learning by linking the act of doing with thinking about doing and thus links to Argyris and Schön (1978) and their concept of deutero-learning, or learning how to learn.

Not all learners use all four stages, which is why some people never seem to learn from their experiences!

LEARNING STYLES

Following on from the work of Kolb, Honey and Mumford (1992) developed a method for categorizing people's learning styles. Using a learning styles questionnaire, they discovered that people fell primarily into one of four styles:

∎ activists, who learn by being involved in tasks such as teamwork exercises, business simulations and work itself;

∎ reflectors, who learn by reviewing what has happened by listening and observing;

∎ theorists, who learn by thinking about concepts and theories;

∎ pragmatists, who learn when they can see a link between new information and reality.

These four styles map directly onto the four phases of the learning cycle. Honey and Mumford used their questionnaire with a large number of people and were able to work out norms. They also found that most people had a dominant learning style and secondary styles.

For a developer or trainer, it helps to know what the preferred learning styles of participants are in order to design events that will appeal to all and that will extend the range of use of styles for all participants. For a manager and learner, it is also useful to know how you and your colleagues learn best; it often accounts for differences in perceptions and ability to absorb new information or demonstrate skills.

ACTIVITY 4.7

If you have not used the Honey and Mumford (1992) learning styles questionnaire, you might like to; it is helpful to see where you have strengths and where you might choose to develop.

SELF-MANAGED LEARNING

Recently there has been considerable emphasis placed on managing one's own learning. There has been a move away from the training directory with the same courses on offer year in and year out and with participants being nominated often without any discussion. Nowadays it is much more likely that people will identify their own learning requirements and find ways of meeting these. This might include a formal course, job rotation, secondments, open learning packages, study via the Internet, or coaching or mentoring.

Learners can go at their own pace and learn in their own time and manner. They may be part of a learning set who meet regularly to review progress and offer encouragement and triggers to learning; and possibly solutions to learning blocks. What the learners 'study' may be directly related to work or completely separate. Some organizations have given workers an amount of money that can be spent on learning anything. The idea is that by encouraging them to learn in one area, they will be more likely to learn work-related items later on. Sheffield Hallam University has a scheme whereby staff in the Facilities Directorate can study anything. Skills learned have ranged from decoupage to swimming, and an increase in self-esteem has been seen. The university also has a scheme where staff can take places on existing courses even if these are not directly related to current job role. Again this has resulted in increased self-esteem and, later, development opportunities (Jumpstart and Headstart). These employee development schemes are receiving wider recognition by employers, including hard-nosed private-sector organizations, notably motor manufacturers such as Rover and Ford.

Many people do not find it particularly helpful to have a highly structured approach to their development. They find the thought of having to construct a learning contract and take responsibility for their own learning unappealing. Other people find it hard to learn from the experiences that they have.

Megginson's (1994) work on planned and emergent learning helps to move this process on. He offers a self-report questionnaire (Figure 4.3) that enables individuals to determine into which of four categories they fit. They can then identify actions they may wish to take to develop their own learning.

ACTIVITY 4.8

You might like to use Megginson's questionnaire and explore your planned and emergent styles. What actions will you take as a result of this insight about your learning?

LIFELONG LEARNING

In February 1998 the British Government published a Green Paper on lifelong learning. The concept is that individuals will 'continually seek

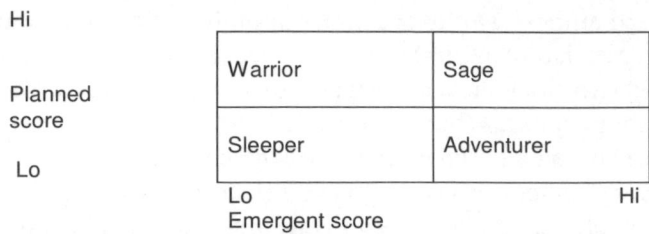

Warrior	Sage
Sleeper	Adventurer

Hi

Planned
score

Lo

Lo   Hi
Emergent score

Learning Strategies Questionnaire

This questionnaire is used with permission of the author

Score each question in terms of your agreement with the statement:

6 if you think it is always true / you totally agree
5 if you think it is usually true / you usually agree
4 if you think it is often true / you often agree
3 if you think it is sometimes true / you sometimes agree
2 if you think it is occasionally true / you occasionally agree
1 if you think it is seldom true / you seldom agree
0 if you think it is never true / you never agree

1		Writing down appraisals of my work performance is an important basis for my development
2		For me, learning is a planned process of setting goals, achieving them and setting new goals
3		In conversation with others I often come to new understandings of what I have learned
4		I regularly prepare a learning contract, development agreement or continuous professional development statement outlining my plans
5		It is important for me to add to/change my learning plans frequently in the light of new information
6		I set goals for my own learning
7		In order to learn from experience I reflect frequently upon what happens to me
8		I set targets for my development
9		It is important to be open to experience; then learning will come
10		I use a learning contract, development agreement or continuous professional development statement regularly to focus on my progress in developing
11		Most of my learning emerges unexpectedly from things that happen
12		You can't plan significant learning

Planned and emergent categories are given at the end of the chapter (page 114)

Figure 4.3   *Megginson's four categories*

to acquire new skills and update old ones with the active help of the state and employers' (MacLachan, 1998: 43). There was a time when the United Kingdom's national training provision was dominated by three key stakeholders: the government, the education system and the employers. To these they are now adding the individual.

While this paper has not received unconditional acclaim, its core proposition is that viewing one's whole life as an opportunity for learning and development opens avenues for change both within the individual and for the individual's career choices. Thought is being given to encouraging 'everyone to invest more in human capital and to recognise that we are moving towards a knowledge-based economy'; it is not appropriate to train people for jobs that no longer exist (David Blunkett, quoted in MacLachan, 1998).

Acknowledging that people start learning in the cradle and continue their learning until they die will help to avoid ageism. One of us recently has had the salutary experience of discovering that they were too old to undertake one piece of training and too young to join the University of the Third Age, and would have loved to do both!

CONTINUOUS PROFESSIONAL DEVELOPMENT

Many professions have a continuous professional development (CPD) scheme that aims to encourage individuals to update their skills rather than rely solely on those they gained when they first qualified. The Chartered Institute of Personnel and Development (CIPD) has such a scheme and provides advice that helps individuals to structure their learning opportunities and reflections. Using the planned and emergent framework provided by Megginson and Whitaker (2003) might help to make the CPD process more readily available to more individuals. It might also help trainers, developers and managers to work with staff on their development. The whole issue of CPD is covered more fully in Chapter 6.

CASE STUDY 4.1 HOW I BECAME THE LEARNER I AM TODAY

One of us conducted a piece of research with some HRD and HRM students and managers (Joy-Matthews, 2003). It was felt to be important to ask an open question in order to elicit from the participants their own views about learning without contaminating their responses with the researcher's own views. So the question 'How I became the learner I am today' was posed. The results were transcribed and analysed. You might like to write your own case study of how you have become the learner you are today. Go back as far as you like, or focus on recent events. Look at work and other parts of your life. What facilitates learning for you? What makes learning hard or even impossible? What conclusions can you draw from your case study? E-mail Jennifer Joy-Matthews (joymatthews@supanet.com) if you would like to know the key categories from her research.

SUMMARY

The intention of this chapter is to provide an introduction to the theoretical basis of learning in a way that supports practical improvements in training and development. Many of the issues covered might, at first appearance, seem to be concerned with alternative ways of learning. On reflection, the reader will recognize that they complement each other.

Knowing what we are doing and why presupposes some theoretical understanding of how people learn, and this is equally applicable to the person learning and to those facilitating this process. Its absence can only limit progress in the search for ways to make learning more effective.

We conclude with Table 4.1, showing some of the key learning concepts. You might like to see with which of them you can identify.

Planned and emergent learning categories for Activity 4.8

Statements are as follows:

Planned   1, 2, 4, 6, 8, 10
Emergent   3, 5, 7, 9, 11, 12

Table 4.1 *Learning theories and definitions*

Year	Author	Theory/Definition/Concept	Uses
1926	Piaget	Four major stages of intellectual growth in children: birth to 2: sensori-motor period 2–7: pre-operational thought 7–11: concrete operations 11–15: formal operations	Explains where we as adults have come from and where we might have become stuck
1927	Pavlov	Conditioned reflexes	Helps us to understand why we and others behave as we do
1929	Whitehead	Inert knowledge	Problem-solving, technology
1932	Thorndike	Law of effect: rewarded action is likely to be repeated	Explains why praise works
1950	Erikson	Psychosocial model	Career development Care of self and others
1953	Skinner	Operant conditioning	Explains why praise works
1955	Kelly	Personal construct theory	Aids our understanding of why we all behave differently and value different things
1956	Bloom *et al*	Taxonomy of cognitive skills: knowledge comprehension application analysis synthesis evaluation	Useful for identifying training needs Design Evaluation
1962	Fitts	Stages of skills acquisition: cognitive associative autonomous	Evaluation of skills development

Table 4.1   *(Continued)*

Year	Author	Theory/Definition/Concept	Uses
1963	Gardner	Self-renewal	Self-development
1963	Harrison	Defences – cannot increase learning by destroying the defences that block it	Need to respect learners' defence mechanisms and understand the purpose they serve
1965	Revans	Action learning sets System beta Survey, hypothesis, experiment, audit, review	Great for solving problems Networking Understanding the learning process
1968	Neugarten	'Major punctuation marks in the adult life' are family, work and social statuses	Life lines Career development
1968	Perry	Continuum of intellectual and ethical development: basic dualism to affirmation of identity	Good for assessing where we or others are in our development
1969	Rogers	Student-centred learning	Explains why tutors should become facilitators in an ever-changing world
1969	Lippitt	Organization renewal (start of the learning company approach)	Organization development
1970	de Bono	Lateral thinking	Problem-solving Creativity
1970	Gagné	Classification of learning: general response to stimulus, chaining responses, combining responses to solve problems	Problem-solving
1972	Bateson	Deutero-learning	Learning to learn
1976	Flavell	Meta-cognition, self-regulated learning	Mathematics
1977	Mezirow	'Personal transformation'	Self-development
1978	Argyris and Schön	Single-loop learning – the detection and correction of deviance from normal performance	Helps us to think through which problem we 'should' be solving

Table 4.1   *(Continued)*

Year	Author	Theory/Definition/Concept	Uses
		Double-loop learning – questioning of the norms that define effective performance	
1978	Ribeaux and Poppleton	'A process within the organism which results in the capacity for changed performance which can be related to experience rather than maturation'	Neat definition that leads us away from age towards experience
1980	Binsted	Lancaster Model – three forms of learning: receipt of input/generation of output; discovery (action and feedback); reflection (conceptualizing and hypothesizing)	Design and delivery of training and/or development; could also be used for designing evaluation
1980	Knowles	Andragogy is the model for adult learning: concept of the learner role of learner's experience readiness to learn orientation to learning	Thinking through how managers and trainers/developers offer learning opportunities critiquing our own performance
1981	Straangard	Model of change: unconscious incompetence conscious incompetence conscious competence unconscious competence	Explains the transitions that we go through during the learning process and why it is so often difficult to explain to a novice how to do something that we are really familiar with!
1982	Boyatzis	Competence: an underlying characteristic of a person that results in effective and/ or superior performance in a job	Training needs analysis Design and delivery Evaluation Accreditation

Table 4.1   *(Continued)*

Year	Author	Theory/Definition/Concept	Uses
1983	Burgoyne and Hodgson	Managers' level of learning: level 1: take in factual information level 2: occurs at an unconscious or tacit level level 3: reflect on conception of the world – how it is and how they can change it	Career development
1984	Kolb, Rubin and MacIntyre	Learning cycle: concrete experience, reflective observation, abstract conceptualization, active experimentation	Self-knowledge Design of learning events to ensure variety
1985	Gardner	Distinction between 'know-how' (tacit knowledge of how to execute something) and 'know-that' (propositional knowledge about how something is done)	Training needs analysis Design and delivery Evaluation
1986	Daloz	A journey from the familiar through 'confusion, adventure, great highs and lows, struggle, uncertainty . . . towards a new world' in which 'nothing is different, yet all is transformed'; 'its meaning has profoundly changed'	Career development Self-development
1986	Dreyfus, Dreyfus and Athanasion	Stage model of skills acquisition: stage 1: the novice stage 2: the advanced beginner stage 3: competent stage 4: proficient stage 5: expert	Assessment Evaluation
1988	Mumford	Barriers to learning: perceptual, cultural, emotional, motivational, cognitive, intellectual,	Design and delivery Coaching Redesign of learning events

Table 4.1 *(Continued)*

Year	Author	Theory/Definition/Concept	Uses
		expressive, situational, physical, specific environment	
1988	Pedler	Quantitative changes: disintegration of old phase leads to discontinuous 'step-jump' to a new phase = transformation: each new phase is more complex, integrating what has gone before	Sequencing learning
1989	Brown, Collins and Duguid	Reflexive contexts	All learners
1989	Brown, Collins and Duguid	Situated cognition	Classroom practice
1989	Jalali	Cross-cultural differences in learning styles: compared Afro-, Chinese-, Greek- and Mexican-Americans in schools in the United States	Understanding diversity
1990	Senge	'Learning organizations are possible because, deep down, we are all learners. No one has to teach an infant to learn. . . Learning organizations are possible because not only is it our nature to learn but we love to learn.'	Organization development
1991	Lave and Wenger	Situated learning and legitimate peripheral participation	Understanding learning communities
1991	Hodgetts	Learning curve: S-shaped – proficiency over time	When to reinforce learning
1992	Honey and Mumford	Learning styles: activists, reflectors, theorists, pragmatists	Self-knowledge Design and delivery of learning

Table 4.1   *(Continued)*

Year	Author	Theory/Definition/Concept	Uses
1992	Snell	Learning from distress	Experiential learning
1994	Megginson	Planned and emergent learning framework: sleeper, adventurer, warrior, sage	Self-development Continuous development
1996	Goleman	Emotional intelligence	All learners
1996	Pedler and Aspinwall	Four types of learning: knowledge skills, abilities; competences; personal development; collaborative inquiry	Organizational learning
1997	Pedler, Burgoyne and Boydell	Learning company – three stages: implementing – does things well improving – does things better integrating – does better things	Organization development
1999	Ainley	Situated learning	Technology
1999	Heron	Ground rules	All trainers and learners
1999	Hmelo	Problem-based learning	Medical education
1999	Wolfson and Willinsky	Service learning	Real projects
2000	Bateson	Five levels of learning	All learners
2002	Beard and Wilson	Learning combination lock	All learners
2003	Joy-Matthews	Personal learning process	All learners
2003	Megginson and Whitaker	Continuous professional development	All professional learners

e-Learning and blended learning

INTRODUCTION

This chapter starts with definitions of e-learning and blended learning and then continues by making a case for their current timeliness and importance. Some case studies demonstrating their use are given and there are opportunities for the reader to engage in a range of e-learning activities. Given that e-learning and blended learning are becoming more popular, it is important that line management and employees as well as HRD specialists have a knowledge of it. A recent study (IES, 2002) concluded that there were over 9 million e-workers in Europe. These people will all be e-literate and will, in the case of home-based teleworkers, use a computer as their main source of contact at work. For such people, the option of attending more traditional forms of work-based learning may be denied.

LEARNING OUTCOMES

By reading this chapter, undertaking the suggested activities and reflecting on the content and your own prior knowledge, you will achieve the following learning outcomes:

▌ an appreciation of the current importance of e-learning;

▌ an appreciation of the importance of blended learning;

■ a knowledge of the history and antecedents of e- and blended learning;

■ knowledge of the key terms and processes;

■ an understanding of who needs to be involved to make e- and blended learning work;

■ an understanding of the relationship of e- and blended learning to knowledge management.

DEFINITIONS

A definition of e-learning that captures its complexity is the following:

> E-learning refers to the use of Internet technologies to deliver a broad array of solutions that enhance knowledge and performance. (Rosenberg, 2003: 1)

The description that we feel captures the essence of blended learning best is the following:

> Blended learning is the most logical and natural evolution of our learning agenda. It suggests an elegant solution to the challenges of tailoring learning and development to the needs of individuals. It represents an opportunity to integrate the innovative and technological advances offered by online learning with the interaction and participation offered in the best of traditional learning. It can be supported and enhanced by using wisdom and one-to-one contact of personal coaches. (Thorne, 2003: 16)

ACTIVITY 5.1 YOUR DEFINITIONS

How does your organization define e-learning? According to Kruse (2003), Google provides more than 40,000 pages related to the definition of e-learning. Try searching for an item by Jay Cross. Do you agree with Jay Cross that e-learning is dead?

Our definition of e-learning is:

electronically mediated learning materials and processes.

Our definition of blended learning is:

learning that makes use of a variety of media and methods and includes some form of electronically mediated learning.

WHY E-LEARNING IS IMPORTANT

According to Charles Clarke (2003: 1), 'e-Learning has the power to transform the way we learn, and to bring high quality, accessible learning to everyone – so that every learner can achieve his or her full potential.' We are already surrounded by e-learning at home, at work, in college or university and in our recreational pursuits. We are starting to find that e-learning is important because it can make a significant difference: to how quickly we learn a skill; to the ease with which we can study; and to the degree to which we enjoy learning. e-Learning also contributes to the British Government's objectives for education: raising standards; improving quality; removing barriers to learning and participation in learning; preparing for employment; upskilling in the workplace; and, ultimately, ensuring that all learners achieve their full potential.

The British Government's vision for e-learning is as follows:

Imagine what our education system could do, fuelled by e-learning:

- Empower learners – With more active learning, people of all ages could take responsibility for what and how they learn, achieving their personal goals as self-directed lifelong learners.

- Be creative and innovative – Teaching could be more creative and innovative, in preparation for the 21st-century global knowledge society.

- Offer flexibility – A more responsive education system would adapt to the needs of all learners, wherever and however they need to learn.

- Achieve better value – Education leaders could develop innovative ways of deploying their resources, exploiting e-learning alongside other teaching methods, to improve quality and economies of scale.

▊ Generate a professional workforce and fulfilled citizens – A community and a workforce for the knowledge society would have a high proportion of people capable of continually updating their knowledge and skills, of managing knowledge transfer, and contributing to practitioner knowledge in all its forms. (Clarke, 2003: 7)

Marc Prensky coined the term 'digital native' to describe those people who are brought up in a digital world (albeit on the rich side of the divide between those who have access to resources and those who don't). It could be true that being a 'native' introduces new cognitive styles, habits and thinking patterns (Gordon, 2003: 30). This has a significant impact on the nature of HRD. If schoolchildren become accustomed to learning for themselves using a computer and other interactive technologies as well as from a teacher, they will have a different attitude to learning from those employees who only learned from a teacher in a classroom. As employees and employers they are more likely to access a range of self-development opportunities.

Governments and organizations around the world are also seeing the benefits of using technology to aid learning. However, as Clarke (2003: 40) says:

At present, the majority of educational software under-exploits the opportunities offered by the technology. It is rare to find materials and interactive programs that make use of the full range of learning technology capabilities, such as automated language analysis, artificial intelligence, adaptive feedback, automated test generation and scoring, virtual environments, remote-control devices, interactive or online gaming models, data capture and analysis, group collaboration facilities, design wizards, etc. There are so many ways in which learners could be engaged, either as individuals or in small groups, in exciting and challenging learning activities of the kind that are impossible without the technology.

One example of exploiting the technology is a course run by the Open University in which students have personalized work space and use an interactive Web site and printed documents to explore the Bloomsbury Group.

THE GOVERNMENT'S RESPONSE

The British Government has suggested that as individuals are likely to change employment throughout their working lives, it would be appropriate for them to have e-portfolios to record their lifelong learning process and achievements. All education and training organizations should contribute to these e-portfolios, thereby supporting learners' development and progression. The Government also suggests that the feasibility of a unique learner number and that the principle of universal lifelong learning online advice, guidance and self-diagnostics for learning, assessment, learning support, qualifications, competences, employment opportunities and citizenship should be investigated. (Clarke, 2003: 35)

ACTIVITY 5.2 E-LEARNING FOR YOU

What learning needs do you, your staff or your organization have that might be met by using e-learning? What help to determine this is already available on the Web? You could use your search engine to help you to find out, or see Activity 5.5 for two sites to get you started.

WHY BLENDED LEARNING IS IMPORTANT

The use of information and communication technology (ICT) to deliver learning is becoming much more commonplace. Trainers and developers are thinking more about how to integrate ICT with more traditional forms of learning (Thorne, 2003). Many learners still find it hard to learn on their own, and much work is being done on the concept of learning communities (Lave and Wenger, 1991). Some communities may be totally virtual but many will meet together in a 'learning space' of some type. The ability to make the best use of other people for the learning process blended with the use of a range of technologies is likely to be the way forward.

Although this may still seem a long way off, it will not be long before it becomes a reality. While we were writing this chapter, the World Wide Web suffered a worm that has had a huge effect on the way it has worked. Not being able to use e-mail and search the Web for a couple of days seemed like a major issue. Ten years ago it would not have been a problem for many people. However, nowadays the Web has become such a part of our normal life that we find it hard to manage without it.

ANTECEDENTS AND HISTORY

We suppose that the 'radio schools' in the Australian outback were possibly the forerunners in the use of wireless technology for learning. These were followed by initiatives such as the Open University, which used radio and television to provide learning packages that students could access in their own time. The advent of the video recorder made this learning more civilized! No longer did the student have to watch television at 4 am to continue their studies.

A range of open learning products (often in book form and generally very poorly presented) followed. These have improved considerably in recent years. A variety of very good videos for learning management techniques became a standard part of many management development programmes. The advent of CD ROMs allowed for far more sophisticated training packages. Then computer packages were designed to provide easily accessed learning, often on company intranets. Web-based e-learning is not yet as sophisticated as CD ROMs, primarily because of a lack of bandwidth. Once this problem has been overcome, the Web-based packages will become more sophisticated.

KEY CONCEPTS AND TERMS

In order to understand the concepts of e-learning and blended learning more clearly, it is useful to know some of the key concepts:

▌ *Synchronous communication* is that which takes place in real time and relies on the use of bandwidth, which is still not universally available, to carry images and sound, eg chatroom, Webcam conference, Internet, phone.

▌ *Asynchronous communication* takes place with a time delay. Prime examples are e-mail, bulletin boards and software user guides. Asynchronous communication is more widely available. Its positive aspect is that it does leave time for a response to be considered. Many of us have made instantaneous responses that we later wish we had not!

▌ *Learning objects* are bite-sized chunks of learning material. These enable the learner to complete a piece of learning at one sitting.

▮ *Web-based training (WBT)* is a type of learning package that is available via the Web.

▮ A *learning management system,* if Web based, will allow the HRD, and in some cases line management staff or employees, to manage the process of training and development. The skills gap analysis can be undertaken online and this can lead to authoring, delivery of content, assessment of learner performance, and feedback to the learner and his or her management. It can also be used to monitor other learning provision that is not online – for example, other aspects of the blended learning. Costs and benefits can be monitored and the success of various packages can be tracked.

PROCESSES

When considering e-learning there are some key issues and processes that need to be thought through:

Analysis

It is really important to get the primary analysis as near perfect as possible, as it is costly to have to redo work later – although, of course, it is even more expensive to reprint paper-based products. The following are some of the questions that need to be considered: What amount of task analysis needs to be undertaken and who is the most appropriate person to do this? How will learning objectives be set? What level will the learners be required to perform at after the training has taken place? A training needs analysis will have to be undertaken; is a training package the most appropriate response to the need? What training methods will be most appropriate? Is a stand-alone Web-based learning package appropriate or is blended learning a better option?

Design

Once the analysis has been undertaken, it is necessary to consider the design phase. What systems need to be available to support the interface? What will an online or paper document look like? What learning strategies need to be developed? How should the content be structured? What are the most appropriate media for delivering the learning package?

Scripting

Once the need for and the style of the learning package have been undertaken, thought needs to be given to scripting: Is there a house style for text on the screen? What questions will need to be asked to monitor learning? What feedback will be given to the learners, and how? The content and style of any input – lectures, narration, dialogue – needs to be considered carefully. What use will be made of graphics, illustrations, photos, animation, video material, links between the elements? What issue will these raise in terms of time to load on lower-capacity computers? What special instructions need to be given for authoring the package?

Production

When all the issues raised above have been resolved, thought then needs to be given to the process of authoring, media creation, programming and testing. This is a crucial phase in the whole process.

Implementation

Once the package has been scripted and tested, it is time to roll out the package. The following stages are part of the implementation process: promoting the course, registering learners, providing tutorial support on- or offline, maintaining records.

Evaluation

Evaluation needs to have been ongoing throughout the whole process of development. Then the first set of learners will need to be very carefully evaluated to determine whether the learning package has met the identified need. This may be through self-analysis by the learners, an online questionnaire, any test results that are available, or the managers' view of the learners' improved performance. HRD staff are also likely to want to evaluate the package against other methods that could have been used, particularly if this is the first online package the organization has used.

This review of the process makes it clear that evaluation is both lengthy and costly and requires a great deal of skill, which is why online learning is not a cheap option. However, if there are a large number of people needing a learning package or there is the possibility that the package can be used over a reasonable period of time, it can be the most affordable option. It is also really useful where there are a large number of learners scattered around a country or the world.

ACTIVITY 5.3 THE PROCESS OF E-LEARNING

If you have been involved with the design, delivery or evaluation of e-learning, spend a few minutes reflecting on the process. What could have been done more effectively?

If you have been an e-learner, how did you find the process? What were the positives and the negatives of this experience? How would you support other e-learners?

WHO IS INVOLVED?

Clearly, a number of different groups of people and individuals will need to be involved in the process of e-learning, from the person who originated the idea of a need for the package through to the person(s) undertaking the evaluation.

Senior line managers and generalists will need to be involved in the decision to make appropriate finances available. They will also need to consider their own involvement in e-learning, perhaps as learners, product champions, managers of learners, assessors, evaluators, etc. These senior managers also need to influence the culture of the organization so that e-learning is seen as an acceptable way forward.

HRD specialists will have a key role to play in determining whether e-learning or blended learning is an appropriate solution for the identified need. They will also need to commission the learning package and work with others on its design, delivery and evaluation. They will probably have to be the product champions for e-learning.

e-Learning providers will probably need to be employed to develop the package, unless there is going to be a considerable demand for e-learning packages, in which case it might be more cost-effective for the organization to recruit appropriate staff. Providers will also need to be engaged in the process of enabling the in-house staff to understand the complexities of e-learning while encouraging them to want to use it.

Line managers will be involved in the process of selecting learners and in enabling them to make the best use of the learning that they have had. They may also be involved in developing the content for the package, mentoring the learners and in evaluating the package and the learning outcomes.

Anyone within the organization is a potential learner, assessor and evaluator of the package, so each individual needs to be receptive to the concept of e-learning. As mentioned already, the 'digital divide' may play a significant role in their receptiveness.

Staff in the IT department will also be involved, as they will have to make the technology available to the learners either at their place of work, in a dedicated learning area or via the Internet at home or on laptops. This implies that IT technicians will need to develop an understanding of the development function. They will encourage other in-house staff in the use of the technology and may need to make them aware of the current inadequacies of the hardware that is available.

ACTIVITY 5.4 THE PEOPLE INVOLVED IN E-LEARNING

Identify people who you know have been or are involved in e-learning and ask them to discuss their experiences with you.

ACTIVITY 5.5 E-LEARNING ON THE WEB

You might like to search for e-learning via your usual search engine, or you could try out the following two sites:

http://www.dereckstockley.com.au/e-learning-definition.html

Try out the e-journey on e-learning and any other part of this site that interests you. What is your view of e-learning?

http://www.e-learningcentre.co.uk

Try searching for inputs on return on investments (ROI) for e-learning and any other part of this site that interests you.

BLENDED LEARNING

Blended learning is a mix of e-learning and more traditional forms of learning. Just as e-learning and traditional learning processes require good planning to ensure that they work well, so does blended learning. While e-learning can provide opportunities for people to work at their own pace and at a time and a place to suit them, and consequently overcomes many of the normally cited barriers to learning, it can also create its own barriers. One of us was recently discussing Web-based learning with a student who is studying for a Master's degree. This course is proving to be most unsuccessful as there is no contact with the student from the learning provider other than online. The student is finding it a very lonely experience and is consequently not progressing very well. This demonstrates that for some, perhaps even most, students there is a need for mentoring or coaching on a more personal level, be it face to face or via e-mail.

One of the key parts of blended learning is to provide face-to-face support and individual coaching for the learners. There are also benefits to enabling the learners to have contact with each other. This contact can be either in a virtual learning space via Web-based chatrooms, conferences and e-mail, or in real life. Another key part of blended learning is to ensure that learners have the opportunity to use their newly gained knowledge, skills or attitudes as soon as possible. www.trainingzone. co.uk ran a poll on 29 August 2003 in which 55 per cent of respondents said that blended learning was essential for making the most of e-learning.

Joy-Matthews and Gladstone (2000: 26) give an example of blended learning taking place with a group of European middle and HR managers from global organizations who have joined together to form the Electronic Communication Forum. The group meet four times a year and use meetings to network, discuss projects and problems, and seek information about leading-edge academic developments that might be pertinent to their professional activities.

The group is composed of members of staff from a range of leading organizations including AT&T, BOC, Compaq, Dell, Eastern Power, Fujitsu, Hewlett-Packard, Hitachi, IBM, IMS Health, MCA, Nortel, Novell, Royal and Sun Alliance, SCO, Sun Systems and the West Midlands Constabulary. Many of these organizations could be seen as in competition, but in this forum they are able to collaborate to mutual benefit. As this example indicates, blended learning does not have to be based around a 'course', but can include a wide range of other options where people learn while using technology and face-to-face interactions.

KNOWLEDGE MANAGEMENT

Knowledge management is the process by which organizations can generate value from their intellectual and knowledge-based assets. This usually involves the organization in sharing these assets among its employees (possibly between departments) and even with other companies so that best practice can be developed and shared. This may – almost certainly does – require the use of information technology, but it is not the technology that is the knowledge; the technology is merely a means of storing, sharing and retrieving it. Some pieces of knowledge are readily shared. However, tacit knowledge (the knowledge that is in someone's head) is much harder to codify and archive. How do we know what someone else knows? So how do we know what questions to ask in order to access that knowledge? People who still feel that knowledge is power may be reluctant to share their knowledge, as it might make them redundant! This is a major issue for most organizations.

During the first conference on HRD research and practice across Europe, which took place in 2000 and was sponsored by EURESFORM and the University Forum for Human Resource Development, it was noted that several papers on knowledge management had made similar points, questioning whether organizations are able to 'manage' knowledge. These papers suggested that organizations needed to accept that each employee uses different learning strategies. They also suggested that organizations needed to accept the socially constructed nature of the learning process and that is it important to recognize and include all the different stakeholders in the learning process. Consideration was given to power relations and the dynamic nature of organizational learning, which generates a need for proactive facilitation. While technology is important, a consideration of 'people processes: especially culture change, training, education and facilitation [is] crucial for successful knowledge management' (EHRD, 2000).

Scarborough and Carter (2000) suggest that trying to manage knowledge by use of intranets, groupware and databases has not led to improvements in performance or innovation and that there is a need for a more people-centred approach that will treat knowledge as more dynamic that just a computer-based asset. Malhotra (2002) continues this theme by raising three myths about knowledge management:

▊ Myth 1. Knowledge management technologies can deliver the right information to the right person at the right time.

■ Myth 2. Knowledge management technologies can store human intelligence and experience.

■ Myth 3. Knowledge management technologies can distribute human intelligence.

Malhotra suggests that a model of a knowledge ecology framework is a way forward. In the XCL case study in Chapter 9, a robust knowledge management system is described, whereby all members of the organization, associates and clients are involved in managing the organization's knowledge. Knowledge management is also covered in more detail in Chapter 8.

Organizations need to work towards more open and collaborative ways of working so that the concept of sharing information and knowledge generation becomes far more commonplace. Once they have done this, they will be in a better position to start to develop a knowledge management system. The system of e-learning and blended material may then become a significant focal point for knowledge management within an organization, but it needs intelligent people to make the connections between what is stored electronically or on paper and the reality of the organization.

ACTIVITY 5.6 KNOWLEDGE MANAGEMENT ON THE WEB

Try using your usual search engine to investigate knowledge management on the web. What information did you discover? How can you share this with colleagues? Do you believe that knowledge can be managed? Do you have an effective knowledge management system at work? Are you a knowledge intrapreneur?

You might choose to access www.brint.com and read some of Yogesh Malhotra's papers. Or go to www.kmnetwork.com/ KnowledgeManagementMeasurementResearch.pdf to look at the balanced scorecard for knowledge asset measurement and management. You could then consider how your department, company or business manages knowledge.

CASE STUDY 5.1: MASSACHUSETTS INSTITUTE OF TECHNOLOGY

In 2001 MIT decided to make available all courses, lectures and reading lists on a Web-based platform called OpenCourseWare (OCW). This initiative was funded by the William and Flora Hewlett Foundation and the Andrew W Mellon Foundation. The faculty at MIT put a great deal of creative energy and time into making their work freely available, and currently over 500 courses are listed on the site. Charles M Vest, President of MIT, said:

> Educators and learners from all parts of the globe tell us that OCW is already having an impact on learning and education. We see OCW as opening a new door to the democratizing and transforming power of education. We hope the idea of openly sharing course materials will propagate throughout many institutions and create a global web of knowledge that will enhance the quality of learning and, therefore, the quality of life worldwide.

To discover the rest of this case study, go to http://ocw.mit.edu/index.html. Follow the links from the home page to

- about OCW
- Our story
- Organization
- Process
- Technology

What issues does such freedom of materials pose?

SUMMARY

The concepts of e-learning, blended learning and knowledge management are becoming increasingly popular, and most people will come into contact with them at some stage in their own development. Many of the concepts and rules that apply to other forms of learning and development and that are discussed throughout this book are relevant. It seems to us that ways have to be found of capturing the tacit knowledge that is held within an organization and making it available to benefit all employees and the organization.

Continuous professional development

INTRODUCTION

Continuous professional development (CPD) is a term used by professions to describe the requirement for members to keep learning throughout their working life. Organizations set the same expectations for their staff and call it something like individual development planning (IDP). The rate of change in practice, technology, legislation and organizational structures is increasing, and this increases the need for continuous development. Individuals taking responsibility for their own careers enhance this trend, as do the engagement of line managers in development and the creation of a coaching culture. This chapter examines the principles of CPD that enable it to make a difference to the careers of individuals and the performance of organizations. It offers practices that individuals can undertake for themselves and encourage in others. The part of e-learning and blended learning in this process is discussed in Chapter 5.

LEARNING OUTCOMES

By reading this chapter and carrying out the activities you will be able to:

∎ identify your own approach to learning and development;

∎ determine a set of principles of CPD that will maximize your own learning and help you to contribute to the learning of others;

▌ Develop a framework for CPD that can be applied at a personal level or be set up for a department or a whole organization.

IDENTIFYING OUR OWN APPROACH TO CPD

When you prepare to carry out CPD, it is as well to get a sense of your own strengths as a learner and also to become aware of how you don't learn well. In a book on being a writer (Goldberg, 1991), the author suggests an exercise of writing for 10 minutes starting with the words 'I remember. . .' – then, after a short break, writing for another 10 minutes starting with 'I don't remember. . .' Bearing in mind how closely connected are memory and learning, one of us wrote the following.

I remember

I remember the conversations that I used to have with my colleagues when I was 25 – they formed my professional identity. I remember writing articles about what I wanted to learn, rather than what I knew, and how this helped me to learn what I wanted. I remember the teachers who were passionate about their subject. I remember the American at university who praised my writing, but I don't remember what he taught me. I remember taking on new responsibilities, and things going wrong, and Kevan helping me put them right with some very direct coaching. I remember taking on responsibility for running the HRM programme – and discovering that there were things that I could do better than others, but there were things that I was *so* reluctant to do; these include detailed administration and being responsible for assessment. I chose roles to avoid these things in the future. I learned how to be a good gardener by doing it, and keeping a gardening diary recording what I have done. I remember learning to identify plants by using Keeble Martin – the pictures combined with core botanical knowledge work just fine. I learned to write by reading authors who write well and emulating them, and by the occasional foray into a short course when the need is urgent. I remember driving 2½ hours to London on a Sunday morning to attend a one-day course. It helped shift me when I was completely blocked finishing my first major book. I also learned by noticing what I didn't like about some writers and avoiding this – mainly impersonality, obscurity, pomposity and lack of clear structure. At least I hope that I have learned that. I learned to lecture by noticing people – most often much younger than myself – who gave brilliant lectures by pushing out the envelope and taking risks. I learned to write poetry by keeping my eyes and heart open and recording what I saw and what I felt. I remember being bowled over by reading Elizabeth David's *French Provincial Cooking*, and being committed to making good food with fine ingredients ever since. I learned to love my friends and family by being loved. I remember my friend Richard just saying, 'I *like* you', emphatically. It seemed a risk at the time. Such a simple thing. So powerfully helpful to me; and a role model for me with others.

I don't remember

I don't remember the structure of government support for small company development, even though it might be useful to me (because I don't think that the authors really believe it will make any difference). I don't remember most of what I was taught in maths; I only got interested in it and found I could understand it when I needed to use statistics in research reports. I don't remember the intention of the change strategies in my organization over the decades. They seemed just to be weaving words that had no heart and no bite. I don't remember anything good about the half-dozen or so people I've worked with whose actions seemed selfish and aggressive. I don't remember how to drive within the speed limit (punishment doesn't seem to help memory). I don't remember to do my tax return in plenty of time – I remember the pain of the last-minute rush but also the excitement. I don't remember nine-tenths of the management books I have read; they lacked the ring of truth, of a story well researched or well lived.

Commentary

It may seem paradoxical to write about what you don't remember, but the example above gives some indication of the ways in which you can get started. Write about bad learning experiences, or about things that you hoped for but slipped out of your attention, about patterns you meant to contradict, but have never remembered to. Use your imagination to find where your unremembered events and intents are lurking. Such an account as this will give the writer (and, indeed, a reader of it) a sense of how the writer learns and develops. It might also highlight gaps that could be filled or compensated for in the future.

ACTIVITY 6.1 I REMEMBER. . . I DON'T REMEMBER. . .

Write for 10 minutes beginning 'I remember'. Take a short break, then go for another 10 minutes starting 'I don't remember'. Compare what you have written with the example above. What would the author of the example above need to do for his or her personal development? How does this differ from the needs emerging from your own writing?

PRINCIPLES OF CPD

This section explores the principles that will enable you to maximize your own learning and help you to contribute to the learning of others. There has recently been a growing interest in CPD, and the topic is dealt with at length by Megginson and Whitaker (2003).

Voluntarism

CPD, like most things, works best if it is undertaken willingly. However, companies and professions often want to make it compulsory. A healthy compromise is to be committed to the principle of everyone doing it, but give the maximum possible freedom to them as to how they do it.

Range of options

Professional bodies, in particular, can be guilty of having a narrow view of what constitutes learning. In the worst cases they require members to attend the profession's short courses for at least a minimum number of hours each year. Our view is that everything can be embraced as a learning opportunity – and it is reflection (see the next main section) that turns this aspiration into a lived experience.

Individual or organization focus

We argue in Chapter 8 that generosity in supporting the individual aspirations of staff for learning and development is amply rewarded by the reciprocal commitment and engagement of the staff, so there is no conflict between individual and organization here. The staff will be more committed to CPD if it is focused on their aspirations rather than a standard package focused on the organization, so we suggest that you start with the individual's dream.

Values-based or pragmatic learning

People can start to meet their dream by developing themselves to act in tune with their values (a principled stance) or to act more along the lines that are rewarded in the organization (a pragmatic position). Either can work, and we do not make judgements in favour of one or the other. The crucial requirement for us is that CPD starting from either position is embraced consciously and includes a critical examination of the effects of the choices made.

Planned or emergent learning

Some people will find it easy to plan; others will struggle with thinking ahead (Megginson, 1996). For planners, CPD systems will come naturally. For emergent learners, it is important to give them scope to be flexible and loose in how they plan, and to allow (in fact, to encourage) them to change their plans as they go along.

Summary

Most of these principles are expressed as paradoxes. And in most cases the way of addressing them is to adopt a 'both. . . and. . .' approach rather than an 'either. . . or. . .' one.

FRAMEWORK FOR CPD

The model presented here has five components, and if you follow these, you can have a lively and engaged sense of progress from your CPD. The five components are:

- purpose and goals;
- sense of self;
- plan;

▌ action;

▌ reflection.

Of course, it is not as simple as that. The stages may fold in on themselves. Finding purpose may well require you to reflect more actively and deeply than you have ever done up to now. In fact, reflection is an inevitable part of learning through all these stages. The final stage is about getting to a new point from reflection – having new thoughts – and may properly be called 'reflexivity' or 'reflecting on our reflections'.

Clarify purpose and goals

The first step in pursuing CPD is to be clear what the intent or goal is for the activity. Where do you, or the people you are helping, want to get to? The focus of CPD can be upon:

▌ doing the current job better;

▌ developing towards the next job;

▌ building career opportunities;

▌ balancing work and other activities;

▌ seeking a purpose in life.

The big question of life purpose is difficult, and it sometimes stalls people. They say, 'I have enough on my plate just getting through each day, without worrying about fancy notions like life purpose.' Nonetheless, we recommend that you reflect on it, because it does not go away, so why not address it now, rather than saving it till nearer the end of your life, when so many opportunities will have been forgone?

Whether or not you find a purpose, it is valuable to set goals. Some people do this as a matter of course, but others find it a very strange idea (Megginson, 1996). They say, 'How do I know what I want to achieve till I see what opportunities come up?' To people who think this way, we just draw your attention to what Csikszentmihalyi (2002) says in his well-researched study of 'flow'. He found that a fairly small proportion of the population set goals (and most of these do not do it all the time and for all areas of their life). However, those who did set goals achieved more, and had greater success and (perhaps even more important) greater happiness, than those who did not.

So, be careful about what goals you set for yourself; you are likely to achieve them. We suggest that you check them for ecological fit and for holistic integrity. What we mean by this is that you ask, first, 'Do they take into account my environment, the people who matter to me, and the communities of which I am a part?' You do not have to be beholden to these outer sources of influence, but you do need to consider them. Perhaps reaching a common goal with members of your work team or your boss or your family is the first task. After achieving this, the rest will be so much easier. Holistic integrity suggests that you pay attention to the balance in your life. Look out for the areas that you customarily neglect and set goals for these too. We use a framework called SPICE to remind ourselves of where we need to set goals:

▌ Spirit;

▌ Physical;

▌ Intellect;

▌ Career;

▌ Emotions.

It is powerful to set goals as affirmations; these are statements of what things will be like when you have achieved the goal. Start them with the words 'I am. . .' Your unconscious will take these as an instruction and will use its power to set out to achieve the state you specify. Then include in your affirmation positive verbs expressing what you will be doing with whom to celebrate the achievement of the goal – for example, 'I am celebrating with my co-authors our delight and relief on completing the typescript, on the due date, and receiving the grateful thanks of the publisher for the timely and high-quality text'.

An alternative powerful format is the SMART goal-setting framework. Here you make sure your goals are:

▌ Specific;

▌ Measurable;

▌ Actionable by you;

▌ Realistic;

▌ Time bound.

Goals set in this way will create a gap between where you want to be and where you are, which again will energize your unconscious to fill the gap. Make sure you specify the date by which you will achieve your goal; 'ongoing' doesn't work – no tension is created. And avoid saying 'I will try to. . .' Put it more positively: 'I will. . .' This creates the energy that leads to action.

ACTIVITY 6.2 PURPOSE AND GOALS

From the writing you did earlier around 'I remember. . . and I don't remember. . .', can you discern any sense of purpose? Make a note of it. If you can't see a purpose in this, then ask yourself some of the following big questions:

- Who am I?

- Why am I here?

- What is my dream?

- What is my unique talent?

- What do I derive joy from doing?

- How can I help?

Then set goals around working towards that purpose. Set them using the SMART framework or using affirmations.

Develop a realistic sense of self

Next it is important to develop a strong sense of self: where you are now, what your current circumstances are. Megginson and Whitaker (2003) list six sources of a sense of self:

- work itself;

- reflection by self;

- feedback from others;

- psychometric and self-diagnostic measures;

■ organizational metrics;

■ professional metrics.

One of the most interesting psychometric frameworks to have come into prominence in recent years is very ancient in its origins. It is called the Enneagram, and it is a model of personality that is both deep and dynamic. The best book we know on it is by Riso and Hudson (1999). This is a helpful framework to use, but Myers–Briggs or a host of others are also useful (see Hirsch and Kise, 2000).

The aim in understanding our personality is not to change it. Personality is too fundamental for this kind of tinkering. Instead, by knowing ourselves well, we can be realistic and loving of ourselves, and not beat ourselves up for not being someone different. The question to be able to ask is, 'Given how I am, what is it that I might achieve beyond what I am doing now?'

ACTIVITY 6.3 WHICH SOURCES OF MY SENSE OF SELF DO I USE?

Looking at the list of sources above, which do you use a lot? Which do you use less? Can you identify what it is that puts you off those that you use less? Think of someone whom you respect who uses the sources you use less and ask him or her about the advantages. Try using this source in the light of what you learn from your informant. Does this new source of information about you throw new light on your strengths, resources or nature? How can you use this new insight in your future development?

Make a plan

Then it is useful to have a plan. The plan represents the tension between the goals you have set and your current reality. The existence of the tension in itself creates a tendency to act, so even if you do not take deliberate action, you may find yourself drawn into filling the gap. Jaworski (1996: 34) speaks powerfully of this planning process at its most vital when he says, 'People are not really afraid of dying; they're afraid of not ever having lived, not ever having deeply considered their life's higher purpose, and not ever having stepped into that purpose and at least tried to make a difference in this world.'

ACTIVITY 6.4 MAKE A PLAN

Conventional plans have columns headed (1) Goal; (2) Resources/ support needed; (3) Target date; (4) Assessment measure. Alternatively, plans can be in the form of a fishbone (see Megginson and Whitaker, 2003: 49–51) or a mindmap. Make a plan in whatever format works well for you. Remember to consider each aspect of the SPICE framework.

Take action

Of course, it is necessary to take action. We need to do new things, but perhaps most of all we need new conversations (Shaw, 2002). Our conversations are where we make sense of the world and thus where we build the springboard from which we leap out into the world. If we have the same conversations ('Ain't it awful. . .', 'I only wish. . .'), then we will be jumping off from the same place. So, we are highly likely to land up in the same pool!

ACTIVITY 6.5 ACTION AND CONVERSATION

Seek out someone whom you work with (or, perhaps even more interestingly, someone you work against). Engage in understanding fully how they see a situation or project you are working on. Make sure you listen hard and long enough to fully understand their position before you say anything about yours. If you were to seek to do everything you could to help them to meet their goals through your project, what would you have to do differently? Does this give you a new perspective on how you need to act?

Reflect on your reflections

Finally, it is crucial in CPD to reflect and to reflect on your reflections. Again Jaworski (1996) has been there before us. He suggests that writing your reflections on your experience day by day helps you to clarify learning and right action in the midst of life. Looking back over past reflections shows how you have moved on. You may have developed a different stance to the circumstances that surround you; you may have changed how you respond. As Jaworski (1996: 33) says:

> This process brought order to my mind and a kind of coherence to my consciousness. It also brought a peacefulness and understanding that I found in no other activity. . . Over time these dialogues within myself became very precious to me. . . I realize that in those moments of silent dialogue – in the void – I gained important insights that helped guide me as I made choices about my life.

ACTIVITY 6.6 REFLECT ON YOUR REFLECTIONS

There are two means of gaining sufficient distance from your customary reflections to be able to use them to have new thoughts and take new perspectives. One is to write down the reflections day by day for a period, and then to re-read them. The other is to voice these reflections to another (a friend who is prepared to challenge you, a coach or a mentor). Have a go at one or the other, specifically seeking out new thoughts or plans in the process.

IS THERE ANOTHER WAY?

So, that's the formal story

How else might you do it? David is on the CPD Working Party of the Chartered Institute of Personnel and Development. The new chair of the Working Party, Jean Floodgate, asked us to bring the CPD record of our development over the past year to a meeting that she was to chair. I thought of my formal, carefully measured plan, set seven months before. That was one story. Another approach could be captured by the 10-minute timed writing approach with which we started this chapter. Ten minutes on what I have learned this year, and 10 on what I have not learned.

What I [one of the authors] have learned this year

I've learned that I can deliver projects on time – even big ones. It helps to make plans and to allocate realistic times for activities (thank you, Ruth). I can even deliver book typescripts on time (first time ever). This may sound small to you, but this is a three-decades-long pattern that I have broken and it will make such a difference to what I can achieve. I have made a small but significant contribution to my local community and it was fun to do. I have decided to leave my job and have successfully set up my own business. I have learned how to manage my business and sort what needs to be sorted and to think of myself as a responsible and active member of the private sector after 34 years in public service. I have written one book, revised another and am launched on the final shaping of a third (you could never do that and be a professor at the same time). I have challenged my own practice as a coach and a supervisor; this was especially learned at the Tenth European Mentoring and Coaching Conference, which I got such a lot from in terms of clarifying (beginning to clarify) my own practice as a coach. And, before that, I had developed as a teacher of coaching (whereas before that I had focused on being a teacher of mentoring). I have learned to use courage, risk and spontaneity within a pattern and a framework. I have learned to write up and reflect upon my professional coaching sessions, and some of my facilitation work as well. I have started re-reading the Bible and the Koran, and deepened my perspective on these traditions.

What I have not learned this year

I have not learned to deliver things on time without a last-minute rush. I put stress on myself, and those around me, by doing things right up against the deadline. It doesn't have to be like that, but it is. The change in my circumstances was meant to make this better and it has, in terms of the perceived pressure on me. What it hasn't done is give me time to do all my projects (I've never been so busy). But the stress is off, and is being replaced by focus and energy. I have not learned to prepare the proceedings of one conference until just before the next one, but watch this space. I have not prepared my tax returns in an orderly and timely way (though I have engaged the support of a local and very helpful accountant). I have not forgiven four people who I felt aggrieved with at the beginning of the

year. I am no more practical in DIY than I was this time last year. My garden is still a mess – a productive mess, but a mess; I haven't learned how to do things at just the time they need doing. I have not (sufficiently) integrated the thoughts and feelings I have about spirituality at work into my practice.

Reflection

Focusing on both done and undone is useful, because the stuff that I have not done represents the germ of a vital plan for the following year. Are the measurables and the dates in there? Not explicitly, but experientially they are vivid and clear.

ACTIVITY 6.7 WHAT HAVE I LEARNED. . . WHAT HAVE I NOT LEARNED?

Try it. Ten minutes on 'What I have learned this year'. Then pause and walk around. Make yourself a hot drink. Then 10 minutes on 'What I have not learned this year'. Would you be willing to submit this to your professional body as CPD evidence? What would you have to do to make it submissible? Would you try it? Or would you read it out to someone you work with whom you trust? Is this your boss? If not, is 'Learn to trust my boss' one of your goals for next year?

CORPORATE CASE STUDY: KELLOGG'S EUROPE

Most of this chapter has emphasized what you can do individually for yourself or for someone you are helping. We conclude the chapter with an example of one company's approach to this area. We are grateful to Kate Howsley, Director, Organization Effectiveness–Europe at Kellogg's for providing this case.

Kellogg's is the world's leading producer of cereals and a leading manufacturer of convenience foods. The case study focuses on the company's Individual Development Planning process and puts this in an organizational context.

CASE STUDY 6.1: CAREER DEVELOPMENT AT KELLOGG'S

Career development is the process used to create opportunities for employees' professional interests and capabilities and to help meet current and future business needs.

Career development at Kellogg's is becoming a more formalized process. The changes for 2004 are subtle and include:

- A new, required form (Employee Profile) to be completed by all Kellogg's non-production employees. The Employee Profile provides a snapshot of an employee's career, including biographical information, work experiences, development plans, and assessment on leadership competences and K-values.

- The Individual Development Plan (IDP) has been incorporated into the Employee Profile. It includes an overview of employee development for current accountabilities and future career opportunities.

- All people managers have a Performance Management Plan (PMP), which concerns their accountability for the development of employees.

Development is a critical process because:

- Change seems to be occurring at a faster rate than ever and employees must learn to change and adapt quickly.

- Relying solely on employees' current capabilities would place the company at a competitive disadvantage.

- Recent survey data indicated that Kellogg's employees have an interest in development.

- Focused development builds stronger teams and attracts and retains the best and brightest talent.

What is an effective development plan?

Development requires more than just identifying the areas or competences that are going to be developed. Just like a project at work, development is more successful when there is a specific plan to accomplish the change in behaviour. Employees will have better success in development if their plan:

- is tied to their PMP accountabilities;

▌ has relevance to the business needs;

▌ is limited to three or four areas for development;

▌ has specific development actions required for each area;

▌ consists of primarily experience-based development actions;

▌ identifies the resources and support needed for each development action;

▌ specifies a date for completion.

Kellogg's philosophy is that the manager and the employee share responsibility for an employee's development. The employee is responsible for keeping skills current and developing skills for future opportunities. Managers make sure employees' expectations are realistic and opportunities to grow are offered and supported.

Table 6.1 *Manager's and employee's responsibilities for employee's development*

Manager's role	Employee's role
Review Employee Profile; Complete the manager's page of the Employee Profile; Review previous feedback and development; Consider possible development actions; Understand what is required to make development more successful; Create key messages to share with employee in meetings; Check with employees intermittently to ensure they are pursuing development; Provide resources, opportunities, and support for development; Offer coaching and feedback at appropriate times.	Take responsibility for own career; Perform well in current role; Complete the employee page of the Employee Profile; Clarify career interests; Determine realistic career goals; Learn more about position requirements; Consider possible development areas to focus on; Plan activities to improve in those areas; Schedule meeting with manager for career discussion; Send all relevant materials to manager (eg self-assessment); Follow up with manager if obstacles are perceived; Present manager with potential solutions; Request feedback and direction.

ACTIVITY 6.8 ANALYSE THE KELLOGG'S CASE

Ask yourself what you could learn from the Kellogg's approach and how this process might be enhanced in the future.

SUMMARY

CPD is a process of development that enables us to gain an unfair advantage over others by consciously propelling our career forward. It means that all the time we are working and doing other things we can also be asking, 'How can I use this? How can I leverage this messy, busy stuff that I am doing to make a difference in my life? How can I carve out just that bit of time I need to start thinking and acting in a way that serves my long-term interests and enables me to make a contribution to the others whom I want to help?'

There are forms, processes and organization practices that enable you to do this, and we have introduced a range of them in this chapter. In some situations you will see your organization, your boss, your professional body as presenting barriers to your doing CPD well. But there is nothing – nothing – that can prevent your doing CPD for yourself. Good luck.

7

Human resource development and change through groups

INTRODUCTION

Teamwork rhetoric is a common feature of the discourse of just about any organization. This may in part be due to the influence of the Total Quality movement, project management and the communication of organizational structure, which emphasize teams. Teams can be regarded as a defined set of people working within a particular context, sharing a common purpose and somehow in touch with each other either face to face or virtually. The general attractiveness of team concepts reflects a reality beyond the rhetoric. That reality is that even if teams are not formally identified, individuals participate in organizational life as members of groups.

Groups may be tightly defined, eg a project team, or only loosely defined. A newer focus is suggested by Wenger (1998), who uses the phrase 'communities of practice' or 'constellations' to identify groupings that are perhaps larger than face-to-face teams and are linked by less recognizable associations (see Chapter 4 for further discussion). Wenger offers the following examples: organizational units; common function; common customer; end-to-end process; critical organizational competence; professional discipline; geographic location; common historical roots; common interests; use of facilities or tools.

> Organizations are social designs directed at practice. Indeed, it is through the practices they bring together that organizations can do what they do, know what they know and learn what they learn. Communities of practice [i.e. groups] are thus key to organizations competence and the evolution of that competence. (Wenger, 2000: 241)

When viewed in this way, groups are an inevitable and unavoidable consequence of organizational life. Therefore, it would seem likely that all workers understand and are able to work with groups (however broadly defined) in order to achieve other conventional aspects of work, eg orientation, culture, communication, learning, leadership, quality, creativity, performance and productivity.

For managers and HRD practitioners, groups provide a practical level of focus. Dealing with all employees individually all the time is neither practical nor realistic. Yet dealing with 'the organization' means engaging with people at some level, and groups provide a practical means of communicating within the otherwise ambiguous construct of 'the organization'. Groups, in all their forms, are therefore a critical focus for HRD.

LEARNING OUTCOMES

As a result of reading this chapter and undertaking the activities, you should aim to progress in your ability to:

- recognize the pivotal role that groups play in organizational strategy;
- understand how group development facilitates change;
- develop your understanding of the dynamics of group interactions;
- identify where opportunities exist to use groups to progress change;
- realize that different groups have different needs.

GROUPS AS STRATEGIC ENTITIES

Groups represent both the heart of resistance to achieving strategy where they are change averse, and the powerhouse for change in dynamic organizations. It is typical for strategy to be formulated at 'top level' and cascaded throughout an organization (Carnall, 1995). However, determining strategy is necessarily complex and dynamic, and ideally would elicit broad commitment by involving all stakeholder groups in its design and implementation.

HRD is closely allied with strategy, the management of change and the management of people as *capital* resources that may be 'developed' in terms of knowledge, capability or simply headcount. HRD can be positioned as a driver of change or as a response to it; either way, groups form a nexus between organizational strategy and individual change.

To focus on groups in strategy is increasingly the wisdom distilled from the experience of many organizations in response to the sort of challenges that they face, which Ulrich (1998: 126) summarizes as globalization, profitability (or performance enhancement) through growth, technology, intellectual capital or knowledge, and 'change, change and more change'.

These challenges to management need imaginative solutions, holistic, integrated approaches and a learning orientation, not just simplistic, off-the-shelf prescriptions. The development of any group therefore must integrate with wider HR policies and practices, and also:

I   make sense strategically;

I   involve an appreciation of the complexities of change;

I   consider how change is facilitated either consciously and deliberately or not;

I   take into consideration that with workforce patterns and boundaries changing considerably from traditional forms, the agents of change may be positioned inside or outside organizations.

Managers illustrate the significance of groups to change and therefore to strategy. The learning necessary to accommodate change, to become institutionalized, needs a readily available critical mass of employees, as is represented by the management group, specifically middle and line managers, because of their direct impact on organizational performance. As J L Alvarez (1996) observes, in an article entitled 'Are we asking too much of managers?' and published in the *Financial Times* (London) on 12 July 1996, 'managers are the best positioned and equipped group to ensure the survival of organizations'.

Managers are critical to strategy, with the potential to bottleneck or even block, but equally to develop, advance, facilitate, roll out and feed back on, strategy. Managers can be the drivers of or restraints on change through their actions. For managers to develop a strategic paradigm is likely to place additional pressure on already stretched individuals. Devolving responsibility for strategy formulation and integration is as likely to be met with suspicion and reluctance as it is to be embraced with enthusiasm.

HRD needs to include all identifiable groups of employees, because in de-layered, flexible and empowered contemporary organizations the distinctions between managers and managerial roles are blurring. Management and leadership are critical to productivity, and many employees increasingly take on a range of management functions even though they may not strictly be called managers (SSDA, 2003). Everyone is a manager of something – not least their own career.

ACTIVITY 7.1 REFLECT ON YOUR PARTICIPATION IN GROUPS

What groups are you part of in your organization? Refer back to Wenger's suggestions for less obvious groupings in the introduction to this chapter to see if you can expand your list.

What development activities are currently targeted at groups within your organization?

As a manager, to what extent are you called upon to facilitate change and to advise on, consult on and develop strategy? Who else is involved?

THE ROLE OF GROUPS IN CHANGE

We have already established the role of HRD in the direction and strategy of an organization, and recognized that groups form important strategic entities. Developing and implementing strategy, the substantive task of any manager, means managing change. We argue, therefore, that groups and their development have a pivotal role in managing change.

The role of groups permeates change management and can be illustrated by reviewing briefly some conventional but still influential perspectives on change, and some more enlightened, developmental perspectives.

Change viewed as something that can be planned and controlled owes much convention to Lewin's (1951) core force field analysis methodology, which models change as moving from a position of stasis (*unfreez-*

ing) through a linear process back to stasis (*re-freezing*). Conventionally, change is also viewed in terms of scale, degree or scope. King and Anderson (1995) discuss smaller-scale *morphostatic* change compared to larger-scale *transformational* change. Kanter, Stein and Dick (1992) contrast quickly initiated *bold strokes* with the sustained effort of *long marches*.

These conventional views of change, however, rather conveniently avoid the thorny issue of people: their role as agents of change, their response to it and the management of the process. These questions can be addressed pragmatically by focusing on groups.

The group of people affecting and managing change, conventionally, are regarded as *change agents*. The role of change agents can be described in terms of: project management, participative management and the political perspective (Buchanan and Boddy, 1992). *Project management* (discussed in more detail in Chapter 3) requires skills of project managers and teams in planning and control to ensure that the change the project brings about is as predicted. *Participative management* places much more emphasis on organizational members affected by the change. Involvement and ownership are key strategies in effecting change and eliciting the commitment of the people required to work with it. The *political perspective* recognizes political and cultural aspects of change as not lending themselves to linear or prescriptive frameworks. Organizational politics is about the needs of groups within the organization. In this model, the senior management group is required to be sensitive to the power and influence of key individuals and groups.

All three models describe groups of people, whether the identified agents of change (ie managers) or the organizational members who are involved in the change. So, even as established wisdom on change asserts that it can be planned, groups emerge as an agent of change. Group development supports change through the provision of the right groups of people with the right skills in the right place at the right time.

Contemporary perspectives on change management emphasize that change necessitates learning, and learning can form a pragmatic basis for organizational strategy through policies that foster a developmental approach and exploit the communities of practice (or groups) within.

> The high failure rate of organizational change programmes of all kinds is well known. To work they need to integrate in a people centred business model, working as a system to learn and improve customer offerings. Learning is critical as a means of raising the aspirations and capacities of both individuals and groups in parallel. (CIPD, 2001: 5)

A cornerstone of organizational learning, for the renowned management author Peter Senge, is what he calls *team learning*, which he defines as 'transforming conversational and collective thinking skills, so that groups of people can reliably develop intelligence and ability greater than the sum of individual members' talents' (Senge *et al* 1994: 6).

Learning, and hence HRD, can drive change. As Leavy (1998) discovered in his review of strategic writings, the development agenda has contributed to change by:

▌ Informing the understanding of competitiveness through experience. The capacity to learn is a core competence in an ever-changing world.

▌ Illuminating the links between strategy and structure, diversification and vertical integration. Organizational ability to share learning is central to the capacity to change the dominant logic of the management group.

▌ Harnessing the small incremental changes and the more dramatic ideas that lead to innovation and the transferring of insights.

▌ Offering advantages over strategic planning, limited by uncertainty and turbulence in business, by taking a more emergent approach.

▌ Practising whole-systems perspectives and learning organization theory has had an impact already.

These observations reveal that organizational members are engaged in learning as an integral aspect of contemporary working. The challenge is to manage learning to balance individual development for current roles and careers with organizational needs now and in the future. HRD focused on groups, we assert, is a realistic and achievable path to change.

The role of the development of groups therefore can be both to support planned change and to drive emergent change in organizations. Groups provide an opportunity to access the relationships and associations that generate the realities of culture and political climate. Organizations are faced with the challenge of engaging in learning that is dominantly responsive and based on a deficit approach to 'identifying training needs', or one that is more proactive and exploratory of future possibilities by inquiring appreciatively into strategic characteristics and through opportunities to generate 'creative tension'. Within a developmental perspective on change, as with more conventional views, groups emerge as strategic entities.

ACTIVITY 7.2 READINESS TO LEARN

Like people, organizations vary in their readiness to learn. Some are more closed and wary, others eager to acquire new knowledge and welcome novel perspectives. Which of the following statements is 'very like us' or 'not at all like us'?

- We have a strong vision of the future.

- Our vision acknowledges old values and identities as well as new possibilities.

- We involve as many people as possible in the process for arriving at our vision and other key decisions.

- We have a strong interest in the education and self-development of all the people in this organization.

- Learning and contribution rather than position or status are rewarded here.

- We encourage experiments, pilots, trials as well as being very clear about the need to 'stick to the knitting', ie our main purpose.

- We rely a great deal on trusted business partners to deliver our best services and products.

The more the statements are 'very like us', the more likely it is that you have the conditions that support further individual and organizational learning. The more statements that are 'not at all like us', the more work there may be to do to enhance your organization's readiness to learn.

MANAGING CHANGE THROUGH GROUPS

Change is a concept and a reality that attracts many different perspectives. In a general sense, it is a defining characteristic of organizational life. Change may be used creatively and as a positive force, but change initiatives are frequently regarded as negative experiences. Change may bring opportunities and advantages; it can also have associated problems and costs. However, change can be managed effectively through groups.

Change may be packaged and presented in different ways and, while an analysis of change will lead to a better understanding of the phenomenon, the reality for managers and business is that change needs to be defined and sold, and even controlled and managed at some level. Groups provide this opportunity, although experience is often more 'messy' than the models or accounts of change programmes portray.

One characteristic of effective organizational change is learning. Carnall (1995) suggests four stages that relate to a general cycle of organizational change.

Each of the 'activities' listed in Table 7.1 suggests group-level interventions in order to achieve the change 'processes' Carnall identifies.

Table 7.1   *Stages of organizational change*

Stage of learning	*Stage of change*	*Activities*	*Process*
Thinking	Beginnings	Diagnosis Brainstorming Assessment	Getting started
Addressing	Focusing	Training Recruiting Piloting	Building capability
Doing	Cascading	Champions New skills New structures	Building and sustaining change
Sensing	Roll out	Team building Celebration Feedback	Evaluation

Change processes may meet resistance from individuals, which can be expressed in a variety of ways and with different characteristics, and which can manifest itself at group level. The phenomenon of 'groupthink' (Myers, 1996) refers to over-conformity, which is conservative and limiting and can lead teams to collude in self-protection and inertia. However, such resistance can itself be useful and tell us things about our change processes and decisions (Perren and Megginson, 1996). Emphasizing learning may help to overcome resistance to change.

Steps that may be taken to encourage the integration of learning into programmes of change include group interventions such as:

■   building relationships and networks, because effective change brings people together in a structured way, ie in groups;

■   creating project groups, because effective change avoids preconceived ideas and options;

■   focus on training and development for groups, because effective change elicits involvement;

■   career management, because effective change allows time for learning, to get the right, lasting solutions.

Change can elicit strongly negative experiences in people when it is imposed by external agents. Negative responses may be inevitable to a degree, but are generally mitigated to an extent if the need for change is generated from within, encouraging a sense of ownership. Change is likely to elicit a range of responses in individuals and groups involving shock to euphoria, through frustration and depression, and eventually, with time, to acceptance. Helpful actions for managers to take with groups with regard to the feelings generated by change might include listening a lot, empathizing, providing extra support, informing and consulting.

In the foregoing paragraphs we have established why groups are so critical to change in organizations. We suggest that it is also useful to have some understanding about the dynamics of how groups work and then to have a range of strategies for all kinds of groups.

ACTIVITY 7.3 STORIES OF CHANGE

Recall a relatively recent story of change that you have knowledge of. Use Table 7.1 to analyse this story. What stages can you recognize? What activities were carried out? What processes can you identify?

What can be done in future change episodes to create a critical mass of people committed to making the change?

SOME IDEAS ABOUT HOW GROUPS WORK

Group development

In reviewing the literature on group development, a psychologist, Barry Tuckman (Tuckman and Jensen, 1977), noticed that groups were seen to go through a process of development. He neatly summarized the stages that had been noticed time and again by researchers in the memorable sequence shown in Figure 7.1.

Figure 7.1   *Group development sequence*

In essence he said that groups go through a phase when members' concerns are about who else is in this group; how will I fit in; what's it all about? (*forming*). When they are settled in, members have time to consider who is in charge; how do I get my say; how can I protect myself from attack? (*storming*). After this rather turbulent phase the group can settle down and establish processes and procedures, acceptable and unacceptable behaviours, how things work around here (*norming*). Only after this, so the theory goes, can the group get down to working well at its task (*performing*).

Boydell and Leary (1996: 146) propose an alternative six stages to a team's development, adapted in Table 7.2.

Table 7.2   *Boydell and Leary's stages of team development*

Stage 0	Getting ready and coming together
Stage 1	Getting started and exploring each other
Stage 2	Getting going and adapting to each other
Stage 3	Getting results and meeting each other
Stage 4	Getting together and working effectively
Stage 5	Getting through and being creative
Stage 6	Ending or dissolving and moving on
Stage X	Getting on with others (may happen throughout)

It may be helpful to a group to take stock of where it 'is' on such a profile, which may in turn stimulate exploratory conversation about different perceptions of the stages of a group's development. Groups can require development for a number of reasons:

■ They may need to establish themselves in their current stage.

■ They may be ready to step through the threshold to the next stage.

■ They may need to work on unresolved questions, issues and tasks from earlier stages.

S and W activity

If members of a group set to work before they have gone through the development sequence, then they will often engage in apparent work rather than real work. Reed and Palmer (1972) referred to this as S and W activity. Apparent work, S activity, refers to 'self-survival' activity: looking busy but not actually being productive, holding lots of meetings at the expense of taking action. S can also refer to 'splitting', where the group justifies itself by seeing itself as wholly good and other parts of the organization as wholly bad. An example of this would be a group whose members say, 'We've got all sorts of ideas but we can't implement them because no one ever listens to us.' Absolute words such as 'no one' and 'ever' are good indicators of S activity, as is dividing the world into heroes and villains. S activity, however, also includes maintenance activity, socializing, caring, team-building and fun – important behaviours in the right balance.

In contrast to S activity there is W: 'whole' or work activity. This is where the group is doing real work, and is committed to making something happen, rather than merely justifying its position, or dealing with unresolved conflicts among members. It is characterized by attention to task, role and achieving objectives. Individuals, or groups, engaged in predominantly one type of behaviour may be difficult to communicate with about another. It may be necessary to resolve the presenting problem before communicating about the real issue.

Defensive behaviour

Groups and individuals can exhibit behaviours that are easily experienced by a facilitator as defensive. Some of the more common include:

- identification – with one particular heroic character;

- depression – involving retreating from the issue and denial;

- sublimation – acceptance without question;

- projection – attribution of feelings to others;

- reaction formation – adopting the originally opposing view;

- fixation – remaining focused on one thing;

- regression – retreat to an earlier stage or infantile state; game playing.

Such labels can assist in identifying behaviours as a first step to doing something about them.

Content and process

The content of a group's deliberation is the subject matter – what is being talked about. The process is the way it goes about its discussion – how the content is being dealt with. Being aware of this distinction is important for managers, because often when group members have difficulty with something you say, it will be not just about its content, but also about the process by which you put the material forward.

Proficient groups are able to move into a brief discussion of process, and then quickly get back into content with renewed vigour and purpose. Inept groups wrangle over content, not noticing the process issues or not having a language to address them, or, if they do get onto the process agenda, do so in a blaming way or at interminable length, thus reducing commitment and direction.

A useful tool in understanding process is the behaviours that members can use in progressing discussion. It can be quite instructive to ask each person in the group to nominate who does the most of each of the following behaviours:

- propose – suggesting a course of action;

- build – adding to someone else's proposal;

- support ideas – saying 'yes' or 'I agree' or some brief comment like that;

- support person – valuing others for themselves or their contribution;

■ disagree – showing disagreement with an idea;

■ attack/defend – going for the person, rather than that person's idea;

■ open – acknowledging responsibility for a mistake;

■ summarize – bring ideas together;

■ test understanding – try out understanding of an idea with a question;

■ seek information – any other question;

■ give information – anything not covered above.

The group could then look at which behaviours they do a lot of; which seem to be neglected; which are done by just one or two people. They could then make plans for developing skills that are currently in short supply. All the behaviours above, with the exception of attack/defend, are useful, so if any are omitted, then the group can usefully consider how to increase the frequency of their use. In our experience (and according to Rackham and Morgan, 1986) the following behaviours are underused in European organizations: *supporting person*; *open*; *summarize*; *test understanding*; *seek information*.

Groups and teams can be seen as a vital link between the individual and the organization. Thus initiatives taken at group level can act as a catalyst for the development of both. With this acknowledged, the development of the management group (bearing in mind its associated ambiguities) is an increasingly important focus for organizational and individual performance enhancement.

Dialogue

Within organizations, people do a lot of talking in order to accommodate diversity, change and complexity. Managers in particular spend up to 75 per cent of their time in conversation. Much of this talk is skilled and instrumental, and is different from the type of talk that is done more naturally in non-work settings, where ideas grow and learning takes place readily. This more developmental style of talking, 'dialogue', involves people collectively constructing new meaning with the purpose of uncovering what is tacit, making manifest that which is taken for granted, and testing reasoning.

In work, although dialogue topics such as effective listening and communication have a high profile, they are frequently underachieved.

Dialogue is somehow constrained so that conversations at work are not as developmental as in other situations. If people are not themselves at work, then how can 'selves', and consequently systems and organizations, develop? Increasingly, the organizational response to this dilemma is to establish the characteristics of effective dialogue, set ground rules, build on existing capabilities and create forums and conditions that promote dialogue practices in organizations.

Dialogue can be incorporated into work practices where a number of conditions are satisfied, principally:

■ empowerment of the group, with support from management and all necessary information available;

■ equality among participants: a diminished role perhaps for management and emphasis on self-management;

■ collective intelligence: no experts or consultants;

■ mixed interaction: alternate small- and large-group interaction.

There are a series of behaviours that individuals engaging in dialogue exhibit and a collection of conditions under which these behaviours are exercised. Dixon (1998) refers to the behaviours as speech acts and the conditions as situation variables (Table 7.3).

Examples of group settings that provide opportunities for dialogue, explored in the next section, are team meetings, away-days, action learning sets, project teams and virtual teams.

ACTIVITY 7.4 GROUP DEVELOPMENT

Think about two or more groups or teams of which you are a member or leader. What stage is the team at? What are the particular challenges facing the team at present? What direction would you like the team to develop in? How does your group measure up against Dixon's behaviours and conditions for dialogue in Table 7.3?

Table 7.3 _The conditions for dialogue_

Speech acts (behaviours)	Situation variables (conditions)
Accurate and complete information	Freedom from coercion
Feelings	Equal participation opportunities
Own position	Heterogeneous participants,
Explicit reasoning	diversity
Invite inquiry	Minimize deference
Inquire	Meetings without purpose or
Test out assertions	agenda
Voice alternative perspectives	Positive outcome
Illustrate and publicly test	interdependence
inferences	Means interdependence
Concrete examples	
Exert effort	
Acknowledge similarities and	
differences in ideas	
Reflect critically	
Objectivity	

USING GROUPS TO PROGRESS CHANGE

In this section we consider briefly various types of group that you can use to make your part of the organization dynamic and change oriented. If you do not have many of these sorts of group, it would probably be a mistake to start introducing them all at once. Start with one – one that makes sense given the task of your part of the organization and its way of working. Use this as a pilot to try out ideas and see what works for you.

Team meetings

Jon Katzenbach (1997) defines a real team (as opposed to a mere group) as 'a small number of people with complementary skills who are committed to a common purpose, performance goals, and an approach for which they hold themselves mutually accountable'. He argues that the litmus tests as to whether you have a team working appropriately and well are that:

▌ They shape collective work and products of clear value.

■ Members share leadership roles according to the task being carried out.

■ Members are mutually accountable for the group's results.

When you are forming groups, these are useful criteria to bear in mind. If teams have collective work and mutual accountability, then the possibility of conflict will never be far away.

Some recent research by Eisenhardt *et al* (1997) illustrates how this can best be addressed. They found that teams that dealt with it most effectively:

■ worked with more, rather than less, information and debated on the basis of facts;

■ developed multiple alternatives to enrich the level of debate;

■ shared commonly agreed-upon goals;

■ injected humour into the decision process;

■ maintained a balanced power structure – the leader having more power, but each member having substantial power, especially in his or her field of expertise.

■ resolved issues without forcing consensus – if it can be achieved, that is the best option; if not, the most relevant person makes the decision, guided by input from the rest of the group.

If you are involved with conflict in any of the teams you play a part in, these guidelines could act as a checklist to examine how you work. You don't have to reach a consensus on how you are doing, of course! You just have to share perceptions and agree areas for improvement.

Team meetings are the most basic form of gathering that you can establish for your people. If you do not run them already, they are probably best set up on a regular cycle, with the frequency depending on the nature of the group's responsibilities (long time span: less frequent meetings) and the geographic spread (dispersed groups: fewer meetings).

If you already run team meetings and are not wholly satisfied with the way they are running, then you might like to use the brief questionnaire in Activity 7.5 (page 169) as a means of investigating how they could be improved.

Another activity that you can use to develop teams is the Post-it planning process. This one can be used on a regular basis. The value of

Post-it planning is that it facilitates focusing on objectives, sharing information and reviewing progress.

Away-days

Away-days are what they say: team meetings that take place off-site. These are particularly useful to teams that get interrupted all the time if they meet at work. They are useful periodically for all teams, however, to review direction and re-energize. The activities for team meetings can be used on away-days, as can many of the questionnaires and activities in other chapters of this book. Away-days can be useful as preparation for a particularly hectic period of change. When planning such an event, aim to include the following elements:

■ a look at the future from someone who knows: you, a senior manager, someone in your team who has investigated what is about to happen;

■ a review of the past – including celebrating achievements;

■ customer input – something on what your internal or external customers want;

■ a fun activity – this can be an experiential exercise (see Fletcher *et al*, 1992);

■ a planning process to specify next steps;

■ a review of learning to capture and share what people have learned; this creates the habit and expectation that things will be learned from such gatherings;

■ time for leisure and informal discussion is also important; this can usefully be combined with a shared meal if the budget will stretch to it.

Action learning sets

Action learning (Pedler, 1996) simultaneously involves personal and organizational development through small sets of people (around six) engaging with a difficult task or problem in the company and acting to change it. Bringing the results back to the set for review and learning, at intervals of 2 to 4 weeks over 6 to 12 months, supports and challenges colleagues. Sets may have sponsors or facilitators, or alternatively may support each other as 'comrades in adversity' (Revans, 1998). To do this you need to have a process for checking in and out, a process for sharing time and a process for drawing out the learning.

The process seems simple enough but requires commitment from participants and willingness to take risks with their learning. It also requires companies to allow employees the necessary freedom.

The problem that individuals address can be in their sphere of influence, or they can bring fresh insight to another. Building expectations from the start that senior management are interested in outcomes, and will hear a report on what has been achieved at the end, will encourage commitment.

Project teams

In action learning sets, each member deals with his or her own unique problem. In project teams, the whole group address one problem, and have a collective responsibility. Increasingly, organizations are being organized more on project lines, so people have to divide their time between several activities. This means that the old certainties about having one boss and knowing exactly where you fit in are things of the past.

For a partly project-based organization to work well, team members need to learn about how to manage upwards as they will be reporting to different people – line managers and project managers – in the matrix. Competing demands on resources and people's time can soon lead to turf battles. Project managers and teams need to remember they are part of the same larger team and learn to improve processes rather than only adopt defensive behaviours.

Virtual teams

De-layering, globalization, round-the-clock working and the technology of digital communication have all contributed to the growth of virtual teams. Virtual teams fit Katzenbach's (1997) earlier definition of real teams, but do not meet face to face. There is much work dedicated to 'computer-mediated cooperative work', and developments in this field are coalescing with new understandings about dialogue.

Virtual working is demanding new skills of groups (Joy-Matthews and Gladstone, 2000), but also some old ones. For example, Charles Handy (1995) emphasizes the crucial role of trust in managing virtually. He makes the following suggestions:

▌ Trust needs boundaries. Members need competence and commitment. Give them self-contained work and encourage teams to solve their own problems.

- Trust demands learning: all members have to be encouraged to seek new opportunities and new technologies.

- Trust is tough: if people do not perform or seem deceitful, action has to be taken.

- Trust needs bonding: virtual teams have to commit to contributing to a wider goal to align their efforts.

- Trust needs touch: paradoxically, the more virtual teams become, the more the members need quality time together on special occasions to build trust and a shared culture.

- Trust requires leaders: all members need to be able to act as leaders or followers as the task, and people's skills, demand.

ACTIVITY 7.5 QUESTIONNAIRE ON TEAM MEETINGS

1. What do you value about your team meetings?

2. What don't you like about them?

3. What do you see as their purposes?

4. What should their purposes be?

5. What could you do to make them better?

6. What might prevent you making them better?

Get all your team to answer these questions and feed back. Make deciding what to do about it an agenda item for your next meeting (an example of giving attention to process as well as content). Set yourselves some actions and review regularly, but don't expect miracles. Find out what has been achieved before getting into problems; celebrate these achievements. If you think your group isn't into celebration of achievements, all we can suggest is 'try it'. You don't have to do anything fancy; just say, 'I think we have started well, and I'm particularly pleased that you have. . .' Seek out what else has to be done in an action-oriented rather than a blame-oriented way.

DIFFERING NEEDS OF GROUPS

There are many areas where different development needs may be expressed in organizations, eg teams, core and peripheral workforces, as well as more specific groups, eg professional, geographic, gender, age and ethnic groups, international managers and executives. Needs will be dependent on issues such as:

▌ the number of people involved;

▌ timescales;

▌ existing development initiatives and opportunities;

▌ existing and desired capability or performance;

▌ barriers to or enablers of learning;

▌ priorities;

▌ diagnostic approach adopted.

Needs are also defined by groups at different levels, eg corporate, business unit, operational, or in relation to specific groups, eg teams, team leaders, supervisors, line managers, or may have more general application. Some needs are defined around the timing of development, particularly if viewed in the context of a performance management system, eg induction, promotion, redeployment.

Different development needs of groups lie within the context of the emergent demands of business strategy, and change, within the workplace. Diagnosing and responding to needs is therefore contingent. Internal and inter-organizational learning networks may be particularly important in relation to achieving strategic thinking and capability, and influence the direction of the organization through time.

The internationalization of business has changed the meaning of development and expanded it to include more, and increasingly complex, managerial situations. The challenges presented to management by today's global business environment and the tensions created by balancing more local needs place demands on managers that are rarely attended to proactively. In Chapter 10 we consider some of the developmental challenges for different groups of managers.

ACTIVITY 7.6 GROUP MEMORY

Get your group together to set its agenda, to evaluate its experience or to address specific questions relating to its purpose. Use large media to record a 'group memory', such as sheets of paper on the wall or floor, flipcharts on table tops, or modern specialist facilitation boards if you have access to them. For larger groups, use more.

Designate different areas of wall/table/board to specific questions, hand out marker pens and invite written contributions on each subject. Establish priorities by voting with ticks or sticky dots. Move people on to consider each subject and read what others have said. Allow opportunity to seek clarification and create action plans as a result. Arrange for the sheets to be reproduced, eg as digital photographs.

The sort of questions posed in Activity 7.5 could be explored in this way.

CASE STUDY 7.1: REALITY CULTURE CHANGE PROGRAMME, 'WE DELIVER THE GOODS'

The company

The Reality Group provides customer services and logistics fulfilment to catalogue brands: Great Universal, Kays, Choice, abound, Home Free and Marshall Ward. The Group also provides a national home delivery service to some of the best-known names in the United Kingdom.

The organization's massive infrastructure includes the United Kingdom's largest parcel home delivery network, formerly known as White Arrow Express, one of the largest networks of contact centres, and a warehousing operation capable of sorting 30,000 parcels per hour. The company employs over 14,000 staff.

Reality had experienced considerable change over a period of several years, meaning that it was vital that people were clear on where the organization was moving as a business. Towards the end of 2002, the board established the direction of the company and articulated this through a statement of business purpose and values that the organization should aspire to. This was, in a sense, the senior management group taking stock of the business situation, learning from the company's experience and creating a vision of how things could be.

Business purpose: service at the right time, in the right place, at the right price, in the right way.

Reality values:
We achieve through teamwork.
We encourage and reward each individual's contribution.
We have a competitive will to win.
We are customer focused.
We add value to our clients' business.

These statements represented the first step in achieving alignment of corporate and individual agendas – or, in other words, establishing a culture oriented towards mutual success. Genuine culture change, it was decided, would be signalled by meeting customer expectations. This would require commitment to these values throughout the company, and that commitment would be more likely to be developed through employee participation in making them real, rather than just telling employees what they were. Only when the purpose and values were embraced by every person, and embedded in every business process from recruitment and selection to performance management and communications, would the culture change be recognizable.

The expression of vision led to an initiative culture change, which became branded as the 'We Deliver the Goods' programme. The programme had three objectives:

▪ to ensure that everyone in the business understands exactly what Reality is trying to achieve, ie the business purpose;

▪ to define the behaviours and the style of management necessary for Reality to provide service at the right time, in the right place, at the right price, in the right way;

▪ to establish where efforts should be focused in achieving the desired culture.

The programme

Sharing the vision and demonstrating leadership
Initially, the board shared the vision with their direct reports and some operational management, in total 50 people, via an away-day. From this group of senior managers, 12 people volunteered to form a project team, 'The Driving Force', with the remit of maintaining the direction and purpose of the initiative.

Learning how things are
Five 'Leading the Way' workshops were held for 300 voluntary attendees from all across the business (a representative group). These attendees were informed about the programme and consulted about behaviours that would be consistent with the values. The 300 employees and the 50 senior managers (collectively regarded as a group of Champions) also took part in a culture survey designed to create awareness generally and to enable the board and the Driving Force project team to learn how things actually were compared to the desired culture.

Learning what can be done and how to get there
The Champions conducted 750 local 'We Deliver the Goods' workshops across all areas of the business, which involved every employee, from all levels. These workshops asked employees to define behaviours that they would stop, start and do more of to achieve the culture change.

Sharing the learning
The Driving Force project team recognized the need for more champions to continue the momentum and interest in the programme. Six 'Action Groups' were formed, representing the main functional units of the business and whose membership was selected against carefully thought out criteria. Nominations were also made against set criteria, to identify Advocates in each key business location and corresponding to functions within the business. Advocates and Action Group members are drawn from various levels within the company.

The results of the culture survey demonstrated remarkably consistent messages about how the prevailing culture was experienced in the workforce. The results of the survey were fed back to the board, to the project team and then to the operational management group to develop specific objectives and plans.

Workshops were also run for the original 300 volunteers to communicate the results of the culture survey and share ideas for what the next steps would be.

Taking action
The Action Groups maintain momentum by refreshing initiatives across the business and seeking achievement of the desired culture. Action Groups hold monthly or bimonthly meetings that consider how the gap between prevailing and desired culture is being bridged, share creative ideas for how to live the values and articulate 'how we do things around here'. The Driving Force project team continues to meet regularly to feed back and cross-fertilize good practice.

Human resource development
The outcomes of these various group interventions that make up the 'We Deliver the Goods' culture change programme have included a number of implications for further human resource development in the company. A comprehensive training needs analysis for the strategically important group of first-line and middle managers was conducted to begin to clarify the management task and consider how to lead people into the desired culture. The analysis, when mapped against the core values, recommended a programme of development supported by interim coaching sessions. Managers would receive training in managing and supporting learning, giving and receiving performance feedback and coaching.

Recruitment and selection practices within the company incorporate the values in role profiles and translate them into competences that can be assessed at the selection stage.

A Performance Management system was established, whereby performance is partly defined in terms of the behaviours identified during the 'We Deliver the Goods' programme. The emphasis is not just on what is done but also on how it is done.

A Succession Planning system was established that dovetails Performance Management criteria with potential.

Evaluation

Reaction to the culture change programme was characterized by general positive engagement with this and other initiatives in which people have fun at work, eg theme days and charitable activity.

Behaviour change included greater awareness and activity in cross-functional working whereby employees can learn about other parts of the business by undertaking visits. There is a sense that employee motivation, confidence and job satisfaction all increased.

The performance management architecture now includes behaviours linked to objectives. This has meant first-line managers changing to an emphasis on leading people rather than being overly task focused.

The company enjoys improved relations with unions. Ideas are shared more willingly as a result of the culture change programme, and employee participation and involvement at all levels generally increased. Organizationally, staff retention levels increased, because a better fit at selection was achieved now that values were incorporated into the recruitment process.

Service level impact is considered difficult to quantify. However, it is believed by senior management that behaviour and attitude are fundamental to achieving results through people and that this ultimately has a positive effect on the bottom line.

During the life of the culture change programme, a change of ownership of Reality further challenged the company's employees. However, this change was accommodated by individuals noticeably more readily than in previous such experiences.

Further action, to continue to build on the positive climate, confidence and determination to succeed that have been created by the culture change programme, will include continued open communication, sharing of ideas, and regular review and development of the culture change process.

Keeping the Driving Force project team feeling fresh and alive will require continual review of progress, further assessment of culture compared to desired culture, and appropriate action. The benefits of benchmarking with other organizations will also be engaged to enable broader learning.

This case study illustrates the role of groups throughout a strategic process, the use of groups to achieve culture change, the different types of groups involved, the role of reaching a critical mass of people, the management group as strategically important, diagnosis and implementation through groups, and how HRD supports change.

SUMMARY

Organizational strategy implies change; change requires development of organizations and individuals; groups form strategically pivotal entities; and therefore development focused on groups is an effective and practical way of achieving organizational strategy.

Both conventional views and more contemporary views of change management highlight the importance of learning. When viewed as a series of broad stages, change is facilitated by activities at group level. However, it is important to understand some of the dynamics of how groups work and be ready to lever the different group opportunities that exist.

8

Organizational learning

INTRODUCTION

An increasing number of hard-headed business leaders have been saying that 'the ability to learn faster than competitors may be the only sustainable competitive advantage'. In this chapter we will examine what is involved in 'learning faster'. A learning company is described as 'one which facilitates the learning of all its members *and* continuously transforms itself as a whole' (Pedler, Burgoyne and Boydell, 1991). We use the term 'learning company', rather than the more inclusive 'learning organization', not because we have a private-sector bias, nor do we think that public-sector organizations cannot aspire to become learning companies. Instead we use the word 'company' because it smacks of 'companionship', rather than the more mechanistic connotations of 'organizing'.

This chapter examines the levels of learning that occur in a learning company. Whereas all organizations engage in 'single-loop learning', learning companies also address the challenges of 'double-loop learning' and 'deutero-learning'. These terms are defined and illustrated in what follows. We examine the central role of the line manager in generating the learning company approach, and we provide a process by which readers can examine how they might progress the learning ability of their organization.

LEARNING OUTCOMES

By reading this chapter, examining the frameworks in the light of the case studies presented, and reflecting on the connection between the examples here and your own situation, you will be able to:

▌ see the competitive advantages of working as a learning company;

▌ differentiate between single-loop learning, double-loop learning and deutero-learning;

▌ characterize your own organization and others in terms of learning company models;

▌ decide on what you might do to increase the organizational learning capacity of your own organization.

LEARNING FASTER AND COMPETITIVE ADVANTAGE

Two people are going along a twisting corridor. One is drunk and the other sober. The drunk bangs against a wall, then lurches across to the other side, and only changes direction again when contact is made with the other wall. The sober person, in spite of the twists and blind corners in the corridor, never touches the sides. He seems to know when to slow down, how to avoid potential blind spots ahead, and when it is safe to accelerate. When there is congestion, he deftly negotiates his way through the mêlée.

Both people may get to the other end of the corridor, but the drunk takes longer, causes more human damage and more damage to property. If there are glass walls or precipices ahead, the drunk may not make it at all.

Organizations can be seen in a similar light. The learning company is like the sober individual. It makes the small, moment-by-moment decisions smoothly. It tends not to make sharp turns. It can see ahead and predict when the corridor looks as if it will get congested; it can move to the other side and keep alert to avoid any obstructions. At a wider and deeper level, the learning company has decided that the strategy of staying sober is the one that gets you down corridors. People in a learning company are clear which route they want to take from among a range of options, and they know why. The learning company has the time to engage in alliances on the way and to conduct business while keeping moving.

On the other hand, the non-learning organization is a bit like the drunk. It seems to face a lot of crises calling for sharp changes in direction. Often onlookers are amazed at its agility in making spectacular recoveries, but these only seem to bring on the next crisis. In these imbroglios a lot of people get hurt, and damage is done to property and productive capacity. If our non-learning organization gets involved with another company, then progress stops while the two cling together, having intense conversations whose purpose and progress it is hard for an outsider to make sense of. Often the non-learning organization moves on again only after an acrimonious break-up.

So how can managers make their organization or the part of it for which they are responsible more like the image of the aware learning company? The answer comes in three parts.

First, they need to accelerate and open up single-loop learning. This is equivalent to not hitting the walls of the corridor. Then they need to notice changes in the offing and watch how they negotiate them and how they make the decisions about steering a new course. The new direction is found by a second process known as double-loop learning. Third, they ask and answer the big questions 'Who are we?' and 'Why are we here?' Perhaps most difficult and demanding of all, they address the question 'How do we decide how to answer these questions?' This may sound somewhat abstract, so in the next section we illustrate the three kinds of learning in relation to Frank Lord, the boss of Appleyards of Chesterfield, a very practical example of a manager working towards the learning company.

SINGLE-LOOP LEARNING AT APPLEYARDS

Frank Lord wants to make sure that he and everyone else in the company know how they are doing. He gathers a lot of comparative data – how they are doing *vis-à-vis:*

- other garages in the Appleyards group;

■   other garages in the area – the Derbyshire town of Chesterfield;

■   other Peugeot dealers in the country.

All staff then examine sales, turnover and profitability. Everyone has access to the figures. They are reviewed most intensely at the cycle of thrice-yearly Quality Improvement Teams, when everyone in the company has half a day working in cross-functional teams to examine areas for improvement.

Frank is delighted with progress in all areas in spite of the difficulties that have faced the motor trade since he opened up in Chesterfield in 1988. Interestingly, for a big, results-oriented businessperson, Frank says that he pays more attention to customer feedback results than he does to bottom-line figures. He says:

> The customer feedback is more immediate, and it is also closer to the root cause of our success than the management accounts. If customers are satisfied, then we know we will get the business. If something's going wrong here then we need to act immediately, as this will affect business in the next quarter, as the word gets round.

Of course, customer satisfaction does not just affect short-term satisfaction. It also has a crucial long-term influence on customers: when they consider buying their next car, for example.

So single-loop learning is *learning that enables an organization to examine the extent to which it is meeting existing norms and standards.*

DOUBLE-LOOP LEARNING BY TECHNICIANS AT APPLEYARDS

Initially Frank gathered customer feedback, analysed it and presented it to mixed-function 'Quality Improvement Teams'. The car mechanics (Frank calls them 'technicians') in these teams said, 'This information is out of date – publish it widely and at once.' So the actual cards returned by customers giving their views on the service that they had received were posted in the canteen as soon as they were received. Again the technicians complained, 'We still don't know which sheets refer to which technician; can't we have our names on the top?' So they did. Notice that the pace for making public this information about individuals' performance was set by the individuals themselves. Note also that it is published as soon after the event as possible. Frank awards a cut glass goblet to the technician of the month. This is not the person who has got the best scores in the feedback, but the technician who has got the most feedback sheets in. He thus avoids the trap highlighted by Deming (1989) of rewarding the best at the expense of (relatively) punishing the rest. All have a responsibility to improve, and the reward comes to those who generate the most data to help everyone to improve.

This is an example of double-loop learning as not only is the company learning from the data, but also it is learning how best to generate data and what to do with them when they are generated. Naïve interpreters of the idea of double-loop learning sometimes assume that it is about changing targets – moving from 7 per cent gross profit target, say, to 8 per cent. The process is more subtle than this, however. To engage in double-loop learning you also have to develop a way of determining new targets, and one that can be sustained and supported by those it affects. Just turning the screw a notch or two tighter is not double-loop learning.

So double-loop learning is *learning* to *change norms and standards, and to do so in a way that takes into account the views* of *those affected by the change.*

DEUTERO-LEARNING IN CHESTERFIELD

A shorthand description for deutero-learning is learning to learn. It involves people in a company saying, 'Let's look at the way we work things out round here, and let's see if we can find a better way.' It involves not just seeing trends and determining which are the significant ones and which indicators need watching; this is double-loop learning. It also entails influencing the environment in which the company exists – being generative, to use Senge's term (1990).

Frank Lord is generative in that he can create within Chesterfield a climate in which he sells 17 per cent of all the cars, compared with 8 per cent for Peugeot nationally. Is this anything to do with the over 100 charitable ventures he and his staff have supported in the first four years since he founded the garage? Appleyards' charitable activities constantly provide news for the local press. They have led to a visit from the Duke of Gloucester; and to a salesperson from one of his competitors coming to him for support for his pet charity, then confessing where he worked. Frank asked the salesperson, 'Why didn't you ask your own company?' He said, 'I did: they said no.' So now, six weekends a year, a salesman from another garage borrows Frank's parts van, which isn't used at weekends and has Appleyards' name in big letters on the side, and goes doing charitable work at a site where lots of people will come and watch. Some will know the salesman and will say, 'I didn't think you worked for Appleyards.' He will say, 'I don't, but. . .' Frank's argument is that he supports charities because it reflects his values (bringing love into the world) and (by encouraging staff to nominate their own charities) it enables them to integrate the work and personal aspects of their lives. All this is true. Is it good for business? Unquestionably, yes. While sceptics can disparage the act of 'doing well by doing good', the rest of us can merely sit back and wonder what kind of society we would live in if every employer with 55 or more staff supported over **100** charities in each four-year period.

This practice can be related to the learning company by considering Peter Senge's three levels at which a leader can influence people to view reality, shown in Figure 8.1.

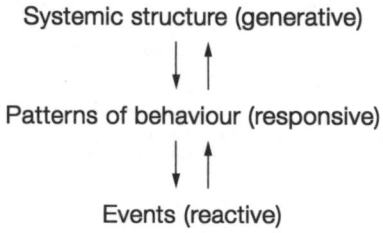

Figure 8.1   *Senge's levels of influence*

Frank's action in altering the perception of people in Chesterfield to his organization is a long-term, consistent, values-driven process of generating an environment in which people will 'think Peugeot, think Appleyards' when it comes to buying or repairing cars. No wonder he can ride out the recession without putting larger and larger advertisements in the local papers. He knows that 33 per cent of his sales come through recommendations and 19 per cent from repeat business, while only 14 per cent come from advertisements. He also knows that 96 per cent of his staff say 'Yes' to the question 'Could you explain to someone who does not work here what the organization is trying to achieve?'

Thus deutero-learning is *learning to learn, by examining the long-term effect of actions in the organization and making the organization influential in generating the environment in which it can thrive.*

A POSTSCRIPT ON FRANK LORD AND APPLEYARDS OF CHESTERFIELD

Since the bulk of this chapter was written, Frank has moved on from Appleyards of Chesterfield. First he was promoted within the Appleyards group, and then he moved out into another phase of his career. What has happened to his legacy in Chesterfield?

Managers who were of a more conventional style succeeded Frank. They found much to admire in what he left them – an organization performing well on all the financial measures, with motivated and dedicated staff and satisfied customers. They also found things that must have mystified them. Why were staff so independent, acting on their own discretion when they should have checked what was permitted? Why was money being spent on an education initiative that wasn't directly related to bottom-line needs (the Appleyards Learning and Education Centre, ALEC)? So, they exercised proper control and cut out the excess. Paradoxically in the eyes of these well-intentioned and conventionally capable managers, their actions seemed to make things worse rather than better.

Some of the keenest supporters of Frank's way found the new style unsupportable and left for organizations and jobs where they felt they could adhere to the principles they had experienced and come to value with Frank. Others remained and did what they could to support the learning approach in circumstances that had become less propitious. The once successful company became less successful and was sold twice in the years that followed.

What are we to learn from this outcome? A number of points come to mind.

▌ Is there a danger in relying on charismatic leadership? Does the changed culture melt away like summer snow when the leader disappears? Does it engender a form of dependency rather than learning?

▌ Leaders in a learning organization have to give as much attention to those who manage them as to those being nurtured under their wing. As well as seeking sanction and understanding of what they are doing while they are there, they need to ensure that their managers understand and accept what style of managing is necessary for the organization to prosper after they move on.

▌ It could be argued that learning companies are ephemeral, and can be swept away by a change in one person's job, but the outcome in this case may offer a different conclusion. Features of what Frank built remain at Appleyards of Chesterfield. There are also a number of other organizations fortunate to have people who are working for learning ends whom they have inherited from Appleyards (like the loosely flocking bluetits referred to later in this chapter).

▌ What has happened to individuals, in terms of concrete skills, self-esteem, career opportunities, cannot be taken away. For example, a young man who was a painter at Appleyards sought and took the opportunity to move into sales, initially by working at weekends. He is now successful in a sales role at another Peugeot main dealer. Others have moved into much more senior roles in other organizations and continue to practise the principles they learned with Frank.

▌ The learning company idea is not a magic formula guaranteeing success for ever. There are no such formulas. It offers a way to work on important matters for particular work communities where there is a critical mass of interest, drive, skill and goodwill. This is all that can be expected of it.

MOVING THE WORKPLACE TOWARDS BECOMING A LEARNING COMPANY

Table 8.1 gives you a self-exploration questionnaire to help you consider how you currently engage in learning company behaviours and plan how you can take on more learningful processes.

For each of the items in the questionnaire ask yourself how important it is to carry out the action in your part of the organization, and how satisfied you are with the quality of your action in this area. Score each item from 0 (low) to 5 (high) on both importance and satisfaction.

When you have explored this questionnaire, what are you tempted to do with it?

▌ *I wouldn't complete it.* This may be a sign of reluctance to engage in active learning.

▌ *I'd complete it and forget it.* This may emphasize a need to develop single-loop learning as a starting point. See below.

▌ *I'd use it to plan what I would do differently, then get on and implement my plan.* You may want to look at the section on double-loop learning below.

Table 8.1   *Self-exploration questionnaire on learning company behaviours*

Item	Satisfaction	Importance
1. Having good-quality information about results.		
2. Having good-quality information about internal customer satisfaction.		
3. Having good-quality information about external customer satisfaction.		
4. Having good-quality information about staff satisfaction.		
5. Having clear specifications for standards of work.		
6. Knowing when we deviate from work standards.		
7. Having means to review results with staff.		
8. Having means to review standards with staff.		
9. Having means to review satisfaction with internal customers.		
10. Having means to review satisfaction with external customers.		
11. Having means to review satisfaction with staff.		
12. Having means to improve results constantly.		
13. Having means to improve standards constantly.		
14. Having means to determine core purpose and vision, and adapt if necessary.		
15. Having means to share and explore purpose and vision.		
16. Having processes whereby staff and managers can learn from experience and mistakes.		
17. Having means to learn with suppliers.		
18. Having means to learn with customers.		
19. Having plentiful means for staff to learn.		
20. Having ability to influence the community in which we exist.		

▌ *I'd work with my people on how we might go about sorting out the main areas of need.* Try the list under double-loop learning again.

▌ *I'd ask staff and colleagues to complete a similar form and compare results.* Try the list headed deutero-learning.

▌ *I'd seek similar information from suppliers, customers and other key stakeholders.* Congratulate yourself. Consider how able you are to initiate action on your own behalf. If this raises difficult feelings in you, look at the single-loop learning list. If not, press on with the deutero-learning ideas.

Ideas for developing single-loop learning

1. Look at your scores for items 1–6 in the questionnaire. For which was the score for importance the most above satisfaction? Start looking at the biggest gaps first.

2. Identify skills that you or your staff lack in generating and analysing data. Make plans for bridging this gap.

3. Ask, ask, ask, ask, ask. These are five good ways of generating single-loop learning, from which a habit of openness to what you hear can develop. This can lead to double-loop learning in time, because, as you get used to hearing others' points of view, you begin to see things from their perspective rather than simply asking questions to pursue your own agenda.

Ideas for developing double-loop learning

1. Look at your scores on items 7–13 in the questionnaire. Look for the big gaps between level of importance and level of satisfaction. Plan with your staff how you could act on these areas.

2. Even better, give the questionnaire to staff to complete, compare their scores and yours and agree areas where there is a high priority for action. Then act, treating anything you do as an experiment to be learned from, rather than a management decision to be defended. This kind of upward feedback has been used in many organizations, including BP and W H Smith.

3. Look at the bluetits and robins box below and ask yourselves the questions, 'To what extent do we behave like robins in our part of the organization, to what extent like bluetits? How can we develop more bluetit characteristics?'

BLUETITS AND ROBINS

Why do bluetits know how to peck through milk bottle tops to get at the milk and robins haven't learned this trick? It is to do with the structure of their respective organizations. Bluetits gather in loose flocks, so they have opportunities to observe each other's behaviour. The flocks have shifting membership, so if the practice had taken hold in one flock, then members would go off and mix with other flocks and spread the news. Robins hang around gardens too, and have the opportunity to get at milk bottles. However, even when an individual robin does get the idea, there is no process for the skill to be shared. Robins are solitary and aggressively territorial. It is interesting that (from a review of any pile of Christmas cards) they seem to be Britain's favourite bird!

In what follows we give some further examples of double-loop learning applied in practice.

Frank Lord of Appleyards of Chesterfield has a system of job swaps. He works as a telephonist for a day, a technician works in the parts department. After the first run of swaps, they changed the system at Appleyards and had nominated job swaps. If someone had not kept records, say, and that had made it hard for the person whose job it was to process the documents to do their work, they could nominate the non-record keeper for a job swap, so that they see the situation from the point of view of their internal customer.

An unusual bluetit strategy that Frank uses is to *encourage* people if they want to leave to further their career. He then continues to act as an informal mentor to them. This means that any new learning from the Appleyards way of doing things being applied in a different place with different people can be fed back and tried out.

Another way of loosening inter-departmental barriers is to run developmental programmes over an extended period – say six to nine months

– with small groups of staff from a range of departments meeting together periodically in learning sets to address work-related concerns or personal and career dilemmas. Sometimes these groups are set up as action learning sets with the focus on the resolution of urgent and intractable work problems. In some cases, however, like Cable & Wireless's corporate Self-Managed Learning Project, the objectives are more open, so participants take ownership of the development that they want for themselves in a thorough way.

This is a high-risk, high-pay-off strategy and is not for the fainthearted, who may want to keep their action learners focused specifically on work-based projects. However, experience with an open self-development direction for groups, both at Cable & Wireless and with managers in Customs & Excise, has shown that groups, given this kind of freedom, act with extraordinary responsibility in doing things that develop both themselves and the organization.

If appraisal and making individual development plans is a fruitful form of single-loop learning, then 360° feedback is an enrichment that can generate double-loop learning. As the name suggests, 360° feedback is given by peers and superiors to a manager. The areas that differentiate effective performers from others are identified and staff are asked to rate the manager on how important each item is and the extent to which the manager delivers it – using a similar format to the questionnaire earlier in this chapter. Further details of this approach can be found in Chapter 4 of Megginson and Pedler (1992).

Ideas for developing deutero-learning

1. Review your own and your staffs scores on items 14–20 of the questionnaire. Decide which other stakeholders of your part of the organization could best be involved in your discussion. Invite them to join in with a view to your delighting them consistently in the service that you provide.

2. Hold an 'organization mirror' meeting once a year at which you invite representatives of all your main stakeholders (internal/external suppliers/customers, top management, board members (dare you?), community representatives, activists concerned about your product or service) to an off-site meeting where you look at trends for the future for your product or service (possibly using a distinguished external speaker, if you can generate the funds or goodwill to find such a speaker; if not, make it a project for one of your people to raise

the issues themselves); then examine ways in which your part of the organization could be even more responsive to the needs and requirements of your stakeholders.

3.   Seek support from someone outside your team to examine how you make decisions, what you attend to and what you miss. Emphasize that in this team-building activity your own behaviour is up for examination, and so too is that of others. Do this in a blame-free environment. This means that questions of 'Whose fault was it?' are not relevant; but exploring 'What went wrong? What can we learn from this? What can we do differently in the future?' becomes the way of life.

In the next section of this chapter we introduce another questionnaire. It is based around the 11 features of the learning company identified by Pedler, Burgoyne and Boydell (1991). These 11 features are listed in the box below, and the questionnaire illustrates each in turn with further questions which you can use to examine your own practice in these areas.

FEATURES OF THE LEARNING COMPANY

1.   *Learning approach to strategy* – examine your part of the organization's strategy with staff, make small changes which you treat as experiments.

2.   *Participative policy-making* – open decision-making, taking into account the views of all stakeholders.

3.   *Informating* – maximizing the sharing of information, using information technology to make this easy, instant and fun to use.

4.   *Formative accounting and control* – accounting, budgeting and reporting systems designed to assist learning and self-regulation.

5.   *Internal exchange* – delighting internal customers and maximizing the overall win–win outcome of negotiation for the organization as a whole.

6.   *Rewarding of flexibility* – considering the basis for pay differentials and debating this openly; identifying and agreeing to the use of non-financial rewards.

7. *Enabling structures* – having flexibility, space and head-room for development.

8. *Boundary workers as environmental scanners* – people in contact with customers gather information, which is collated and acted upon.

9. *Inter-company learning* – sharing, stealing shamelessly (and letting others steal ideas from you), benchmarking (cooperative and joint ventures are part of the spirit of the learning company).

10. *Learning climate* – questioning ideas and actions, seeking feedback from others, valuing mistakes as learning opportunities, relishing difference as a generator of new ideas.

11. *Self-development opportunities for all* – people encouraged to take responsibility for their own development and given ample and flexible resources to pursue this development.

DEVELOPING THE LEARNING COMPANY IN YOUR WORKPLACE

The following checklist provides a means of thinking in practical terms about what you might do about building a learning company where you work. Mark each item with *Y* if you do it, *N* if you don't, ? if you are not sure, and *D* if you don't know.

Photocopy the questionnaire and give a copy to each of your staff, and seek their feedback.

Three ways of getting this feedback are:

1. From the whole team at once in a team meeting, which maximizes the exposure for you as the manager – this method does provide a chance for synergy and the development of ideas by the team.

2. One-to-one from each of your staff, possibly to balance up a session where you are giving them feedback and coaching, eg an appraisal or personal development planning meeting.

3. Anonymously returned questionnaires, so you can aggregate the scores and discuss the overall pattern with the team.

This kind of discussion in itself helps to engender a learning company climate. It provides for upward feedback, openness to having your views examined, and a sharing approach to making improvement.

ACTIVITY 8.1 CHECKLIST FOR MOVING TOWARDS A LEARNING COMPANY

Action	Y	N	?	D
1. Agree and adapt strategy in consultation with staff.				
2. Try out new strategies with staff and consult them about the impact.				
3. Share policy decisions.				
4. Encourage open debate and the voicing of differences.				
5. Provide the maximum possible availability of information for all.				
6. Encourage others to use this information for decision-making.				
7. Design information systems that are fun and easy to use.				
8. Use accounting and control systems in a way that encourages self-control.				
9. Encourage this part of the organization to see itself as an internal supplier to others.				
10. See managing as 'providing an internal service of management' to staff.				
11. Reward staff equitably within authority.				
12. Change structure and roles to enable learning and growth.				

13. Organize jobs swap.

14. Consult those staff who are in touch with internal and external customers about our service.

15. Learn and apply ideas developed elsewhere.

16. Use mistakes *and* successes as learning opportunities.

17. Don't blame.

18. Accept that people are doing the best they can *at the time*.

19. Encourage staff to examine and give feedback on managers' actions.

20. Encourage staff to reflect on and examine their own behaviour.

21. Make resources for learning available for all staff.

22. Encourage staff to set goals for learning before beginning a learning activity.

23. Review learning and plan action with staff after learning activity.

24. Encourage staff to set a development plan for themselves regularly.

25. Evaluate effects of learning/training development regularly.

RESEARCH ON THE 11 CHARACTERISTICS

The Royal Institution of Chartered Surveyors (RICS) funded some research at Sheffield Hallam University, which examined the relationship between adoption of the 11 characteristics (see page 189) in surveying practices and the success of these companies. The report of this research is of particular significance as surveying practices are examples of knowledge-based firms, which are seen by many authorities as the organizational form which is going to predominate in the future (Matzdorf *et al,* 1997).

The firms represented in the survey were drawn from two populations – which we called 'successful' and 'random'. The successful firms were those judged to meet our success criteria by a large sample of leading members of the profession. The random firms were then selected from a database of all firms in the profession from which these successful firms had been removed. Our survey had 281 respondents, 148 from 'successful' and 133 from 'random' firms. An impressive result from this research was that the successful firms reported a higher level of activity with all 11 of the 11 characteristics. The probability of this result being obtained by chance was tiny, so it seems that there is some real link here. Of course, correlational studies do not prove causality, but we were strongly encouraged to find the 11 characteristics being associated with success.

We asked our respondents about not only the level of the 11 characteristics present in their firm (the 'is' measure) but also how much of the characteristics they would like (the 'would like' measure). We then examined these measures in relation to the size of practice (very large, large, medium and small) and in relation to other variables, including the level of job of the respondent. We found that three characteristics were given high 'is' measures by all size categories. These were 'internal exchange', 'learning climate' and 'self-development for all'. The lowest 'is' scores were given to 'participative policy-making', 'reward flexibility' and 'inter-company learning'.

With 'participative policy-making' we found that there was a sharp difference in the scores for 'would like' between partners in the firms and their staff. In effect, staff wanted a lot more of this and bosses thought that there was already enough. This issue of organizational power is one of the key reasons for the difficulty of introducing learning company practices. They challenge the vested interests of current power-holders.

'Reward flexibility' is found to be one of the most difficult and intractable areas in all surveys of the 11 characteristics that we have come across, and represents a major challenge in designing learning organizations. This survey was exceptional, however, in the low scores for 'would like' allocated to 'inter-company learning'. For all the talk of being a profession, which is posited on maintaining and sharing standards, in practice surveyors found such sharing very undesirable. This again represents a sharp challenge to these and other professional service firms. We conducted some detailed case studies of firms in our successful sample, and one exception to this rule of non-sharing seemed to be the practices in a small, relatively isolated town. Even here our respondents said, 'We share a lot with all firms in Lincoln except one.' So, there were limits to their openness, and a firm that was seen to be predatory and aggressive was left out of this network. It may be that for firms in other places inter-company learning would best be initiated between related organizations that were not direct competitors – such as a law firm and an accountant, or surveying firms that were geographically distant.

Among the contrasts between firms of different size, one of the clearest was about 'boundary workers as environmental scanners'. Very large and large firms found they had less of this and wanted more of it than medium and small practices. This may illustrate an advantage of smallness. It may show that in a small office, bosses can be tempted into feeling they know all that is to be known, so they do not need insights from receptionists and technical assistants. The result poses interesting questions for large and small organizations alike.

In fact, this is the main value of frameworks like the 11 characteristics, and research programmes like the RICS survey. They pose new questions that can lead people in organizations to set up a process of dialogue and exploration to find what needs to be changed.

CASE STUDY OF A HIGH-GROWTH KNOWLEDGE-BASED COMPANY

This chapter so far has been built around a low-technology company, where one man's vision had a powerful impact on the nature of the company while he was at its head. The case study of Nexor offers a contrast in that it is highly knowledge based, with over half the staff having PhDs and university research experience before they join the firm. It is also a case study of a long-term successful relationship between a consultant (Wyn Williams, Director of idm Group, a strategic change consultancy) and the top team of the company, including Irene Dovey, Business Improvement Manager of Nexor, who collaborated in the writing of this case study.

ACTIVITY 8.2

Case Study 8.1 below gives some background about Nexor, a company situated in the Science Park at Nottingham University. It then describes some of the organizational learning and development that the company has undertaken. Use the frameworks in this chapter to analyse the development of Nexor. From your interpretation of the case, what are examples of single-loop, double-loop and deutero-learning? Which of the 11 characteristics of the learning company seem best developed? What more can be done?

CASE STUDY 8.1: NEXOR – A LEARNING COMPANY

Nexor is an information technology business with its headquarters in central Nottingham. It was formed out of a research project conducted by the Computer Sciences Department at Nottingham University in 1990. It currently has a turnover of £5.5 million, employs some 80 people and is navigating an ambitious plan for growth.

The company specializes in messaging and directory solutions for use in high-risk, complex environments where security and reliability are paramount. The Ministry of Defence uses Nexor for all messages classified as 'secret', the European Central Bank transfers billions of euros a day using Nexor, the front-line information infrastructure used during the Kosovo conflict was built around a Nexor product and Nexor is used to circulate the Prime Minister's weekly cabinet briefing.

The Nexor Improvement Programme (NIP) was set up some six years ago to ensure that the organization remains at the forefront of a rapidly evolving industry and makes the most of the talent and expertise it has within the business. The initial aims of the NIP included:

■ to introduce and embed current best practice into the organization;

■ to encourage learning, innovation and improvement;

■ to build an infrastructure for growth;

■   to promote and retain the organization's culture as the business grows and develops;

■   to integrate a number of initiatives into a single framework.

The NIP now incorporates a number of initiatives that underpins its 'way of working':

Corporate audit

During the mid-1990s the company had three separate false starts in introducing ISO 9000 into the business. Managers believed that ISO was an important control needed to steer the organization's growth. However, feedback from staff highlighted that the bureaucratic, compliance-focused systems that were introduced detracted from the culture that had been developed, which was based upon challenge, innovation and experimentation.

A programme of 'corporate audit' was developed out of this feedback. This approach, whereby a team are drawn together to check standards, review process and question overarching company policy, is viewed as a challenging, participative and congenial approach to quality and continuous improvement, with the audit team making operational and policy change recommendations. Audits have become a welcomed part of the management process and are seen as an important tool with which to confront established conventions and develop more innovative approaches.

Additional external challenge based upon established best practice is brought to the process through accreditation to ISO 9001, Investors in People and BS 7799 standards.

Balanced scorecard

The balanced scorecard was adopted as a 'change control' mechanism. The starting point for scorecard development is a management away-day when organizational strengths and weaknesses are matched against emerging market developments and threats. This analysis is combined with the growth aspirations of owners to produce a high-level business plan. The business plan is translated into a simple scorecard through asking:

- What do we need to do with our customers to achieve financial ambitions?

- How do our internal processes need to adapt to meet our customer ambitions?

- What do we need to learn in order to implement the required process changes successfully?

Indicators and targets based around the answers to these questions are then cascaded to the relevant functional departments, which specify how they will achieve the required process innovations in their area. Systematic and continuous feedback during the year is used as a basis for problem-solving and predicting future performance at all levels of the organization.

Nexor Improvement Board

An Improvement Board was established to steer and provide added impetus to the NIP two years ago. The board comprises six employees from across the organization, who are invited to join for a 12-month tenure, with three members changing every six months to ensure continuity. All board members are given comprehensive training in business improvement on appointment, and initial meetings use both performance information and company audit feedback to pinpoint improvement projects for the organization. Cross-functional improvement teams are then set up to manage these projects, and the project leader reports progress monthly to the Improvement Board. Participation on the board is seen as a valued responsibility, and each member receives an additional £1,000 on his or her salary. The board has directed a number of significant projects in the business, including time recording, project management and company infrastructure.

The Nexor Grid

The Nexor Grid was introduced as part of the NIP to bring a higher degree of consistency in performance management and to ensure a much greater emphasis on values and behaviours during feedback.

The grid measures two aspects of people's contribution to the organization: how they perform against business objectives and how they approach and carry out their role. Before each six-monthly evaluation meeting, the manager will identify where he or she believes the staff member is positioned on the Nexor Grid. The manager will first use the strict criteria to establish whether the employee has demonstrated that he or she has behaved outstandingly, satisfactorily or unsatisfactorily. These behaviours are tightly specified around the five Nexor values: customer focused, communicative, team player, innovative, flexible and accountable. Second, the manager evaluates whether performance has been outstanding, satisfactory or unsatisfactory against measurable objectives that have been cascaded from the balanced scorecard.

The manager then positions the employee on the Nexor Grid.

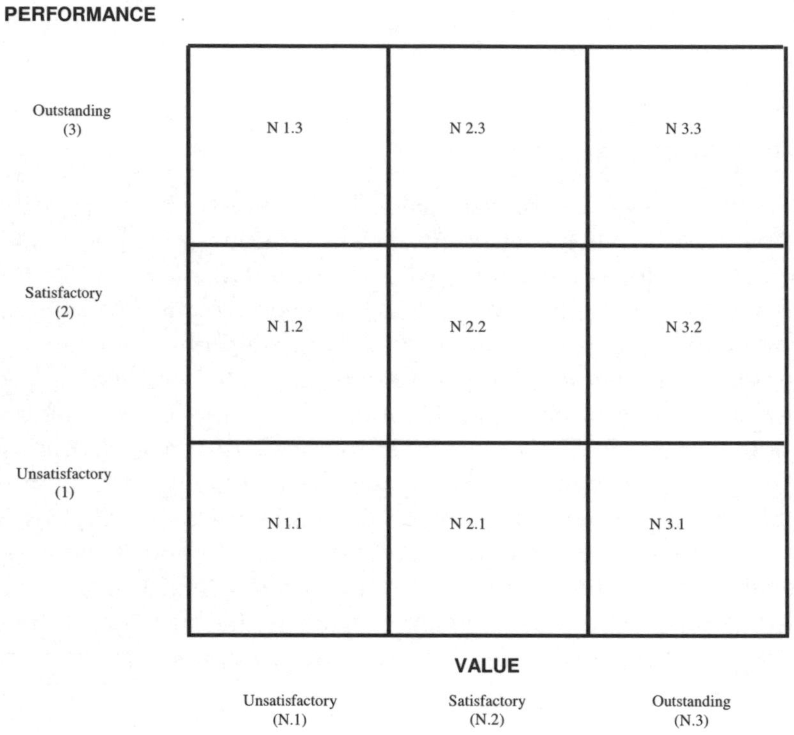

PERFORMANCE

	Unsatisfactory (N.1)	Satisfactory (N.2)	Outstanding (N.3)
Outstanding (3)	N 1.3	N 2.3	N 3.3
Satisfactory (2)	N 1.2	N 2.2	N 3.2
Unsatisfactory (1)	N 1.1	N 2.1	N 3.1

VALUE

Figure 8.2   *The Nexor Grid*

The grid is underpinned by a number of important principles that the whole organization understands.

The majority of staff will cluster around satisfactory/satisfactory (the criteria used dictate this), and that is all the organization expects.

Special interest will be paid to a member of staff who is ranked outstanding/outstanding (this will be about 4 per cent of the workforce). Performance problems can easily be addressed if the employee is demonstrating the required behaviours – for example, through additional training or guidance.

Potentially, the most damaging employees are those who score outstanding for performance but act in a manner that detracts from the organization's values (unsatisfactory).

The Nexor Grid has also been linked to the pay and reward system to further reinforce the culture.

Company meetings

All employees are invited to a quarterly company meeting. Each meeting begins with an honest appraisal of company performance delivered by the Chief Executive, who then invites challenging, open and frank feedback and appraisal of the leadership team from the entire organization. The meeting is facilitated to ensure a positive conclusion with agreement reached on where senior managers can provide further direction and support and how employees can exercise greater operational leadership.

The Friday seminar

Every Friday, employees are invited to a one-hour seminar on a relevant topic area. These seminars were set up to promote sharing of knowledge across the business and to encourage collaboration across functional areas. Attendance is voluntary, and after five years of seminars, the majority of employees still participate every week. Recent topic areas have included new security standards, what the company's major clients are doing, product innovations being tested and company templates explained.

Commentary and further questions on the case

Is the corporate audit simply single-loop learning? Or does it go beyond compliance (doing things right) to creativity (doing right things)? Similarly, where would you place the balanced scorecard?

Is the Nexor Improvement Board an example of deutero-learning, or is it 'only' double-loop learning? IT seems to throw into question deep assumptions about only the board making decisions about processes and infrastructure. But what would happen if the NIB came into direct conflict with the board of the company? Would this shadow board just be a shadow?

Does the Nexor Grid represent a source of learning and development or is it a control mechanism? How should it be developed?

Do company meetings have a chance of shaping the direction of the organization, or are they an opportunity for the top to talk to the rest? Deutero-learning or single loop?

Similarly, are the Friday meetings just knowledge sharing (single loop) or is something more fundamental taking place?

The purpose of inviting you to consider this case is not to come to a judgement about Nexor. It is to encourage you to think deeply about organizations in your sphere of influence. What kind of learning goes on in these at an organizational level? Which of the 11 characteristics are best developed and which are most in need of further development? Recent books on organization learning that we have valued include those by Christensen and Raynor (2003), Collins (2001), Darwin, Johnson and McAuley (2002) and Shaw (2002). Christensen and Raynor focus on innovation and in particular the potency and challenge of what they call disruptive innovation. Collins, in a well-researched study, illuminates the processes that enable companies to make major long-term development 'from good to great'. Darwin and colleagues have a deep look at various ways of understanding and therefore creating change, and Shaw addresses the power of developmental conversations, which are means for participants to shift the web of constraints in which they are enmeshed (Shaw, 2002: 51).

SUMMARY

The learning company is not simply a checklist for action. It is a demanding and life-changing way of relating to self and organizations. In this chapter we have offered a range of ideas on how to begin to develop this approach. There are no simple recipes. Instead, we encourage you to seek out your own way of adding the learning ingredient to your organization's menu.

9

Diagnosis and evaluation in human resource development

INTRODUCTION

'Diagnosis', when associated with health care, means 'determine the nature of [disease] by means of symptoms'. The term has currency in the field of HRD too. Caring for the 'health' of an organization will involve giving some consideration to its condition. This will almost certainly involve some kind of investigation or assessment, decision or judgement, and, finally, action or intervention. Action and intervention may involve some developmental process, possibly even training, but may equally involve some other aspect of management. So, diagnosis is necessary if HRD is to be positioned effectively within the realm of management activity. The implication here is that diagnosis represents a rigorous approach to HRD, more so than, say, identifying training needs, which may presuppose that training is the solution.

Evaluation, in the context of HRD, literally means 'find the value of', and is readily conceptualized as the final stage in a sequence. Indeed, systematic models of training do this explicitly (see Chapter 3). However, an organizational development consultant may, for example, use evaluation at the beginning of the process of identifying performance elements that can offer maximum influence and leverage. There are some searching questions to be asked about evaluation. For now it is sufficient to note that diagnosis and evaluation are interlinked.

LEARNING OUTCOMES

As a result of reading this chapter and undertaking the activities, you should aim to progress in your ability to:

▌ understand the close relationship between diagnosis and evaluation in HRD;

▌ determine the nature of organizational situations and problems towards which HRD may contribute constructively;

▌ understand a range of diagnostic methods;

▌ demonstrate the worth of HRD practices;

▌ appreciate the value that evaluation itself adds to the learning process and the field of HRD.

DIAGNOSIS

Any thorough diagnostic process, however initially concerned with HRD, may actually conclude that some other aspect of management is the real concern. Different organizational contexts give rise to different management priorities, which in turn can lead to different approaches to HRD (see Chapter 3). How prevailing management perspectives are formed will depend on any number of variables linked with the interplay between different parts of the organizational system. Thus early in any diagnostic process, it is useful to bear in mind the different aspects of organizational systems. So-called systems models (eg the 7-S framework of Waterman *et al*, 1988) attempt to present a whole picture of an organization, its issues and the interdependence between one subsystem and another in the fashion of the model shown in Figure 9.1.

For Senge *et al* (1994: 6), systems thinking is necessary to understand 'the forces and interrelationships that shape the behaviour of systems', and is an essential discipline in the pursuit of any development initiative in organizations. In contrast to the rather structural model presented above, Senge describes his view of organizational systems in terms of discrete sets of behaviours or disciplines: personal mastery involving self-development, sharing of mental models, shared vision, team learning and systems thinking.

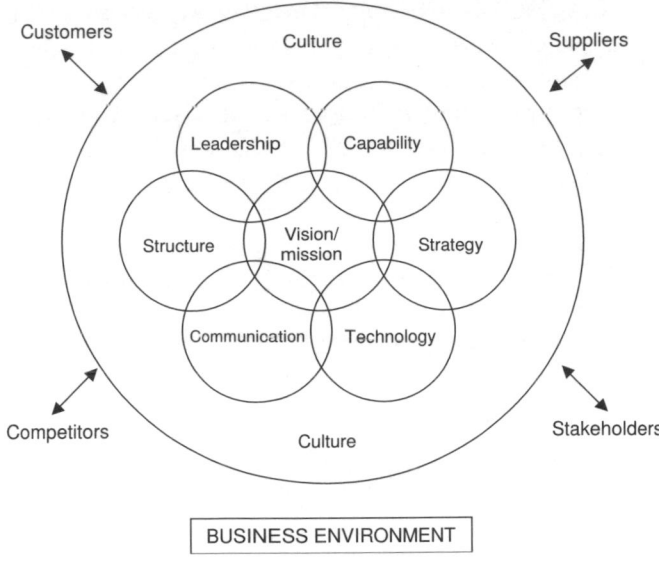

Figure 9.1 *Model of organizational subsystems*

Whether from a perspective that views organizational systems in terms of structures or generic disciplines, or both, any diagnostic effort will benefit from an appreciation of the whole system. 'Selection of any one solution is dependent upon the cause and nature of the performance problem, and the criteria used to evaluate a solution must include its potential to make a measurable difference in the performance system' (Rothwell, 1996).

There may be multiple solutions to human performance issues. Thus being able to accurately diagnose reasons for performance problems (ie looking beyond the symptoms) is significant to HRD. Clearly establishing the nature of the underlying problem is critical: misdiagnosis could lead to inappropriate responses, which become destined to fail.

Diagnosis is not just about looking for problems; it is equally concerned with seeking opportunity. Methods associated with 'identifying training needs' tend to concentrate on a 'deficit' model of analysis – that is, identifying gaps in performance that can be filled with suitably designed interventions. However, an alternative stance is represented by the notion of appreciative inquiry (Cooperrider *et al*, 1995) – that is, considering characteristics and their potential for growth, envisaging an enhanced future and doing what is necessary to move towards it, rather than constantly seeking to move away from undesirable aspects of the present.

By the time an individual manager or HRD practitioner gets involved with a performance issue, to an extent the diagnosis may have already been made, in however crudely and politically loaded a way. It is therefore important for the practitioner to know and understand how the diagnosis was arrived at. Reverting to the health care analogy, treating the 'presenting complaint' may not address deeper systemic concerns.

> When it is done well, diagnosis clearly points the organization towards a set of intervention activities that will improve organizational effectiveness. Diagnosis is the process of assessing the functioning of the organization, department or job to discover sources of problems and areas for improvement. (Cummings and Worley, 1993: 84)

ACTIVITY 9.1 SYSTEMS THINKING

Think of an issue that is affecting your organization; it may be associated with a particular subsystem, a discipline or an as yet unrealized opportunity. Note down your understanding of the present state of this issue in relation to each aspect of the system, perhaps using the systems model in Figure 9.1.

Now, for each aspect you have described, note your thoughts on the preferred different state. In each case, what human performance enhancements will achieve the desired state? What measures are beyond the gift of human performance?

Organizational diagnosis

Diagnosing organizational requirements concerns the performance of the organization as a whole and performance at various levels. Categories of performance provided by Boydell and Leary (1996) – implementing, improving, innovating (see Chapter 3) – provide a helpful framework from which to consider levels of performance and diagnosing requirements. Diagnosis will require information about current performance in the form of objective data, feedback from others or self-assessment, and about future changes. This information may come from stakeholders, environmental sources or feedback received internally and externally.

Different people may be involved with diagnosis: those with whom the need is associated (primary roles) and those involved in providing the information (secondary roles). The people involved may include learners, colleagues, line managers, senior managers, clients, customers, suppliers and budget holders. Whatever their relationship to the diagnostic process, there are likely to be various influences and perspectives that are bound up in the unavoidably political context of organizations. Therefore, various skills are required for diagnosis, generally comprising:

- process skills, eg making plans, setting goals, reviewing and evaluating;
- relationship skills, eg supporting, listening, empathizing, challenging and confronting;
- content skills, eg data collection, information handling, analysis, interpreting and summarizing.

These various contingencies indicate the potentially complex and difficult associations of diagnosis. However, from a more systematic perspective, the overall process of diagnosis may be summarized into six key stages.

1. Define and redefine the boundaries and chart the processes that define the organization or part thereof where performance is up for analysis.

2. Collect detailed data to illuminate the situation.

3. Establish comparative levels of performance required.

4. Identify the cause of the current limitations on performance where the effect is a system-wide phenomenon rather than individual.

5. Prioritize the causes, perhaps by involving everyone in the system, or a representative sample.

6. Propose and prioritize possible solutions.

Where the focus for concern for organizational performance is to meet current objectives (ie implementing) or to improve existing operations, assessment and judgement need to be based on well-informed data. Objective data, whether qualitative or quantitative, may come from benchmarking, feedback say in the form of customer and supplier surveys, feedback generated internally (eg attitude surveys) or organizational learning climate surveys.

Where organizational performance is concerned with innovating and making fundamental strategic decisions about organizational purpose and direction, diagnosis may involve assessing an organization's stage of development – for example, from pioneering and entrepreneurial through formalized and bureaucratic to integrated and synergistic. Here diagnosis can be aided by using, as a basis for detailed exploration, various elements of success such as main ideas (represented in purpose, vision or values), the reality of relationships, processes and resources, and the bridge between ideas and reality that is formed by people.

In diagnosing learning and performance at a strategic level, increasingly there is a shift away from involving solely senior management. Organizations engage with processes that bring together larger numbers of people from the whole organization, or system, to discover common ground and share the formulation of action plans (so called large-group interventions).

ACTIVITY 9.2 CAUSE AND EFFECT: FISHBONE DIAGRAM

Think of an issue in how human resource development is carried out in your organization. This could be a problem or some success, but a problem might be more generative here. Consider this the effect.

Now think of the major contributors to this issue and make these the first branches on your fishbone (see the example in Figure 9.2). For each of these 'causes', think through, and add as sub-branches, the things that contribute to them. As you explore deeper into each cause, look for recurring themes.

Do these themes represent the underlying causes of this issue (and others)? Which themes can be addressed by HRD? Which are beyond the scope of HRD? What are you going to do about it?

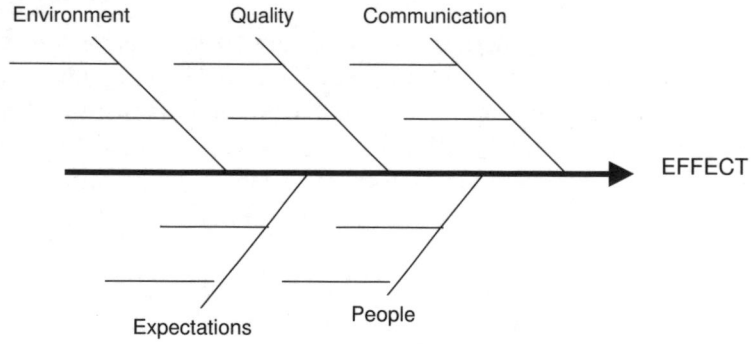

Figure 9.2 *Fishbone diagram with examples of headings*

Methods for diagnosis

Research

An appropriate approach to take to diagnosis depends on the sort of contextual factors discussed above. However, the methodologies available tend to be similar to those used by managers when investigating complex problems. In some situations it may be appropriate to use quantifying measures such as performance indicators, surveys and questionnaires, particularly if there is a large population in the organization whose performance, attitudes or views need to be understood. If the issues under consideration are at all sensitive, it may be more appropriate to use more qualitative processes such as feedback or interviews. This is particularly so when the diagnosis is viewed as part of the learning process in itself and contributors themselves make connections they had not made before.

However, diagnosis is not an end in itself; it is there to provide information on what action can be taken. So, while diagnosis needs to capture perceptions and understanding reasonably accurately, it does not necessarily demand the rigour of a scientific investigation. Ethically, there are also issues of confidentiality to consider.

Broadly, two extremes of diagnostic method can be identified in terms of degree of prescription between directed (focused) and undirected (open) research (Nevis, 1987). The characteristics of these types are summarized in Table 9.1.

Table 9.1 *Characteristics of directed and undirected diagnosis*

Directed (focused) diagnosis	*Undirected (open) diagnosis*
▮ Relatively easy to establish	▮ Requires a great deal of searching
▮ Pursues an agenda	▮ Responds to issues as they arise
▮ Work from a position	▮ Avoids prior assumptions
▮ Narrow, specific consideration	▮ Values all data, lets themes emerge
▮ Emphasizes measures	▮ Emphasizes meaning
▮ Values objective data and benchmarks	▮ Values discovery and subjectivity
▮ Rational, scientific approach	▮ Holistic approach
▮ Expert consultancy	▮ Facilitation

Source: Adapted from Nevis (1987)

Good practice would involve some blend of these two positions, making progress in an accountable way while remaining open and able to accommodate all relevant data. In this respect, diagnosis is similar in form to the field of action research.

Action research
Action research is a developmental, formal, systematic and cyclical process by which initial research provides information to guide subsequent action and further research (French and Bell, 1990). The benefit of this approach is that it not only diagnoses and implements planned change but also helps to develop the skills to deal with future problems. Collecting relatively objective data, sharing those data through workshops, generating meaning collectively, action research involves movement from diagnosis to implementation.

Business development as diagnostic activity
Business plans vary in form and content depending on what they aim to achieve, over what timescale and for what audience they are intended. Undertaking a business development plan at any stage in an organization's growth can be used to take stock, refocus and provide direction for the future, as well as to engage the 'current' team. The degree to which any plan represents real intent or just aspiration depends largely on the autonomy of the organization and how much uncertainty surrounds it.

Business planning, in general, concerns the relationship between the purpose of an organization and the environment in which that purpose is pursued. Purpose can be a key diagnostic issue, either creating or providing an understanding of existing statements of purpose. The environment includes that which is represented by stakeholders and their interests as well as political, economic, social and technological (PEST) environments.

The analysis of purpose and environment provide data for development planning questions such as: what do we actually do, how do we do it, and how do we need to develop what we do? Thus a plan is a process of mapping out the situation, sharing perspectives, generating ideas and taking action.

Systems approach: challenging questions
Previously this chapter considered the notion of a systemic approach to diagnosis. Associated with this, searching diagnostic questions may need asking about any of the elements or disciplines that make up the system:

■ Culture: how do people describe the atmosphere in the organization?

■ Communication: how do people describe the formal communications?

■ Purpose: can people express a shared vision?

■ Strategy: what do you need to do to respond better to your customers or competitors and create unique value?

■ Technology: does the technology enhance communication or make it more private?

■ Leadership: what style of management is really valued?

■ Capability: how does your organization develop its people?

■ Structure: does the structure reflect the needs of customers or internal power needs?

Research, business development and systemic questions all represent analyses that need to be synthesized and clearly communicated. Some tools for doing this are force field analysis, change analysis, 'U' process analysis, SWOT analysis and feedback.

Force field analysis
Force field analysis is an analytical tool that graphically represents Lewin's (1951) forces for change and forces for maintaining the status quo. All such forces are identified and can be prioritized and action-planned (see Figure 9.3). As much attention could be paid to reducing the influence of restraining forces as increasing forces for change.

Change analysis
By judging activity in line with four general categories, change analysis establishes a sense of priority and appropriate action:

■ must dos: processes critical to success, could need major change;

■ keep stable: core processes but not a priority for change;

■ areas for innovation: future success dependent on change here;

■ subsidiary activities: maintenance activities – should be few.

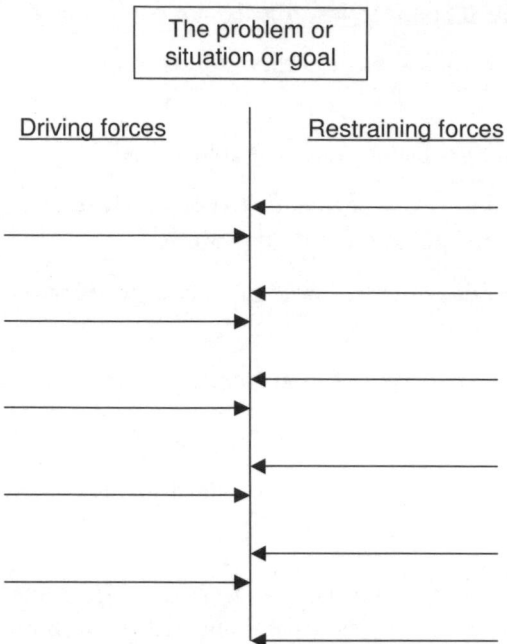

Figure 9.3   *Force field analysis*

'U-process' for diagnosis and action

The 'U-process' involves reflection on past actual experiences, moving to defining the present situation and through to conceptualizing the future and finally making concrete proposals for action. The process is illustrated in Figure 9.4.

SWOT

Another widely used diagnostic tool worth recalling is a SWOT analysis, which can be used by individuals, groups, departments or whole organizations to consider their strategic position. The meaning of the acronym is given in Figure 9.5.

Typically, each of these sets of characteristics would be populated with ideas, which are then evaluated and action-planned. Collective contribution of ideas (brainstorming) often begins this process.

Feedback

Other techniques that may be used to diagnose conditions centre on getting feedback from others. At organizational level this may be feedback

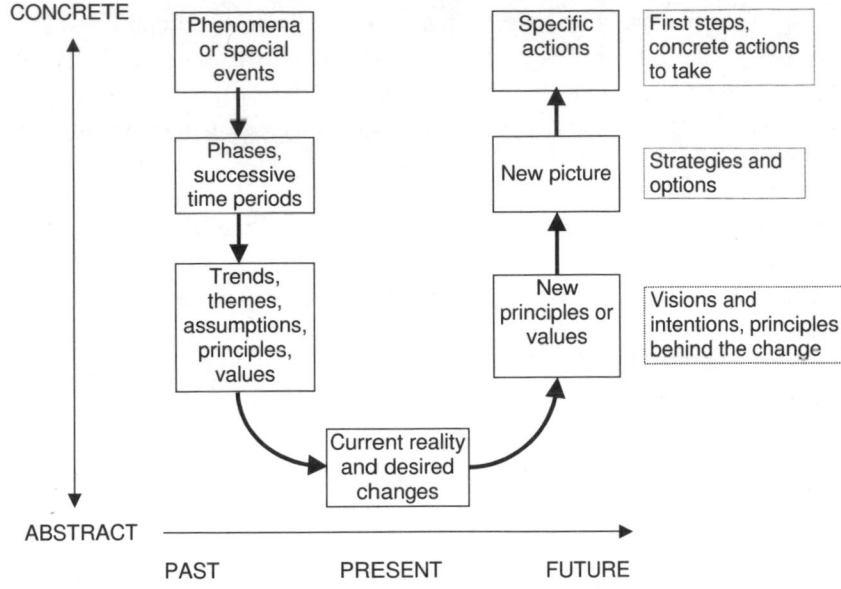

Figure 9.4   *'U' process for diagnosis and action (adapted from Megginson and Whitaker, 1996)*

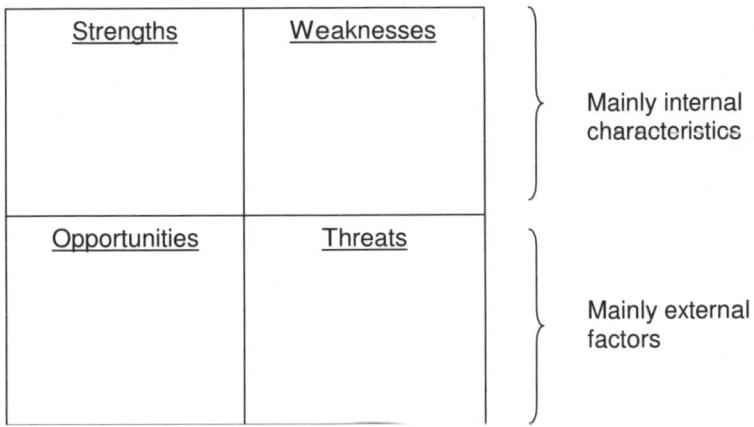

Figure 9.5   *'SWOT' analysis*

from suppliers, consumers, other departments, audits, etc. At individual level it may be staff, managers, colleagues, etc. In principle, feedback is relatively objective, neutral and factual. In practice, it is often value laden, assumption ridden and subjective.

The best generic guidance on feedback we have encountered is embodied in the notion of 'characterization' (Locher and van der Brug, 1997). This accepts that there cannot be pure, objective feedback – that the observer becomes part of what is observed by virtue of his or her own cognitive filters and mental maps of the world. Feedback given should aim to focus on the defining characteristics of what is observed, while feedback received should concentrate on the essence of the message – what is intended.

There is a risk that others will take the opportunity to express their views as therapy for their own angst, to be spiteful or even to exorcize their own sense of inadequacy. Feedback does not have to be accepted without question; in certain circumstances, clarification or substantiation may be required – things that require evidence. However, an appreciative acceptance of feedback, constructive or otherwise, is likely to elicit in the giver the confidence to offer more. Even malicious or deluded data may have some relevance; extract what is valuable and let go the rest.

ACTIVITY 9.3 USING METHODS OF DIAGNOSIS

Think of a problem or issue in your organization. Using the principles of action research described above, formulate how you would organize the collecting of data to give a useful diagnosis.

Do you have a business plan, or similar document, to provide direction to your activity? Whether you do or you don't, try answering these questions: What do we actually do? How do we do it? How do we need to develop what we do? Then try asking someone else to answer these questions, eg a customer, supplier, another department. The answers can be revealing.

Use one of the more graphic methods, eg force field analysis, U process or SWOT, to analyse a problem or situation.

Diagnosing training opportunities

Training methods are varied. However, the process of choice may be guided by considering the present and envisioned levels of learning within the organization and with reference to the type of learning involved. Four types of learning are proposed by Pedler, Burgoyne and Boydell (1997: 59): learning about things (cognitive), learning to do things (affective), learning to become yourself (self-knowledge) and learning to achieve things with others (interpersonal). This is the basis for a framework that may be used as a strategic tool for exercising appropriate choice of specific actions, summarized in Figure 9.6.

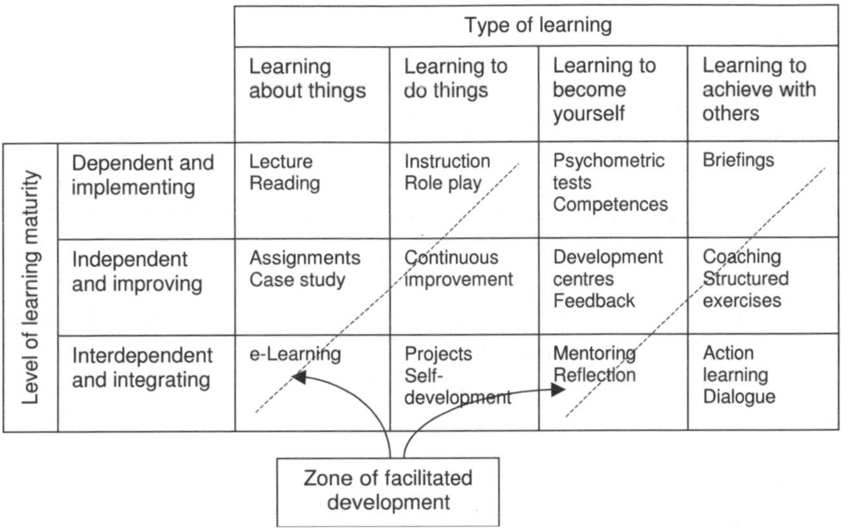

		Type of learning			
		Learning about things	Learning to do things	Learning to become yourself	Learning to achieve with others
Level of learning maturity	Dependent and implementing	Lecture Reading	Instruction Role play	Psychometric tests Competences	Briefings
	Independent and improving	Assignments Case study	Continuous improvement	Development centres Feedback	Coaching Structured exercises
	Interdependent and integrating	e-Learning	Projects Self-development	Mentoring Reflection	Action learning Dialogue

Zone of facilitated development

Figure 9.6 *Strategic framework for choosing development methods, with examples*

The resulting progression towards a vision is characterized at the immature end by a training paradigm that may involve methods such as lectures, structured exercises, guided reading, etc. The mature end of the spectrum is more characterized by organizations that 'self-manage' learning. Between the two extremes (and illustrated arbitrarily in Figure 9.6) is the field of facilitated development, which includes many methods. Particular methods may be better suited to different fields within this framework; for example, the sort of methods that might be most appropriate for the mature end of the spectrum are summarized below:

Action learning	SWOT analysis
Projects and assignments	Large-group interventions
Dialogue tools	Role negotiation
Self-development groups	'U' procedure

Managers are, potentially, suppliers of development opportunities to their staff so that staff:

▌ develop themselves and feel better about their work;

▌ work together with managers to improve work performance;

▌ contribute to the development of the organization.

Managers as developers are required to be not only proactive and planned in the development of their staff, but also ready to capitalize on development opportunities by providing support, encouragement and direction. This requires alertness (to the opportunity), knowledge, and creativity to organize formal opportunities and to grasp informal (and perhaps less expensive) opportunities. Opportunities will exist within every manager's scope and authority. An initial step is to identify existing opportunities. However, identifying development opportunities can be ambiguous and hence relatively difficult compared to, say, training needs analysis based on a readily identifiable deficit.

Work-related development opportunities are frequent if the developer is ready to take advantage of chances as they arise. These different opportunities can be classified according to their degree of formality and whether they are dominantly work based or off-the-job, as illustrated in Figure 9.7.

Formal (work based)	Formal (off-the-job)
Informal (work based)	Informal (off-the-job)

Figure 9.7　*Classification of work-related development opportunities*

■ *Off-the-job* training normally comprises formal events away from the normal work environment, often in specially designated areas. Participants are expected to apply this experience to their own personal work situation.

■ *Work-based* development opportunities arise from the execution of, and improvement in, work tasks. They may consider a specific work area or have a wider scope.

■ *Formal* training involves specially arranged courses or events with a particular purpose, either specific or general.

■ *Informal* training involves development opportunities that arise in unexpected, unplanned ways.

Off-the-job development might include formal appraisal systems and training courses already established as development opportunities in an organization. Such experiences can be made more developmental by linking them with individual work or personal needs. Managers can facilitate this process by debriefing staff and helping them to link the experience to work. It is important that managers are well informed about existing development opportunities.

Work-based development requires particular skills from managers, particularly the ability to delegate, mandate and facilitate. It is also useful to gauge staff preferences for development, through discussion, for which the following checklist of work-based development opportunities might be helpful:

■ modelling, emulating or copying;

■ planned discovery: observing others' behaviours then applying in own situation;

■ unplanned discovery, trial and error, experiences with reflection;

■ experimentation, with a deliberate learning intent;

■ instruction: practical demonstration of an approach or idea;

■ discussions, to share ideas and experiences;

■ recording of information, facts, ideas, impressions and events.

ACTIVITY 9.4 CLASSIFICATION OF TRAINING AND DEVELOPMENT ACTIVITY

Consider the various development opportunities that exist in your area. Use the foregoing information as a prompt and add any of your own to complete the table in Figure 9.7. Do you need to move some of your development activities towards the formal boxes in order to make them more planned and systematic? Do you need to move any towards the work-based boxes in order to make them more directly relevant?

CASE STUDY 9.1: XCL LTD – DIAGNOSIS IN A CONTEMPORARY PRIVATE-SECTOR COMPANY

XCL Ltd is a small UK-based company providing training and development services to clients ranging from individuals and volunteers to work teams and large organizations. Uniquely, XCL's portfolio of services includes development consultancy, facilitation, international expeditions and corporate events. As well as diagnosing HRD for others, the company applies its approach to diagnosis to itself too.

▪ The company employs only three people; however, it is really made up of a close network of 'associates', the core team of which voluntarily take responsibility for development of the business, strategy formulation and implementation. Autonomy, interdependence and a strong psychological and moral contract are the 'glue' of this organization.

▪ Diagnosis is treated as an ongoing business process. As well as frequent (often self-critical) review at a company level by associates, the purpose and values of the company, created by the people involved, are regularly checked for validity. Customer and colleague feedback is actively sought and acted on as part of systematically managing work assignments. New possibilities are explored by enquiring appreciatively into what people can offer.

■ The plan for further development of the business is regarded as a learning opportunity for the team and individuals within. Ownership and responsibility for different aspects of the plan is offered, and regular communication and mutual support act as enablers. Problems of unexpected change, service quality and performance are considered collectively and always in relation to the company's strategic context.

■ Customers and suppliers are viewed as part of the system and are often consulted on changes and ideas. Their development is considered to be part of XCL's purpose. Through the expedition arm of the company, individual customers are offered the chance to progress through a leadership development programme in which the transfer of learning to their occupational lives is actively supported.

■ The company supports individual learning with opportunities for experience, resources, time and finance, although it remains judicious in its spending, checking out potential value with key stakeholders and alignment with business plans.

■ Personal development is explicitly valued and viewed as integral to company development. Self-development is a key supporting principle and is part of how individuals can fit with the general ethos of the company. Individual learning is given voice through regular in-house training and knowledge-sharing sessions.

■ Specific development activity is diagnosed through a combination of core team initiatives, associate feedback, client enquiry, customer surveys, workshops and individual needs and offers. For example, with associates, the core values of the business are shared, opinion is sought on the behaviours that will represent those values, and these desired behaviours are reviewed against achieved behaviours. In this way, opportunities to develop behaviours are identified.

■ Often, with customers, in relation to particular projects or periods of time, mutual expectations are explored and made explicit through descriptions of roles. Individuals are invited to assess their own strengths and weaknesses in relation to these role descriptions, by reflection and with feedback from others. Strengths reveal opportunities to learn from each other; weaknesses reveal potential training needs. Where possible, these opportunities and needs are built into the project.

❚ This case study illustrates how this company diagnoses development by emphasizing ownership and involvement, flexibility and
respect. Needs are given the opportunity to be expressed and
offers are made in the context of a mutually agreed direction for
the company. This provides a robust framework for managing
knowledge, whereby employees and associates walk the talk.

EVALUATION

Evaluation is, in a sense, the determination of how useful a management
activity, an intervention or experience, in this case HRD, is to an organization. Evaluation may be concerned with both what has been the effect and
why the effect was what it was. However, the links between HRD and
business performance are complex and possibly indirect. Proving the
value of HRD in a direct 'cause and effect' sense may often be less realistic
than establishing a significant association.

Evaluation is concerned with establishing the value or 'worth' of
something (Bramley, 1996), and in the context of HRD may also be
concerned with the assessment of learning. By introducing the term
'worth' we recognize that 'value' is not always limited to financial value
added. However, this begs a number of questions: Worth in terms of what,
pleasure, desirability or utility? Worth to whom? Is it shared 'worth'? Isn't
'worth' subjective anyway? Is it the result that is valued or the process
that produces the result, or both?

In addition to these rather awkward questions, evaluation is often
regarded as burdensome or even threatening, with little genuine commitment being shown to it as a result. One possible reason for lack of serious
commitment is the risk that evaluation may so vividly demonstrate a lack
of value. It might also be reasonable to ask: why bother? If an organization
is successful, is evaluation a rather contrived concept?

Despite these difficult questions, evaluation is an integral aspect of
HRD, not least because initiatives do get evaluated routinely, albeit
through the subjective rationality of people's personal judgements. For
example, you have been evaluating this book ever since you first saw the
cover. We offer a number of possible reasons why the profile of evaluation
remains high in HRD:

❚ There is a general trend towards increasing interest in demonstrating
the impact of development.

■ There is a perception that too little evaluation is carried out, considering the rising investment in training.

■ There is a greater emphasis on outcomes.

■ There is increasing competition in the field of provision.

There are also a number of significant implications of evaluation:

■ It consumes resources, especially time.

■ It can fuel premature decision-making.

■ Inherently it is a political process.

■ There are different perceptions of evaluation as objective or as subjective.

In order for evaluation to be credible, authoritative and convincing, it must address the reasons for, the purposes of and the interests in evaluation.

Accountability and measurement

Most organizational processes and the associated management disciplines have at least a degree of accountability. Such accountability in HRD provides one possible reason for evaluation. In everyday language this is about determining outcomes, comparing results against expectations and providing measures of effect. However, the realities of organizations can render the determination of outcomes of HRD problematic. These realities include:

■ the continuous nature of change;

■ a changing organizational environment;

■ change occurring at different levels;

■ changes occurring at a variety of points in time;

■ different perceptions of change;

■ differences between espoused and actual change strategies.

These 'realities' create ambiguity in the specific outcomes of HRD as well as in the outcomes desired. Such uncertainties may be increased by the

Table 9.2   *Summary of the main arguments for and against measurement*

For	Against
▮ Helps credibility	▮ Can be disruptive and demoralizing
▮ Provides objective data	
▮ Provides a reflection of reality	▮ Outcomes are subjective
▮ Enables 'marketability'	▮ Difficult to prove cause and effect
▮ May help to maintain quality	
▮ Demonstrates success	▮ Motivation may be political
▮ Emphasizes financial measures	▮ May diminish trust
▮ Links with setting goals	▮ May breed complacency
	▮ Not necessarily human performance
	▮ What gets measured gets done

diverse ways in which outcomes can be measured and who does the measuring. Table 9.2 summarizes some of the main arguments for and against measurement.

Various management authors have also offered their perspectives on measurement. In *The Empty Raincoat*, Charles Handy (1994) described what he termed 'the Macnamara fallacy':

▮   The first step is to measure whatever can be easily measured. This is OK so far as it goes.

▮   The second step is to disregard that which can't easily be measured or to give it an arbitrary, quantitative value. This is artificial and misleading.

▮   The third step is to presume that what can't be measured easily really isn't important. This is blindness.

▮   The fourth step is to say that what can't be easily measured really doesn't exist. This is suicide.

In Senge *et al* (1994: 46) the physicist David Bohm points out that the Western word 'measure' and the Sanskrit *maya* appear to derive from the same origins. Yet in the West, the concept of measuring has come to mean 'comparison to some fixed external unit', while *maya* means 'illusion'.

Conventional approaches to measurement may involve techniques derived from accountancy, marketing or quality management, eg quantitative cost–benefit analysis, auditing, attitude surveys, professional standards or benchmarking. However, the variety of organizational forms and of working practices that are present in business mean that approaches to HRD are unlikely to be consistent, and therefore the measurement of its effects is also contingent. The diversity of business creates many different contexts in which HRD might be situated and measured.

ACTIVITY 9.5 QUESTIONS ABOUT MEASUREMENT

Consider the following questions about measurement:

1. What environmental pressure might produce a need to measure the outputs of HRD?

2. What would be the arguments against measurement?

3. What are the benefits of measurement?

Aims of evaluation

Contextually, the reasons or motivations for evaluation set the scene and determine at the most fundamental level how successful evaluation will be. It is important to ask why one should evaluate, or what the aims of evaluation are. In general, evaluation typically aims to:

■ demonstrate contractual compliance;

■ legitimize the approach to development;

■ demonstrate worthwhile benefit in relation to cost and provide feedback on investment;

■ drive change.

In organizational contexts, determining development or assessing the extent to which the experience of an event or episode 'transfers' something constructive beyond the event itself equates to determining its value or worth, or some form of evaluation.

In organizations, however, there are other influences that may restrain learning, eg inertia, autocratic opposition, bureaucratic procedures, work overload, interpersonal relationships, vested interests or insecurity. Evaluation therefore needs also to take into account background, context and inputs that will impact on transfer.

Evaluation provides opportunity for appraisal of the investment in a developmental activity, feedback to providers, improvement, reinforcement of learning, and identification of further needs. Which of these goals is uppermost in any one context, along with decisions about who is evaluating what, may affect perceptions of transfer.

Given the variables that will influence evaluation, or at least influence the perception of evaluation, asking why or what is the true purpose of an evaluation may be the most crucial step. The answer may be different for different interests (worth in terms of what, to whom?). The following three ideas offer frameworks for considering the aims of evaluation in organizational, individual and group contexts:

■ Organizational motivation to evaluate can be identified with one or more of the following categories: prove; improve; learn; control (Easterby-Smith, 1994).

■ Individual value in evaluation is demonstrated in the taxonomy of learning adapted from Bloom *et al* (1956): awareness – knowledge – comprehension – application – synthesis – evaluation.

■ The worth of evaluation in a collective or group context is demonstrated with reference to experiential learning theory. The question 'what is this worth?' has a future orientation to it: 'what will this be worth in the future?' In this sense, evaluation has a pragmatic purpose and can be used to appeal to those of a strong pragmatic learning style while mobilizing the pragmatic stage of the learning cycle for others.

Bee (2000) offers the following general guidance on how to approach evaluation:

1. Begin at the objectives-setting stage. Know what is aimed for and by what criteria this will be judged.

2. If objectives were not well formed at the outset, then form them retrospectively or 'operationalize' them, ie look for indicators.

3. Be 'utilization focused' – that is, information produced should be of use and should make a perceivable difference.

4. Involve stakeholders in agreeing purpose and methods, reaching conclusions and taking action.

5. Engage line managers in setting objectives, involve them in the whole learning process and brief them on the purpose of evaluation and their role.

6. Celebrate changes; feed back and publicize changes and improvements.

A clear purpose and durable general approach to evaluation provide a sound basis for evaluation. Further rigour in how to tackle evaluation is provided by some best practices that have become established in the general field of development and training.

ACTIVITY 9.6 AIMS FOR EVALUATION

Evaluate a recent developmental experience for yourself, for example a recent training event, coaching session or something you've read (this book, perhaps). Take as your starting point the question why? Why evaluate? What will your evaluation achieve? Will you hope to prove that something happened, to improve how it happens next time, to control it if it is still going on or to reinforce your learning at some level – but what level? When you achieve the aim of your evaluation, how will this be of use to you in the future?

   Repeat this same process for a development experience you have (or someone else has) yet to undertake.

Best-practice models of evaluation

Traditional models for evaluating outcomes comprise a hierarchical series of levels. Variations on this theme generally resemble Buckley and Caple's (1990) model based on the work of Whitelaw (1972) and Kirkpatrick (1967).

   Hamblin (1974) suggests a more deductive approach to determining results. In his complete framework, at each level of evaluation an outcome is hypothesized or, in other words, a specific objective is set against which the effects of the learning intervention may be tested. These hierarchical models are summarized in Table 9.3.

Table 9.3   *Hierarchical models of evaluation*

Levels of evaluation (Reid and Barrington, 1997)		The deductive approach of Hamblin (1974)
Level 1	Reaction	Reactions objective . . . Reactions evaluation
Level 2	Learning	Learning objective . . . Learning evaluation
Level 3	Job behaviour	Job behaviour objective . . . Job behaviour evaluation
Level 4	Departmental gain	Departmental objective . . . Departmental evaluation
Level 5	Ultimate level organizational	Ultimate value objective . . . Ultimate value evaluation

Although influential in training evaluation, this model type fails to explore the full scope of evaluation adequately. Learning outcomes, for instance, may be considered in terms of knowledge, skills or other attributes such as beliefs and values, all of which may need to be evaluated very differently. Organizational outcomes may be perceived in different ways, eg financial, customer satisfaction or internal processes.

Also, the context and inputs to development are antecedent to the transfer of learning and therefore need to form part of evaluation. Warr, Bird and Rackham (1970) suggest a model for evaluation which encompasses all these dimensions: C – Context, I – Inputs, R – Reaction, O – Output, where output encompasses all levels from learning to ultimate value.

Ultimate value may extend beyond the organization. Development contributes to an industry as a whole (skills available in the employee market, workforce availability, etc) to society and ultimately to the future of the global environment (IRS, 1998: 23). Ultimate value, expressed in these terms, is contingent upon innumerable extraneous factors and may therefore be difficult to determine. This difficulty may contribute to a general lack of serious evaluation beyond reaction level despite its potential value to an organization (Badger, Sadler-Smith and Michie, 1997: 321). This extended range of evaluation levels is illustrated in the descendent model of Figure 9.8.

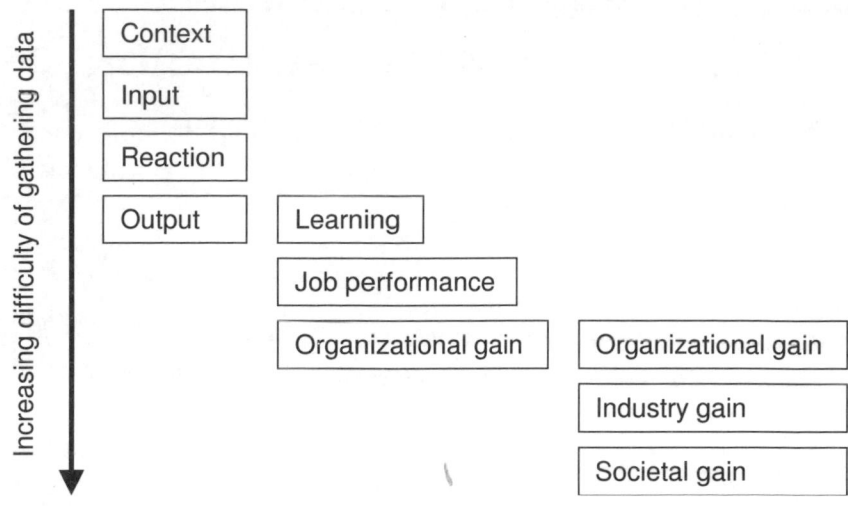

Figure 9.8 *Model illustrating the levels of development evaluation (adapted from various hierarchical evaluation models cited in the text)*

The general overview of evaluation provided in Figure 9.8 usefully illustrates the tension between scale of importance and difficulty of procurement of evaluative data. Which level is appropriate to consider is likely to be a function of context. This framework therefore provides a useful jumping off point from which to consider more specifically the evaluation of HRD interventions.

An alternative for evaluation involving an experimental design and the use of a control group for comparison is represented by Solomon's variation (Figure 9.9).

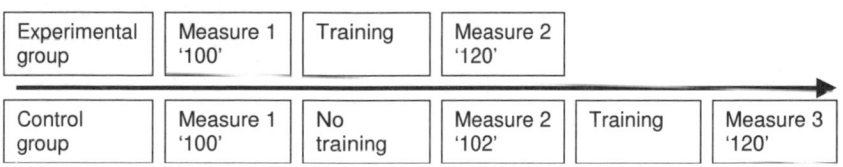

Figure 9.9 *Experimental design for evaluation*

ACTIVITY 9.7 LEVELS OF EVALUATION

Recall the same experience you used in Activity 9.6 and ask yourself what you have learned as a result of this particular experience.

Whatever your answer, now ask yourself why it is that this is the case. Refer to Figure 9.8 and extend your evaluation back through how you felt at the time. Recognize the inputs that generated those feelings and the context in which the whole thing took place. Now extend your evaluation beyond yourself. How is your learning manifest in your behaviour or beliefs? Where is your development contributing to your organization? Is the benefit of your development felt beyond your organization?

Gathering, processing and presenting data

The practice of gathering, processing and presenting data for evaluation is akin to management research. The field of management research is greatly informed by both scientific and social research and benefits from considerable literature on the subject (Gill and Johnson, 1997; Hussey and Hussey, 1997). Detailed consideration of research theory is beyond the scope of this book. However, when engaging with evaluation (and diagnosis) as practitioners and managers it is important to recognize some of the key limitations and implications of our approaches.

HRD practitioners, managers and many employees will be familiar with the 'end of training course questionnaire'. This common aspect of evaluation should not be derided too quickly. While it is true that such instruments can be manipulative, routine and of little consequence, it is also true that they can be pragmatic and focused, and can provide valid data. Other instruments that commonly feature in evaluation initiatives include surveys, tests, follow-up questionnaires, interviews, focus groups, reviews, reports, line manager assessment and projects. The choice of evaluation method will be influenced by both practical and contextual factors. Practical questions include:

▌ What will be the degree of access to the 'research population' and the nature of sampling that allows?

▌ Whose interests are being served by the evaluation and do therefore some fairly pragmatic criteria need to be adopted?

▌ How general, valid and reliable are the results expected to be?

▌ Where will the evaluation add real value to HRD?

▌ How can information overload be avoided?

▌ How can the evaluation be kept 'user-friendly'?

Contextually, we have already encountered the importance of establishing the aim of evaluation and the level of focus. It is also important to recognize that any approach to evaluation makes assumptions – for example, assumptions that culture and diversity (organizationally and ethnically) will not adversely affect perceptions and responses; that evaluation can be objective and neutral; that development can be 'measured'; or that perceptions can be rationalized.

Evaluation of a particular process or 'event' assumes a link between the two in a broad 'cause-and-effect' manner. However, there are many other factors, or variables, that may intervene to influence development, particularly with the passage of time. This realization may make a highly scientific approach to evaluation less valid than one that is descriptive and interpretative. There are strengths in both dominantly scientific approaches and more subjective approaches. It is legitimate to combine methodologies to enhance the rigour with which evaluation is undertaken.

Practitioners carrying out evaluation need to be aware that their own beliefs, views and habits will influence (often unconsciously) how they view others. Our own deeply ingrained values influence our assumptions about people, about what is and is not observable, about what can be reduced to simple cause-and-effect relationships and about what is human nature.

Individual methods of data collection tend to rest within one set of conceptual assumptions or another. The practitioner who is aware of this can also, therefore, be informed about the limitations of any evaluation exercise. The relationship between certain methods and assumptions is summarized in Table 9.4.

Quantitative data are those that can be subject to mathematical or statistical treatment that aims to summarize, illustrate frequency, draw meaningful comparisons and valid conclusions, and enable understandable presentation of data when they are gathered in large quantities – typically, numerical data. Common methods of presenting quantitative data involve graphic displays, eg bar charts, pie charts or graphs. Legiti-

Table 9.4   *Evaluation methods and associated assumptions*

Scientific methods	Phenomenological methods
Surveys	Ethnography (being closely
Experimental studies (control	involved)
groups)	Action research
Questionnaires	Projects
Longitudinal studies (over time)	Manager/colleague feedback
Assumptions	*Assumptions*
Reality is concrete and measurable	Reality is a projection of imagination
Objective world	Subjective world
Observer independence	Observer is part of what is observed
Science is value free	Science is driven by human interest
Limited number of variables	Locally grounded rich description
Emphasize quantitative data	Emphasize qualitative data

mizing conclusions by demonstrating statistical significance can be aided by using computer statistical packages.

Qualitative data are, typically, words, either of the data source, eg learners on a programme, or of the data gatherer, eg a facilitator, or of some third party, eg the manager of the learners. Although collected and processed using different techniques, qualitative data can be reduced, displayed and analysed with as much rigour as can quantitative, numerical data (Miles and Huberman, 1994). Qualitative data summaries and displays include tables, matrices, flow charts, affinity diagrams, frequency counts and representative quotes.

ACTIVITY 9.8 GATHERING DATA

Refer again to the experience you recalled for Activities 9.6 and 9.7 and the conclusions you reached about your development and its impact. How do you know? What data support this? Is your perception accurate? Who else would have a view on this?

How can you ensure a thorough, clear and authentic determination of the worth of the next development initiative you are involved with?

Auditing and added value

Considerations of what is meant by evaluation, accountability, establishing the aims of evaluation, systematically doing it, and rigorously gathering, processing and presenting data are all valid whether the focus of your evaluation is a specific event, or is an evaluation of organization-wide HRD.

An evaluation of current organization-wide HRD practices may be appropriate at any time. To borrow from the language of accountants, an 'audit' can aim to establish what is happening, how it is happening and what value is added. Such auditing exercises can therefore be used to refocus effort into areas of need or areas of opportunity, but, as with any evaluation exercise, it is critical to establish the true purpose of the audit first.

We have heard it said, 'Rather than think about the value of doing this thing, think about the cost of not doing it.' Possibly true, although this may not satisfy organizational accountability processes. However, it may be useful to determine the value of HRD interventions before they have taken place – in other words, make a business case. Readily available sources of perspective on this will be customers, colleagues or the line managers who are supporting, ordering or requesting the intervention. Asking them to clarify how value will be added is tremendously empowering and pre-empts some of the barriers that can hinder the transfer of learning from one context to another.

Benchmarking

Benchmarking is a principle that has grown among organizations that look beyond their own boundaries to test their performance against that of others. The principle is straightforward: examine what others are doing, identify new ways of doing things and set a development agenda. The risks of this mechanism include establishing only that the organization is no worse than competitors, is achieving only the minimum required, playing to the lowest common denominator and reinforcing inappropriate long-term strategy.

Nevertheless, comparisons with other organizations can provide an element of objective data that can then support organizations in meeting current objectives of learning to do things well, implementing performance standards and beginning to improve performance by setting new objectives. Benchmarking can compare performance in a number of ways – for example:

▮   internally, between departments, divisions, etc;

▮   externally, with specific competitors or the industry in general,

▮   externally, with non-competitors whose processes or problems are similar and might generate ideas;

▮   against standards, eg the European Foundation for Quality Management (EFQM) Business Excellence model; ISO 9002; the Investors in People quality standard in the United Kingdom.

The benchmarking process requires managing, should recognize success as well as shortcomings, and may be iterative rather than a one-off event.

ACTIVITY 9.9 AUDIT YOUR ORGANIZATION'S ACTIVITY

What aspects of learning and development is your organization good at and which does it neglect? It may be helpful to classify current activity in terms of two dimensions:

▮   *competence*: learning to do things in the required way to meet current specifications; or *development*: expanding capacity by learning to face future needs or to take personal responsibility for self-development;

▮   *efficiency*: doing activities well, reducing costs; or *innovation*: doing new things, finding a better way.

List up to 10 major activities that your organization is undertaking that contribute to learning, development, education or training. Use the matrix in Figure 9.10 to classify each activity accordingly.
    What do you conclude from the results you have recorded? What can managers in your organization do to initiate any improvements?

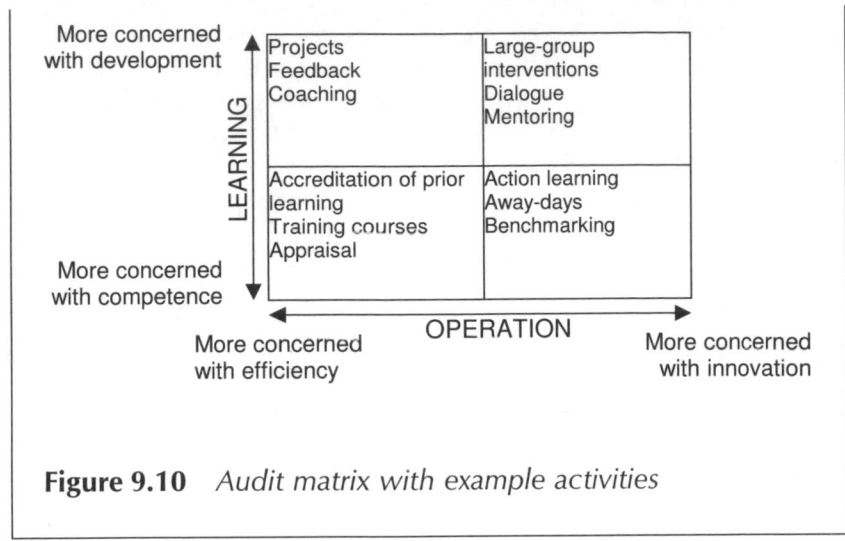

Figure 9.10 *Audit matrix with example activities*

CASE STUDY 9.2: CONNEXIONS' OUTDOOR DEVELOPMENT PROGRAMME

Context

Connexions is a service provided to young people (aged 16–19) by the UK Government Department of Work and Pensions through a network of offices around the country. It provides help, advice on jobs and training, and the support of professional personal advisers. The service aims to help young people engage in learning, achieve their full potential and make a smooth transition to adult life, and places great emphasis on building strong links with local businesses and training organizations.

Connexions is organized regionally, with considerable autonomy given to how each region approaches helping young people navigate decisions about studying, jobs and careers. Young people are assigned a personal adviser, who gives close coaching and support over a sustained period of time, exploring positive and exciting ways of developing their talents and interests.

The service is for all young people, helping them to make decisions about their future, aiming to energize them, encourage them to believe in themselves and putting them in control of their own learning and development. Central to Connexions' approach is a theme of learning: young people learning about themselves and how organizations work, and being offered equality of opportunity to continue to engage with learning after 16. The organization's literature states that

> Youth work helps young people realise their full potential by developing a wide range of skills. These include building self-confidence, relating to other people from all walks of life, developing team work and leadership skills. This will often involve learning in different and informal settings and the chance to take advantage of personal development opportunities such as arts, drama, sports and international exchanges.

An outdoor programme piloted in one region of Connexions aimed to complement its work with young people. This innovative approach to Connexions' aims involved a partnership with a local commercial training company. A rigorous evaluation of this initiative provided evidence to suggest that this style of intervention could be used to augment similar young people's programmes in the future.

Inputs

The Connexions region began an initiative to facilitate the progress of young people in the area, which involved the use of outdoor management development techniques. The local manager sponsoring the initiative informed the training company that they wanted not only to integrate outdoor development with the work of personal advisers but also to evaluate the initiative thoroughly.

The training company created the outdoor programme and evaluation process, recognizing that traditional classroom-based education did not appeal to many young people and leaves them unsure of their next steps after school. The challenge for the company was to offer something different and engaging for young people that transparently supported the wider work of Connexions and personal advisers.

The outdoor programme itself would not be unfamiliar to many outdoor providers: a series of activities to explore different themes such as initiative, teams, problem-solving, communication and responsibility. A variety of metaphors, journeys and challenges were used to engage imaginations in light-hearted and inclusive ways. Active reviews throughout the programme encouraged participants to reflect on their experiences and link them to the context of their lives.

Experienced facilitators and personal advisers accompanied the young people through their experience and joined in as equal partners. In this way, while participating as part of a group, they were able to provide individual attention, supporting the key principles of Connexions' approach of meeting individual need and overcoming barriers to learning.

Approach to the evaluation

The central theme of learning was taken as the main focus of the evaluation, although, in accordance with good practice in evaluation, data were also gathered on the context of participants and the inputs to the process as well as more immediate reactions to the programme.

Certain limitations to the evaluation process were recognized from the beginning. These include the specific nature of the results to the particular population involved, the absence of a control group for direct comparisons and the broad nature of learning as an outcome. Key to the approach therefore was a semi-structured questioning regime that allowed the young people to express the sense they made of their experience in language that they chose to use. The approach also, crucially, involved role set analysis through the participation of personal advisers before, during and after the outdoor programme.

The character of the population was recorded mainly in the form of quantitative data gathered on the participants' profiles, and included demographic data, background, educational achievements, motivations and priorities. These data were gathered from both the participants and their personal advisers, so they could be used to account for the potential effects of extraneous variables such as age, academic ability or peer group.

Since learning was the objective and can broadly be thought of as a qualitative change in someone's life, it was decided to seek qualitative data. The perspectives of participating young people and personal advisers were recorded and analysed in accordance with recognized qualitative data analysis techniques.

Reactions

The reviews conducted with the young people during the outdoor programme, coupled with unsolicited data in the form of spontaneous feedback, indicated enthusiastic reactions to the programme from both the young people and the personal advisers. A general view from the personal advisers was that the programme readily integrated with their work with the young people.

Outcomes

The findings of the evaluation fall into two categories: those learning outcomes that are reported by the young people themselves, ie their own views; and those reported by personal advisers, ie observed changes in the young people. Within the second set of findings, personal advisers witnessed behaviours that directly related to some of Connexions' key objectives such as relating to other people, developing teamwork, developing self-knowledge, and building self-confidence and self-esteem. The young people themselves tended to emphasize interpersonal learning outcomes such as relating, teamwork, awareness and trust.

While perhaps unremarkable to anyone working in the field of outdoor development and training, these outcomes, it should be noted, represent the sense that the young people themselves made of their experience. The outcomes also reflect sustained changes witnessed by their role set, ie personal advisers, based on their knowledge of the young people prior to, and after the programme.

In an exercise that was integral to the data-gathering before, during and after the programme, the young people's perspectives were also sought on their priorities for their immediate futures. Personal advisers further corroborated the consistent intent of the young people to seek further training and employment, thus supporting Connexions' aim of helping young people become active citizens.

Ultimate value added

The outdoor development programme demonstrably supported the aims of Connexions. Key to this was the close involvement throughout of personal advisers, a rigorous evaluative framework and a partnership approach.

The nature of the learning outcomes highlighted may not in themselves sound surprising to anyone familiar with the usual claims made for outdoor development. However, the uniqueness of the Connexions programme was to provide a thorough analysis and to value the perceptions of the young people for whom the organization exists.

This case study illustrates the care with which evaluation needs to be approached in order to provide valid and reliable information. By building evaluation in from the very beginning, a number of key aims were addressed and data were gathered and processed in a thorough and rigorous systematic fashion.

SUMMARY

In this chapter we have sought to establish a rigorous approach to HRD through the closely related areas of practice of diagnosis and evaluation. In diagnosis we recognize that the antecedents to successful HRD strategies are complex, but are manageable with the application of certain key perspectives. Systems thinking, performance strategies and personal skills illuminate the subtleties of this aspect of HRD. A number of methods to help with this are offered and encompass the more traditional but limited notion of identifying needs as the first step in a systematic approach. HRD when aligned in a strategic context is proactive, insightful and holistic in intervention.

Diagnosis may begin with an evaluation of the present. Similarly, evaluation may in effect diagnose the present. To varying degrees, and with varying levels of awareness, these processes do go on in organizations. They contribute to the accountability demanded by stakeholders and to the learning process itself at individual, group and organizational levels. A number of ideas about evaluation distilled from wider practice have been reviewed. These can help to conceptualize practice and guide managers and practitioners in how to evaluate appropriately for their context.

10

Management development

INTRODUCTION

According to Hirsh and Carter (2002), there is widespread acceptance of the importance of management development. The often-repeated phrase 'our people are our most important asset' implies that managing those people must also be important. Consequently, how those people's managers are developed is also important.

In 2003 Tom Lester, in a *Financial Times* Management Special Report entitled 'Encouraging talent: an urgent need for good quality mentoring' and published in the paper on 27 October, reported that it was not only a lack of talent or skills within an organization that would prevent it from moving into markets, products or processes but a shortage 'of experienced, hardened general managers, the sort that make the company function through thick and thin and who take years to train'.

It seems to us that it is important to identify the imperatives that are driving today's organizations and to define the management requirements that will enable organizations to flourish in the changing business world. It is also crucial to think through what the ideal manager and 'transformational leadership' are like. Without this understanding we cannot determine what development the managers of the future will require.

LEARNING OUTCOMES

By reading this chapter, undertaking the suggested activities and reflecting on the content and your own prior knowledge, you will achieve the following learning outcomes:

■ an understanding of the deep shift in ideas about what 'management' is;

■ an appreciation of the changes and challenges for management development;

■ an insight into the processes and practices of management development;

■ an understanding of the special requirements of different categories of managers:

   – CEOs and chairs;

   – directors;

   – highly talented people, professionals and specialists;

   – general managers;

   – international managers;

   – graduates;

   – women managers;

   – managers from minority groups;

   – managers with a disability;

   – managers of a certain age.

DEFINITIONS

An early definition (TSA, 1977) suggests that management development is 'an attempt to improve managerial effectiveness through a planned and deliberate process'. Burgoyne (1988: 40) suggests that management development is about 'managing careers within an organizational context', while Schroder (1989: 28) suggests that it is about 'expanding the range of contribution based on competing strengths that a manager makes to work groups'. Krouwell and Goodwill (1994: 18) define management development as the branch of management education

which addresses the 'softer' skills of enterprise, developing managers' competence in the handling of interpersonal matters, getting the best from people through improved understanding of the human condition, and developing as an individual.

However, the definition that we favour most is Woodall and Winstanley's statement that management development is

primarily orientated towards developing individuals in ways which are complementary with the organization and its objectives and appropriate for meeting the individual's own career and development needs. (Woodall and Winstanley, 1998: 5)

ACTIVITY 10.1 DEFINITIONS

Of the definitions that we have cited, which one can you identify with most?

What is your own definition of management development?

Our definition of management development is:

those activities that enable managers to have a clearer sense of purpose about their own development. This involves diagnosis, process and critical reflection. The activities undertaken have to be appropriate for the career development of the manager and to work within the work environment.

THE DEEP SHIFT IN IDEAS ABOUT MANAGEMENT DEVELOPMENT

In the past, management was seen as a necessary evil, something that had to be done but that got in the way of making widgets or dealing with customers. It was often perceived as being a low-status administrative process. Unfortunately, in some cases this view of management still persists. Other people are seeing management as a natural progression in their careers and as an important, strategic role in which their contribution to meeting the organization's needs is essential.

One view of the role of management is that it is about 'transformational leadership': being able to create a sense of vision and purpose in an ever-changing environment, motivating and leading people through the change process and finding innovative ways of working to develop and deliver new products and services. It is not sufficient to ensure that more people have more qualifications and greater skills. If organizations are going to remain competitive, they must focus on the behaviours of individuals.

The research by Guile and Fonda (1998) found that there was a move away from 'command and control'-type management towards flatter and process-based organizations with responsibility devolved to front-line staff and that there was a constant drive towards 'added value'. If we intend to serve the interests of employers in their competitiveness, the interests of individuals for their employability, and the public good by greater social cohesion, we need a clearer view of the capabilities needed in today's world – and of the learning processes that help to develop them (Guile and Fonda, 1998).

This suggests that the type of management development on offer needs to be responsive to this new work environment. Among 20 behaviours identified by Guile and Fonda (1998), the following are highlighted as critical:

■ taking 'ownership' of the results of your own work;

■ planning and organizing your own work;

■ building stakeholders' trust and commitment;

■ team and partnership working;

■ seeking continuous improvement;

■ responding positively and constructively to change;

■ developing creative solutions to problems.

These place a great deal of emphasis on the managers and their line managers engaging in a process of critical reflective practice. Cheryl Hunt (1999: 222) says:

> The main reason for consciously and systematically engaging with the process of reflection is to learn how to identify, articulate, take ownership of, and begin to control that which constitutes 'baggage' – habits, ideas, assumptions, preferences, needs and so on – that would itself otherwise control our thoughts and actions; and to consider to what extent, and with what effect, the influences from our past interact with the requirements of the environment in which we now live and work.

Given all of the above, it is our view that there are at least three types of manager: the administrator, the career professional and the transformational leader. They will have very different management development requirements, and the need for critical reflection is key for all of them.

ACTIVITY 10.2 TYPES OF MANAGER

What type of manager are you?

- administrator;

- career professional;

- transformational leader.

Check your concept of you as a manager with some trusted colleagues: junior, equal and more senior will give you a more rounded view. What development needs do you have? How will you meet them?

What activities have you undertaken (see Chapter 6, 'Continuous Professional Development') and what have you discovered about your management development needs?

THE CHANGES AND CHALLENGES FOR MANAGEMENT DEVELOPMENT

If the concept of management has evolved, so have ideas about management development. The recent context in which management development has been taking place includes concepts such as:

- excellence (Peters and Waterman, 1982);

- lean and mean (Atkinson, 1984);

- fragmented – formalized – focused (Barham, Fraser and Heath, 1988);

- re-engineering (Hammer and Champy, 1993);

- competence and competences (Summers, 1994).

These have brought with them improvements and drawbacks in managerial effectiveness.

Excellence encouraged people to think about the standards of service that customers, both internal and external, had a right to expect and of the issues involved in meeting these.

Lean and mean worked towards cutting out unnecessary processes and layers within an organization. This shortened the 'chain of command' and, in theory, improved communications. Unfortunately, the pruning process often left organizations so lean, almost anorexic, that they did not have the reserves to develop to meet new needs.

The *fragmented – formalized – focused* framework allowed people to think about where their organization was in relation to it and to make the necessary changes. The downside was that people realized just how fragmented and poor their organization was at training and development, and left!

Re-engineering encouraged people to consider the ways in which products and services were delivered and to work towards making improvements. One of us supervised an MBA student who redesigned the lubrication system in an aluminium rolling mill and saved his company £50,000 in the first year.

Competence and competences encouraged people to break down the requirements for a job into even smaller units, and led in some cases to a 'tick box' approach to development as the competences that were easy to identify and categorize took preference over the more nebulous ones.

One way of thinking about the future of management development is to consider how it can address leading ideas (see Chapter 2). Another perspective is to explore the needs that are thrown up by:

- endemic organizational change;

- communicating management development's priorities;

- centralizing or devolving management development or this function;

- the question of who should deliver management development;

- meeting the needs of individuals and the organization;

- an increasingly diverse management group;

- the turnover of ambitious managers and the lack of turnover of unambitious managers;

- fitting the process into people's already busy lives;

- changes in ideas about learning (see Chapter 4);

- changes in delivery methods, including ICT;

- e-learning and blended learning (see Chapter 5);

- evaluating management development – human capital reporting.

We go some way to answering these issues in the rest of this chapter.

ACTIVITY 10.3 MANAGEMENT DEVELOPMENT PROVISION

Think about the management development provision within your organization (or for yourself if you are a sole trader or self-employed). Which of the issues cited above are pertinent to you?

Do you have other issues that need to be considered? How could you meet these needs?

THE PROCESSES AND PRACTICES OF THE DELIVERY OF MANAGEMENT DEVELOPMENT

The processes and practices of the delivery of management development can be categorized into three main groups: formal management training and education, informal learning and personal development, and career development.

Formal management training and education
According to Hirsh and Carter (2002: 2), 'more managers are taking higher education qualifications in business and management, either before they enter employment or later through certificate, diploma or part-time MBAs'.

Informal learning and personal development
Learning at work as opposed to attending a course, by project work, team facilitation, coaching, mentoring, secondments, learning sets and action-centred learning are becoming increasingly popular and are very beneficial for personal development.

Career development

Given the changes in organizational structure, with fewer opportunities for promotion owing to the flatter hierarchies, there is a need for career development to be enhanced. Most managers receive very little, if any, formal career advice or development.

A good management development process will harness all three categories and provide an integrated response to management development needs (Figure 10.1).

Figure 10.1 *Management development: a more integrated approach (after IES, 2002, 387, p 3)*

THE SPECIAL REQUIREMENTS OF DIFFERENT CATEGORIES OF MANAGER

While some of the work of all managers will be the same, different categories of manager will inevitably have different needs.

CEOs and chairs

CEOs and chairs are often in an isolated and lonely position within an organization. They may also feel that because they have reached their

ACTIVITY 10.4 TYPE OF MANAGEMENT DEVELOPMENT

What type of management development have you had in the past year:

■ formal management training and education;

■ informal and personal development;

■ continuous personal development;

■ career development?

How successful has this development been? How do you measure this success?
What development will you be pursuing next year?

current position they may not need any further development. According to Braddick and Casey (1996), this may be because

> they feel that development courses are too theoretical and too lengthy for busy active people. Management development specialists do not help. Many of them regard it as *lèse-majesté* to suggest that board members may need development.

However, this may not be the case. Any new role raises development issues, and as a role grows over time, that also raises development issues. For many CEOs and chairs, one way to receive management development is to be coached and mentored by someone from outside the organization. Alternatively, they could take part in a development programme or action learning set with other CEOs and chairs.

It is important for these senior people to recognize the benefits of management development as they are in a position to champion and promote it. They also play a part in the management development of their directors and boards.

Directors

Directors may be in a less isolated position in that there are usually several of them in an organization, although of course they may perceive themselves to be in competition for the CEO's role. While they feel that in common with CEOs and chairs they are past the stage when they need development, it is suggested that 'the need for training at senior levels has never been more pressing' (Braddick and Casey, 1996). They have needs and opportunities similar to those of the CEO or chair, and they will have additional development needs related to equipping them for their potential future role of CEO. They may also have needs that are specific to their functional role. The Institute of Directors has a chartered director programme, and information about this and a practice exam can be found at www.iod.com.

Highly talented people, professionals and specialists

Highly talented people, professionals and specialists are of vital importance to organizations, especially in this age of knowledge management. In view of the need for organizations to remain ahead of the competition, they need to recruit and keep these people. These are the people who are 'highly desirable' to other organizations and are likely to be headhunted or to leave for career progression.

Both professionals and specialists have a great deal of power. Because entry to their professional body is restricted to those who gain the appropriate qualifications, and through commitment to a professional code of ethics and behaviour, professionals can regulate their services. Specialists by virtue of their knowledge, which is often not codified and consequently not available to others within their organizations, are very valuable contributors. To some extent both groups already have the knowledge, skills and attitudes that they need to progress up the organizational ladder. They are also the type of people who can easily leave an organization and become consultants or self-employed. Therefore they need to be looked after. This all poses great problems for those in an organization responsible for providing their management development.

General managers

General managers need to have 11 qualities or attributes, which can be grouped into three categories, according to Pedler, Burgoyne and Boydell (1994: 23–24):

- basic knowledge and information:
  - command of basic facts;
  - relevant professional knowledge;
- skills:
  - continuing sensitivity to events;
  - analytical, problem-solving, decision/judgement-making skills;
  - social skills and abilities;
- personal qualities:
  - emotional resilience;
  - proactivity – inclination to respond purposefully to events;
  - creativity;
  - mental agility;
  - balanced learning habits and skills;
  - self-knowledge.

ACTIVITY 10.5 WHERE ARE YOUR MANAGEMENT DEVELOPMENT NEEDS?

You might choose to assess yourself in relation to Pedler, Burgoyne and Boydell's 11 qualities and attributes. Where are your strengths and where could you develop?

While all managers, at any level, need these skills and attributes, it is probably when they are at the general management level that they are most likely to learn them. Some will be acquired 'on the job'; others will come through more formal routes: courses and briefings, etc. The remainder will require the manager to engage in some personal reflection. Engaging fully in the continuous professional development (CPD) process will enable managers to develop more fully and will fit them for promotion. See Chapter 6 for some practical ideas on development.

International managers

International managers also need to be developed carefully. A UK television advertising campaign for an international bank showed the difference in culture that people face when living and working in another country. These differences in culture are brilliantly explained by Rosinski (2003). The same differences also face international managers. There seems to be a tendency for some multinationals to attempt to smooth out the differences and to run their organization as it would be run in the home country. This poses problems where the employment laws, customs and practices are different in the host country. It can also raise issues in the management development process.

So not only are there issues about cultural differences between countries that managers need to be familiar with, but there are issues about how the development should take place. The education and learning process might be quite dissimilar in different countries. One of us has run training programmes in Mexico and Kuala Lumpur for managers from an international organization and the delivery of the course had to be redesigned even though the content remained virtually the same.

One of the issues that often needs consideration is about the international manager's partner/spouse and family. The case of the male manager taking his non-working wife and children to live in another country is no longer the only model. It is now quite likely to be the female manager with her husband or partner who is working overseas. Dual-career couples can have major personal issues to resolve before either or both of them can contemplate working abroad. This issue has led organizations to make use of short-term international assignments.

There can be little doubt that the opportunity to work abroad can be a highly developmental process in its own right. There is also greater emphasis on multinational task forces and teams. One of us has had the experience of working as part of a multinational team consisting of a German, a Spaniard, a Mexican and an Englishwoman who did not have a single common language. Out of working hours the conversation was carried out in a mixture of Spanish, French and English. In work time, simultaneous translation or interpretation was used, so an understanding about being really clear about what needed to be communicated came about. All members of the task force gained a huge understanding of the different cultural aspects. Two members of this task force (German and English) were seconded to work in Asia, where the cultural issues were very different, but even so, their experience of the very different culture in Mexico enabled them to get up to speed much quicker.

Not only are there needs to be considered before a manager is sent to work abroad, but there are also issues to be dealt with upon his or her return home. In a piece of research conducted by Uwe G Seebacher as part of a multinational team from seven countries for the European Union, it was stated:

> In regard to the applied MD tools and techniques, for Germany it can be stated, that the organizations are applying a wide variety of tools and techniques. This also causes the use of not effective but very expensive tools such as international assignments or projects. This tool for example is not considered by the managers as essential for their development. Still many companies think that this MD tool is vital for their managers' development. Less is more! (Seebacher, 2003: 1)

Graduates

Graduates are often well catered for in larger organizations that have a graduate development scheme. However, problems can arise. We worked for a major organization that sent its graduates on an in-house MBA programme, and within a few years of completing it, virtually all the managers had left because no thought had been given by the organization to career progression. Another problem with graduate schemes is that those managers who are not graduates often feel, and indeed are, left out.

Women managers

Women managers make up approximately 50 per cent of the workforce in the United Kingdom. Harrison (2002: 145) says that

> their access to development and promotion opportunities is now an area of even greater concern than in the past for employers. The European Directives Sex Discrimination (Indirect Discrimination and Burden of Proof) Regulations 2001 'widen the definition of indirect discrimination under the Sex Discrimination Act of 1975' and 'shift the burden of proof towards the employer'.

This means that employers and individual managers need to give thought to the management development opportunities that they make available to women and, crucially, to the development that they give to male managers so that they realize that they have a role to play in developing women. Woodall and Winstanley (1998: 225) cite Cooper and Davidson's

1983 research, which stated that there were four main categories that potentially contribute to women underachieving:

■ lack of confidence – they do not seek out promotion;

■ competitiveness – they are less likely than men to be self-publicists;

■ family roles – women assume the majority of domestic responsibilities;

■ stereotyping – the notion of the successful manager consists of essentially male characteristics.

Twenty years on and these categories still seem apposite!

Managers from minority groups

Managers from minority groups may also face unfair practices in the workplace and be overlooked for development and promotion. The Office for Public Management is an independent, not-for-profit, public-interest company working with people to develop high-quality management, professional practice and public engagement in organizations that aim to improve their social results. As part of its provision it runs the Routes Programme. This is the management development programme for black and ethnic minority managers in local government who wish to be more strategic and influential in a changing environment. The programme includes:

■ Module 1: *Launch and personal development*: Managing in the new millennium, Introducing the programme, Modernizing local government – the new agenda, Establishing a learning community, Keynote speaker and launch dinner, Personal development and effective management, Management competencies and self-analysis, Learning styles, Your management challenge – identifying and resolving dilemmas, Stakeholder analysis and scenario planning.

■ Module 2: *Strategy, leadership and organizational change*: Environmental scanning, Strategic behaviour, Sources of power and influence, Leadership style.

■ Module 3: *Managing relationships: negotiation and conflict management*: Negotiation, Conflict management, Managing diversity in teams, Interpersonal skills.

▮ Module 4: *Managing the reality*: Financial and information management, Quality and accreditation, Performance management, Career and life planning.

▮ Module 5: *Managing the future*: Equal opportunities and valuing diversity issues for the future, Reframing perceptions, Where next?

More information about this programme can be found at www.opm.co.uk/minisites/Routes/routes_home.html.

Managers with a disability

Managers with a disability are sometimes seen as not suitable for promotion or development. This is often the attitude of individual managers and is not part of the organization's policy. It is essential that all organizations comply with the legislation relating to disability discrimination to avoid costly legal cases and, perhaps more importantly, to avoid missing out on some of the talent within the organization.

Some very helpful suggestions are made on www.yourable.com under three key headings:

▮ 'Training for employees with a disability';

▮ 'Training for existing staff';

▮ 'Retaining an employee who becomes disabled'.

It is appropriate that all employees should have access to development and training opportunities. Management development needs to be accessible and the particular needs of those with a disability need to be taken into account. This may mean providing special equipment or adapting what is currently available. The development activity may need to take place over a longer, less concentrated period of time. Materials may need to be provided in Braille or large print. Sign-language interpreters or personal carers may need to be accommodated. The physical location of development programmes may need to be altered to cope with some of these demands. One of us recently worked on a programme with a profoundly deaf learner who was accompanied by both a note taker and a specially trained dog.

All those who are involved in the management development programme will need to be aware of their responsibilities towards people with a disability. This is as much a requirement for the other learners as for the staff. Some years ago, one of us worked on an outdoor management development programme where one of the participants was a wheelchair user. The group decided as one of their ground rules that they would only do activities that they could all manage. This meant that they could not go sailing, as they were required to be able to swim. The wheelchair user could swim; it was one of the able-bodied people who could not. This was a salutary lesson for all concerned. See the ability, not the disability.

It is possible for an existing employee to become disabled, and care must be given to helping that person to return to work and to making a full contribution. He or she will have skills and knowledge that need to be kept.

Those people involved in Web-based development could usefully view the Association of Disabled Professionals' Web site, which has some very user-friendly features at www.adp.org.uk. The aims of the ADP are:

■ to improve the education, rehabilitation, training and employment opportunities available to disabled people;

■ to encourage disabled people to develop their physical and mental capacities fully, to find and retain employment commensurate with their abilities and qualifications, and to participate fully in the everyday life of society;

■ to improve public knowledge and acceptance of the capabilities, needs and problems of disabled people, particularly in relation to education and employment.

It does this by focusing on the provision of advice and information and by influencing Parliament.

Managers of a certain age

According to Cascio (1998: 351), 'advances in health and medicine make it possible for the average male to live for more than 72 years and for the average female to live for more than 79 years'. This means that there are now many people over the age of 65 who are willing to work and capable of continuing to do so. Unfortunately, there are still many myths about older workers. Cascio (1998: 352–53) lists the following:

■ They are less productive.

■ It costs more to prepare them for work.

■ They are often absent for age-related illness.

■ They have more accidents.

■ They don't get on well with others.

■ The cost of employee benefits outweighs work benefits.

■ They are inflexible.

■ They do not function well if continuously interrupted.

He states that none of these is true. Consequently, there is no reason to have an age barrier for hiring or developing staff. Even so, you only have to look at job adverts to see that age is frequently mentioned. So, if age is deemed a critical factor for engaging a manager, what chance have older managers got of being selected for learning and development?

Of course, younger managers who are deemed not to have sufficient experience to warrant development can also feel age discrimination. The need for managers is to see them as individuals and not to make judgements about them based on age.

One of the major issues is to see the manager as an individual. It is easy to define categories in a chapter of a book, but in reality, any manager may fall into more than one category, and this makes the provision of development opportunities even more complex.

ACTIVITY 10.6 SPECIAL REQUIREMENTS

Which category of manager do you best fit into? Do you fit into more than one category?

What development do you need?

CASE STUDY 10.1: VILLAGE AID

The clue to Village AiD lies in its title. AiD stands for 'aid in development'. Village AiD's mission statement says, 'Village AiD exists to help African rural communities to drive positive and sustainable change in their lives.' A charity based in Bakewell, Derbyshire, since 1990, Village

AiD focuses on four countries: Sierra Leone, the Gambia, Ghana and Cameroon. Village AiD's aim is not to impose Western solutions on communities, but to help them achieve self-sufficiency and their own potential within their own social framework.

In real terms this means that Village AiD supports community workers, literacy trainers and agricultural advisers through a network of partner organizations. It also employs some directly paid staff in Africa. The calibre of African staff is generally high, but there have been several instances where younger, more academically educated staff have left to study for Master's degrees in the United States, or have moved to larger NGOs. One of the two African Programme Coordinators based in the United Kingdom was initially himself a country programme manager in Cameroon.

To build the capacity of African partner organizations, Village AiD will in 2004 initiate a substantial programme of management development. Co-funded by a block grant from the European Commission, this project will strengthen Village AiD's partners' professional skills and organizational capacity. Baseline profiling, participatory monitoring, building in annual and quarterly cycles for review, accounting, target setting and budgeting, and staff appraisals all form part of this management development programme. In addition, new Web sites and Internet access will improve their chances of capturing their own support and funds from outside Village AiD, as well as providing a platform from which to communicate their own message.

Confident and competent management will, also, crucially be better placed to empower village groups in their own political literacy development. From a basic pattern of group formation, learning, reflection and action, on the model first articulated by Paulo Freire, people are already gaining much greater self-confidence and practical skills. If they can sign their name, they can claim a legal identity. If they can use numbers, they can move on to establish micro-credit schemes. Lack of affordable credit facilities is one of the main barriers to economic development in African villages.

One important strand of the work is social drama. Using role play in the village meetings, learning circle members deal with sensitive cultural issues in a way that makes the audience engage, sympathize, and then hear others' viewpoints.

The African Programme Coordinators spend on average six weeks at a time in any one country. Much of this time will be spent in management development and support for in-country staff, as well as visiting communities and evaluating the projects. Formal evaluations and annual reports are required by funders. Factual data to set against aims and objectives have to be collated. From the UK office, much time is spent researching, submitting and then reporting to donors.

The work is hard to explain briefly, hard to 'sell' to casual enquirers, who may hope to see tangible signs of development made immediately obvious: a well, a school, a chicken pen. These things certainly do occur; however, Village AiD believes that the path of development out of poverty, poor health and debt can most clearly be accessed through the processes outlined here. Women's literacy, local business initiatives, educational aspirations for their children, and personal empowerment within their own cultures have come about in more than 280 communities now. Younger people are gaining an economic stake in their villages; there is less alienation, less sense of injustice, a greater sense of real change taking place. In all of this, Village AiD plays a small but vital role.

ACTIVITY 10.7 VILLAGE AID

Village AiD was set up and is run from Bakewell, a small market town in Derbyshire, and works with communities in West Africa. How would you suggest that it develops its UK management team to work with the African staff? And how would you suggest it develops the African staff to work with the UK management team?

What management development do the African beneficiaries from the project need in order to be able to develop their businesses successfully?

SUMMARY

In this chapter we have given an overview of the challenges that management development faces in the ever-changing work environment. We have provided activities to involve you in the management development process and would suggest that you might like to try the activities in other chapters as part of your own management development. If you are a manager, you could think about the development process that you offer to your staff. Is it appropriate for the needs that your organization is facing?

Leveraging the human resource development function

INTRODUCTION

In this chapter we cover the important area of how line, middle and senior managers can harness and develop their own ability to make the HRD function work more successfully for them. The word 'leveraging' is related to power and influence, and these topics form a major part of this chapter. It has been suggested that

> Staying ahead of the competition and coping with the increasingly turbulent environment are issues that challenge most managers, thus, focussing on the development of themselves and their staff has to be of major importance. (Joy-Matthews, Andrews and Firth, 1999: 455)

LEARNING OUTCOMES

By reading this chapter, undertaking the suggested activities, and reflecting on the content and your own prior knowledge, you will achieve the following learning outcomes:

▌ an understanding of managers, management and the relationship to the HRD/learning function;

■ knowledge about how to manage HRD professionals so they work to your specification;

■ skills in how to harness HRD professionals' expertise to achieve your goals;

■ knowledge about how managers can enable the organization's strategy to drive the development process and vice versa;

■ an understanding of how to ensure that any development process is what is really needed and not just what is easily available or has been used before;

■ an insight into how to gain clarity about what you as a manager want to achieve for yourself, your staff, colleagues and your line manager;

■ an appreciation of what you need to know about HRD, who you need to know, what you need to use and what you need to develop;

■ an insight into how you can keep up to date;

■ an understanding of ways to change mindsets and thus enable everyone to continue learning.

MANAGERS, MANAGEMENT AND THE RELATIONSHIP TO THE HRD/LEARNING FUNCTION

Given the increasing emphasis on learning and development, it would be understandable if managers began to see HRD as some kind of panacea for all their organizational problems. This is rarely the case. However, the *relative* importance and value of certain kinds of learning activities in support of specific behavioural requirements is high.

Providing opportunities to learn, even if these have positive outcomes, will only provide people with the *potential* to do things differently and better: successful learning does not come with a guarantee that the learning will always be used! Learning is the process that results in an increase in the capacity to perform; the environment in which people are willing and able to use this enhanced capacity still has to be established.

It is as important to know when an HRD response is appropriate to a particular situation as it is to recognize when it is not. Remember the discussion about diagnosis compared to training needs analysis articulated in Chapter 9. The implementation of HRD strategies must, therefore, be based on a clear and accurate understanding of the problems and needs that require managerial action, and of what HRD can realistically contribute to these.

Contemporary management is a demanding and complex task requiring high levels of technical and personal skills, and managers with these skills, particularly in small- and medium-sized enterprises, are increasingly under pressure to take on more tasks and to carry them out to ever-higher standards. Many managers might feel unable to take on additional responsibilities for training their staff, often in circumstances in which short-term production targets are given precedence over longer-term and unfamiliar considerations. Little is usefully served by projecting the importance of this aspect of their jobs if it is at the expense of other legitimate, and often more urgent, priorities.

There is no dilemma! The objective is not to turn managers into development specialists, but to show them that they have so many ways of helping people to learn *in the context of their existing jobs and responsibilities*. Previous chapters have explored the many different ways all managers can contribute to learning and behavioural change. The secret – if there is one – of achieving this lies in changing the perception of what managing people involves.

Old attitudes and excuses for not responding to this challenge and opportunity are increasingly unacceptable, simply because the costs of not developing the capacity to help others do their jobs better continue to grow. Those managers who use lack of time to avoid this responsibility are offering an excuse, rather than a reason, for not acting. Deferring doing something positive until the time is more appropriate becomes a permanent strategy for inaction. Times and circumstances are rarely more favourable, and are never likely to be so for the manager who is determined that they should not be!

This perceptual change in managerial attitudes towards HRD is one that needs to affect every manager. The potential that exists for managers to directly influence the behaviour of their staff is rarely appreciated or acted upon. The irony is that managers offering encouragement, giving direction and taking an active interest in what their staff are doing can often achieve improvements in employee performance far beyond that which any course or training programme can deliver. Jenny's daughter has recently started working for the Healthy Living Project for East Cambridgeshire Council. During her first month of work she was called in to meet the council's chief executive. He likes to meet all new members of staff and sees this as a way of integrating them into the team. A comprehensive programme of induction training was also provided. The result is one very committed employee!

The idea that managers are free to choose whether or not to commit themselves to new HRD activities is no longer tenable. Whether they like it or not, the implications of decentralization and the increasing tendency for CEOs and MDs to commit themselves to major change and quality initiatives inevitably means that managers at all levels will be required to participate.

The evidence cited throughout this book shows quite clearly that managing the HRD function effectively does make a difference to employees, and not simply in terms of job performance: learning can be an exhilarating and liberating experience that has many positive effects. These are also of benefit to the organization in general and lend additional force to the argument that managers really do need to consider how they are contributing to this process.

THE HRD/TRAINING FUNCTION

Many large- and medium-sized organizations have attempted to meet the HRD 'need' by establishing specialized and centralized development or training sections or departments. These have, over time, become institutionalized; some have been in existence for many years and have acquired their own routines, traditions and procedures. Despite periodic 'threats', they have largely survived in one form or another. Small businesses, by virtue of their size and limited resources, are rarely associated with specialist staff functions.

Despite a trend towards changing their designation from training to HRD, the reality for most is that they are still called and known as training departments, and are seen to represent, or claim, the primary if not exclusive source of expertise in this area.

In cases where smaller organizations maintain a generalist personnel function, with relatively few staff, training can be a shared responsibility or seen as the major part of one person's job. Where a single personnel officer is the only tangible expression of a centralized function, training is one of many competing demands on a very limited resource base, with obvious implications for the contribution this can make to HRD.

The institutionalization of the development and training function has undoubtedly had some beneficial effects, particularly in the development of a more rational and coordinated approach to training and, to a lesser extent, development opportunities. Yet despite their existence, too many development and training departments have yet to acquire the respect and recognition of other organizational departments, which, in the light of what has been said about HRD and organizational success, might be thought surprising. Explanations for the actual status and perceived effectiveness of specific training departments have to be sought within individual organizations, but in a more general sense there are three points that may shed some light on this question:

■ Training is *not* the same as HRD. The tendency to equate the two is a fundamental misconception that clouds people's expectations of what to expect from training departments. HRD is more strategic and developmental.

■ Training departments, even where they more narrowly define their role, often fail to provide a quality service. Their ability to operate as effective deliverers and managers of the training function is limited and fails to meet increasing standards and expectations.

■ Training departments suffer from structural and managerial limitations, which means that on their own they can never provide the quality of service and contribution to individual and organizational performance that is expected of them.

One of the most significant and damaging consequences of the growth in specialist functions is that this often results in the intended or accidental shift of responsibility away from line management. There is no doubt that in many cases, line managers have not seen the role of training specialists as a cause for concern, or as a threat to part of their managerial responsibilities. Given what has been argued earlier, they may well have welcomed the tendency for their organizations to create and fill training roles with so-called experts, because this allowed them to disclaim any significant responsibility for training. It became somebody else's problem!

On the other hand, confident and influential training managers may well have created their 'empires' *despite* the resistance and reservations of other managers, who recognized that too much centralized power over training and development might compromise progress in this area.

This debate about respective roles and responsibilities of development and training specialists and line managers is not simply about organizational politics; it is also concerned with the need to improve efficiency and effectiveness, and the appropriate form and location of the training and HRD functions. Certainly, the trend over recent years has been towards decentralization, which may or may not involve the retention of some form of central strategy-making and coordinating function.

Where organizations adopt a general strategy of decentralization, the outcome for an existing training department almost certainly involves the dispersal of training specialists to organizational sub-units, where they provide direct support to line managers. In extreme cases the process of downsizing and decentralization can result in the virtual demise of any specialist, in-house provision.

Organizations that have retained training departments – and there are many such – are increasingly concerned to establish their effectiveness. It is never easy to suggest how they might do so, out of context, but it is possible to put forward four quite different explanations for why training departments are perceived to be less effective than might be expected. Where a particular department does not enjoy high status within its organization, it is likely that one or more of the following points will help to answer the question 'why?'.

▌ There may be misconceptions concerning their role and capability, and unreasonable expectations of their ability to provide short-term solutions to an often ingrained and institutionalized problem.

▌ There may be personal limitations. Specialist staff suffer from the same limitations as managers as others in the organization – perhaps more so!

▌ There may be structural and organizational weaknesses, exemplified by a central department and operating units not coordinating their training policies.

▌ There may be process weaknesses. These could be in decision-making, consultation or evaluation.

The reasons for taking a somewhat qualified position as far as the contribution training departments make to improving the competence and capability of employees are important enough to be considered in more detail. Without denying the respect that some undoubtedly enjoy, the following represent some of the more specific criticisms made against them:

▌ They develop their own agenda and priorities, which can become separate from – and, in extreme cases, in conflict with – other organizational interests.

▌ They lack a sufficiently developed awareness of 'business needs'.

▌ They are staffed by people who, although competent in their own fields, lack appropriate experience and skills of other disciplines and functional areas.

▌ They become 'course dominated' in their thinking. This means that training and development become synonymous with the provision of and attendance on formal courses.

▌ Their criteria for success lack conviction and (often) relevance.

▌ They can become excessively administratively or control oriented.

▌ They do the things that they are good at.

▌ They confuse activity with results.

▌ They fail to change what they do, on the basis of an evaluation of successes and failures.

Raising questions about the effectiveness of development and training departments is not something that implies doubts about the inherent value of their potential contributions. The purpose is to ensure that the practices and activities that characterize their work support pressing, rather than imposed or perceived, organizational needs.

There is nothing inevitable about the realization of this potential. To avoid the process of 'degeneration' into net consumers of resources rather than a major source of added value, they have to be managed in exactly the same way as any other management function: professionally and with a clear sense of purpose and operational accountability. In one sense, this involves making a rational judgement of the value associated with retaining a centralized department, based upon some agreed cost–benefit criteria. These can be quite straightforward: they might even take the form of simple but challenging questions such as:

▌ In what way and to what extent is the department contributing to the development of individuals in ways that support their job performance?

▌ What does it cost to maintain the department at its current level of resource consumption?

▌ Is there a more effective way of enhancing the value of its contributions by changing the way it operates, to make it more accountable and integrated within the line function? What do its customers think?

■ If we didn't have one, how long would it take for people to feel its loss?

ACTIVITY 11.1 VALUING AN HRD FUNCTION

You might want to ask the four questions above about your own HRD function. Check out your responses with other people in the organization.

The idea that a development and training department is the exclusive instrument for individual and organizational learning should, quite simply, be rejected. The reason for this is that at best such departments have only a limited impact, and at worst they can become active impediments to the realization of HRD's potential.

This comment should be seen more as a general critique of an organization's senior management than as a specific criticism of its training department. The question that demands an answer is: whose responsibility is it for ensuring that HRD is conceived, managed and directed in ways that support organizational performance? Senior management's reluctance or refusal to act to improve how development and training departments are staffed and function can have serious and damaging consequences for how the function is perceived within the organization.

Once a department or an individual's responsibility for development and training is established, it becomes much easier for senior managers to use the vocabulary of the righteous. Yes, we do take HRD seriously, and we have a training department to demonstrate this. The next step, of course, is to emphasize someone else's primary responsibility for managing training, often to the exclusion of those who should be seen as the major contributors to an organization's HRD activities: senior and line managers at all levels, working with the specialist support function.

The rhetoric that expresses senior management's formal commitment to the training function, and to HRD, needs to match the reality of what this actually means in and to the organization and its members. Avoiding their real and permanent responsibility in these fields is always going to represent one of the less tangible reasons why the quality and effectiveness of training and development remain worryingly low.

The effective management of training and development requires a clear and *shared* vision of specific responsibilities, which, when taken together, represents the foundation for building a range of learning opportunities. Table 11.1 outlines what these responsibilities might be.

Table 11.1 *The responsibility map*

Level	Role
Senior managers	To establish a broad policy framework, linking HRD with other aspects of human resource management in ways that clearly support current and future organizational requirements
Development and training specialists	To work with senior managers in establishing the policy framework, and to design and implement detailed proposals for learning against specified objectives
Line managers	To ensure that the policy framework and detailed proposals reflect operational requirements, and to actively support staff's learning, with particular emphasis given to its application and utilization
Employees	To commit themselves to their own continuing development, and to support management's attempts to relate this to enhanced organizational effectiveness

Some of the key issues that have been raised and that deserve consideration when attempting to manage the human resource development or training department include:

■ The importance of *integrating* HRD activities within a wider HRM framework. For example, the absence of career and succession planning makes it very difficult to identify longer-term developmental needs. There is a failure to recognize that training and development are *only two*, albeit important, instruments for enhancing performance. Even in their most effective states, they will not overcome limitations and difficulties, which are more appropriately dealt with by other managerial responses. Those relating to improved selection decisions, leadership, and motivation and discipline are sometimes alternatives and/or complementary to a response that concentrates on structured learning to enhance performance.

▮ Realizing the potential that effective HRD offers requires the same kind of *professional management* and commitment as would be expected in any other management function.

▮ Concentrating responsibility for HRD into the hands of *specialists* is not always associated with positive and valued outcomes for the organization.

▮ Unless management is prepared to accept the need for *organizational changes* to facilitate the *utilization* of learning, then newly acquired capabilities will be lost.

▮ While learning and the acquisition of higher levels of competence are important in their own right, the bringing about of *real and significant* changes in individual performance is the acid test of HRD effectiveness.

▮ Finally, enhanced performance resulting from HRD activities must *be recognized and rewarded* by senior management in appropriate ways. If there is no attempt to discriminate between those employees who have made the necessary commitment to their own development in response to job and organizational needs and those who have not, why does personal development and performance matter?

ENABLING THE ORGANIZATION'S STRATEGY TO DRIVE THE DEVELOPMENT PROCESS

Many managers will be familiar with the following:

> a training department run from head office, which offers a directory of courses that have been running for several years, more or less successfully. Every so often, typically annually, managers are asked to nominate participants for these set courses.

Does the above scenario seem familiar to you? Does it really meet the needs of you, your staff or your colleagues? Or do you feel that there has to be a better way?

ACTIVITY 11.2 DEVELOPING STAFF

Review your own contribution to the development of your staff. Write down for each of them what you believe your contribution over the past 12 months has been. Ask them to read it and to give you their reaction. Discuss the results.

What contact have you had with your development and training function over the past six months? Try to identify the specific value of the contacts you have had with them.

Write down the ways you would like to change how the development and training function operates. Think about how you might share these changes in a way that has positive outcomes.

The next time you have a meeting with the CEO or MD, ask him or her when was the last time the senior management discussed the company's approach to HRD and whether they felt satisfied with it. Work out a strategy for promoting more frequent discussions with them on this subject.

It seems vital that HRD should meet the needs of the organization and not be driven by a bureaucracy. This is achieved in many different-sized organizations in the private, public and voluntary sectors, as we shall see.

If HRD is to be truly relevant, it needs to be driven by the organization's strategy (see Chapter 2). This makes each piece of development work a part of the organization's own development, with all participants receiving what they need and in the way in which they need it (Hunt, 1986; Cushway, 1994).

In defence of the HRD function, what often happens is that someone decides to make a change of some sort (eg install a new computing system). A list of criteria is drawn up and the system is bought or rented and installed. Often only at that stage are the HRD professionals asked to provide training, and then usually on a shoestring. It is still, unfortunately, rare for the development of staff to be one of the criteria that determines which system is chosen.

Many managers have to become much better at thinking through what the HRD implications are for the actions that they take. Just as we have to use the organization's strategy to drive HRD, we also have to use it as the vehicle by which HRD can be accomplished within our organization.

> # ACTIVITY 11.3 ASSESSING YOUR ORGANIZATION'S STRATEGIC ISSUES AND CAPABILITIES
>
> What strategic issues are facing your organization now? What are the implications for HRD?
>
> What steps have you taken to ensure the capability of yourself and your staff to meet the strategic aims of the organization?
>
> Does your line manager need developing? Can you help?

RESEARCHING WHAT IS NEEDED

There is often a tendency to stay with the familiar – to use the consultants, video or course that has been successful in the past. Most managers are short of time and this is just the commodity that research consumes voraciously! However, it is worth attempting to identify what will provide an appropriate solution. Once research has been seen to work, it can become part of 'the way we do it around here', and the process of taking things for granted may be overcome.

There is a far higher emphasis on benchmarking now than there was in the past, and it is possible by reading professional journals to see what other managers have done in similar circumstances. See Chapter 9 for a further discussion of benchmarking.

HRD practitioners are also short of time and often have a very limited budget, so they too have reasons for recycling material. One of us worked on an international programme where there was a clear example of using research that had been funded from outside the organization to enable a very thorough training needs analysis to be undertaken. Once this had been completed, further research was conducted to design the content for the learning events. The fact that all the work could be translated into a variety of languages and used throughout Europe saved on the 'reinventing the wheel' syndrome. Much of the material was completely new, and the ability to update it on a regular basis means that this organization will not fall into the trap of using what it has always used!

ACTIVITY 11.4 ASSESSING YOUR ORGANIZATION'S HISTORY AND NEEDS

What has been available historically? Is it still relevant?
What do you need to have available for you, your staff and colleagues?
Who else could undertake the research?

GAINING CLARITY ABOUT WHAT YOU AS A MANAGER WANT TO ACHIEVE FOR YOURSELF, YOUR STAFF AND COLLEAGUES

Before you are in a position to commission the human resource development professionals to provide the solution, you need to know what you need. Alternatively, you may be able to provide the solution yourself by some means other than a course or structured learning event.

It is essential that managers think through ideas for the future strategy for the organization. Where is the organization now and where does it need to be? The gap in between is likely to be where HRD will play a part. Could this gap be met: by changing systems, practices or attitudes? Can the need be met by a course – off the job or at work – or by e-learning or blended learning?

The role of development and training within organizations is changing, and staff have to rethink where the responsibility lies. Nowadays, more managers are finding that their line management role includes a significant responsibility for the development of their staff and themselves (Banfield, 1997). They may also find that there is a role in developing colleagues and their own line managers. Having a clear vision of what appropriate development looks like is essential.

ACTIVITY 11.5 ASSESSING WHERE HRD CAN PLAY A PART

Have you thought through what the gap is and how it could be met?

What changes need to be made? Who needs to be involved in the development process? How much involvement can you have?

WHAT MANAGERS NEED TO KNOW ABOUT HRD

Knowledge

Knowledge is a valuable resource in its own right, and we have talked about this in other chapters. It is, however, useful to consolidate the point here.

You need to know who your participant(s) is and why that person needs development, at this present time. This will link back to the strategy of the organization, although there will be times when a participant may have a very individual need that – because you have a holistic view of the participant – you feel is worth meeting anyway. You need to know, also, whether it is appropriate for you to get involved in a direct way with the development activity or whether it is a case for the training department, if your organization has one. We would argue that a manager always has responsibility for development of self and others, so indirect involvement is of course always required. Knowledge of the organization's strategy linked to the participant's needs should be your starting point.

Knowledge of ways of meeting the need is the next requirement – knowing how directly you should be involved as a trainer, developer, coach, mentor or facilitator. If you decide that it is appropriate for you to have a direct role, you will need to know what learning strategies are available to you.

Research

One way of gaining information is to conduct a piece of research. Compiling data and generating facts and figures about an issue gives you credibility, provided you have used a sound methodology. Gill and Johnson's book *Research Methods for Managers* (1991, 1997) makes an excellent starting point.

There are hundreds of capable and intelligent HRM students in universities and colleges all over the country longing to get an invitation to undertake some detailed exploration of an HR issue in an organization like yours. Why not contact your nearest course leader and discuss with him or her what you need?

WHO YOU NEED TO KNOW

Stakeholders

It is often suggested that people are an organization's most important resource. They can certainly be a manager's best resource when it comes to undertaking HRD. It is useful to carry out a quick stakeholder analysis of who you need to know in order to facilitate the HRD of yourself and others in your organization. It might look something like Figure 11.1. By choosing to work with these people, or some of them, you should be able to gain part of the knowledge that you need in order to implement your chosen development event.

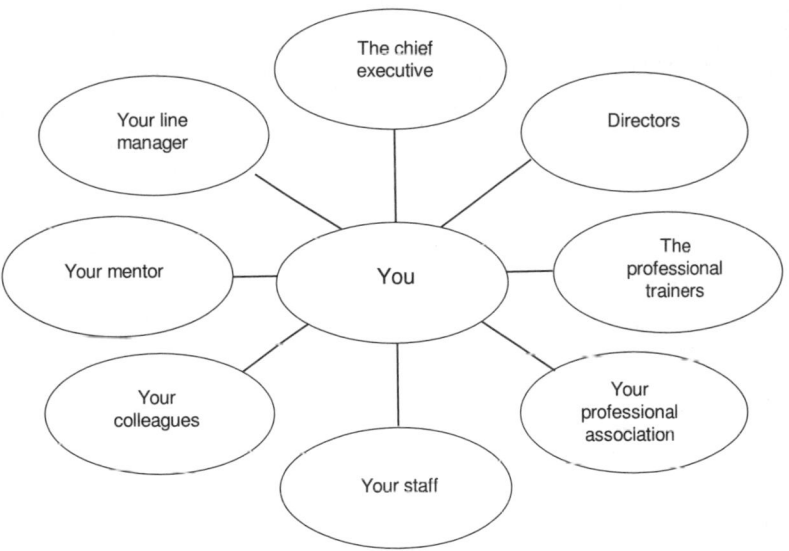

Figure 11.1   *Stakeholders*

Networking

Networking is perhaps one of the most powerful learning strategies available to managers. Peers, other colleagues and managers from other organizations can be a great source of knowledge. Networking informally at meetings and conferences is one way of developing. Networking more formally is another. Getting a group of people together to share learning is a very powerful experience. Much of the information for this book has come from a network of friends, clients, students and colleagues who have shared their ideas, knowledge and concerns with us. In the process we have become far more knowledgeable and competent in many areas. We have also increased the number of people that we can draw on in the future to help us to develop.

WHAT YOU NEED TO USE

Books

Other, obvious sources of information are books. University and college libraries are sometimes open to the public. During holiday periods they will have a wider variety of choice, when their students are not borrowing them so heavily. Other books in this series may help with the content of your chosen training event. Lois B Hart's (1991) neat little book *Training Methods That Work* not only covers the basic principles of learning and how to prepare and use different methods, but provides descriptions of 17 of the most successful and widely used techniques. Given that variety helps people to retain their interest and concentration, this is an invaluable text. Kogan Page also provide some of their books on cassettes, which is useful for people with sight or some learning disabilities. The McGraw-Hill training series offers a comprehensive look at training and development that is well worth dipping into.

Journals

Trying to keep up to date with new books can be an uphill task. However, many journals offer book reviews, which can be a most welcome short cut. Journal articles are another source of relevant and current information. *People Management*, *Management Learning*, *Industrial and Commercial Training* and *Executive Development* – the last two from MCB – are among the most useful general training and development journals.

Your own professional or trade journals may have useful articles about training and development, and attempting to keep up to date with what your competitors are doing can be of strategic importance.

Libraries

Many libraries now have a CD ROM system that will enable you to research specific topics. You need to be selective or you may end up with many thousands of references if, for example, you key in 'development' as your descriptor.

Films

There are a wide variety of films, videos, tape-slide sequences, interactive videos and OHP acetates on the market. Many of the companies hold preview days, sometimes at no cost, when you can look at the material available before you decide to hire or buy. Some material may also be available free.

Directories

Kogan Page publish a number of directories, of which *The Skills and Training Directory* (Jolly, 2003) is particularly useful for anyone engaged in researching or providing HRD.

Computers

Computer-based training (CBT) is defined by Kandola (1998) as 'the delivery of training materials via a computer'. It does not include interactive videos but is a generic term that encompasses computer-assisted instruction (CAI) and computer-managed instruction (CMI).

Being able to deliver training via a computer has both advantages and disadvantages. On the plus side, learners can learn at their own pace and when it is convenient for them. However, it can be expensive to design packages, and many people find training of this kind a lonely experience. See Chapter 5 for a further discussion.

Having a system that can manage the 'paperwork' that is associated with training, and particularly accreditation of competences, is invaluable. Organizations need to keep accurate records of who has received what training, and managers and staff need to have this information too.

Table 11.2　*Computer-based training*

CBT	
CAI	*CMI*
Tutorial	Routing
Drill and practice	Recording
Discovery	Testing
Simulation	Reporting
Modelling	
Gaming	

CD ROMs

CD ROMs have a very wide application in terms of training and development, both for finding information and for delivering training. Systems are becoming more affordable, and with the advent of the ability to write to disks, they will be even more popular.

The World Wide Web

There is just so much information available on the Internet that the problem is more often how to limit the amount than how to access it. Finding key words that aid the search and control the amount of information gained is essential. We believe that learning via the Web will continue to become more widely used in the near future. The concept of the virtual campus or business school is a major development, with people from all over the world being able to access 'local learning' in their home or office rather than having to make ecologically unsound journeys to places of study. This will mean that very high-calibre international experts will be available to virtually everyone with access to a computer, and will mean a radical rethink in the way that we view training and development.

Grants

Development is often expensive. However, there may be grants towards the cost. In the United Kingdom the local Learning and Skills Council may be able to provide some funding or put you in contact with a potential source of grant aid.

The European Social Fund (ESF) is currently providing money towards redressing the balance in the number of female as against male managers and by providing help in some of the disadvantaged parts of countries.

AS A MANAGER YOU NEED POWER

One of the most important resource bases that managers can have is their own power. French and Raven, in a seminal piece of work in 1959, identified that power could be drawn from five distinct bases: reward, referent, legitimate, expert and coercive. Working in the 1980s, Pettigrew, Jones and Reason (1982) also provided five bases: 'borrowed' power, relationships, ability, policies and allies.

We outline the 11 sources of power we see needing consideration for developing HRD in your organization:

■ *Referent power*. Being a role model can be very influential. If your staff look to you for guidance, you can clearly set the tone for your department etc. It can also work the other way. Finding a suitable person to be a mentor can help you to gain power and exposure in the organization, thus making it easier for you to have your ideas championed.

■ *Expert power*. Your technical expertise in performing your particular function in the organization gives you power in determining the training and development required. Your procedural knowledge of 'the way things are done' in your organization gives you similar power.

■ *Legitimate power*. It goes without saying that by this we mean your rightful power to wield influence at work, achieved by using other sources of power ethically. For example, it is more appropriate than coercive power.

■ *Coercive power*. This, unfortunately, is what a lot of managers resort to when they cannot use any other form of power. It is usually the least successful, as it builds up resentment.

■ *'Borrowed' power*. One way in which the training and development practitioners can be particularly useful is that you can borrow their expert, legitimate power and add it to yours. Having knowledge and understanding of the way the training and development function operates within the organization can be a source of power. You can become involved in their operation to the advantage of both yourself and your staff and the training and development department.

- *Relationships*. If you are recognized as 'a good egg' and have a high profile within the organization and are part of an influential network, you will have a strong power base. Looking at your role and completing a stakeholder analysis are also useful. Identifying what your role is and who the key players are gives you the opportunity to focus on areas where you may wish to develop. Perhaps there are key players whom you should cultivate as 'friends'.

- *Ability*. Having a good track record, being acknowledged as an able person, can often extend your power within the organization – and beyond, if you present papers at conferences, for example.

- *Policies*. Policies can be a useful starting point or back-up. However, hiding behind the policy is no substitute for real power. What is necessary is the ability to translate a policy into practice.

- *Allies*. People in high places with whom you are aligned are a great source of power, partly because they will be supportive of you and also because what you wish to implement almost certainly supports or drives the organization.

- *Reward*. Training and development can often be perceived as a reward. It may provide the chance of better things to come, once new skills and knowledge have been gained.

- *Personal power*. This comes from a combination of the above and is mainly to do with self-belief. As Henry Ford is reputed to have said, 'If you think you can or you think you can't, you're probably right!'

The ability to persuade other people is invaluable and is therefore well worth cultivating. There are many books on the market that aim to help managers become more powerful. Working on assertiveness skills is one interesting approach. Developing the ability to use interpersonal skills more effectively and to develop a fit between what you would like to do and what the organization requires is essential, as is using power for the good of the organization rather than for personal gain.

ACTIVITY 11.6 POWER ANALYSIS

Using the 11 categories of power just referred to, determine from where you derive your power and identify the areas in which you could develop your power base.

WAYS TO KEEP UP TO DATE

If you are a line or senior manager, you are unlikely to be, in the formal sense, a trainer or developer and you may not have all the very latest tools at your finger tips! There are, however, ways to gain knowledge of the tools that are currently available. While looking for suitable tools it is important to keep up to date. There is often a tendency to remember the course or video screening you attended years ago – but although it was right then, that does not necessarily mean it will still be appropriate now (although there are some classics that have stood the test of time and should not be dismissed out of hand).

There are a variety of journals that cover the field of HRD. Some are free and it is comparatively easy to be added to the circulation list; others need a subscription. They may be available from the HRD department or a local library.

Most professional HRD organizations will be pleased to add you to their circulation lists – but be selective, or you could end up buried under a mountain of course directories etc. The Association for Management Education and Development (AMED) is keen to recruit line managers interested in development to its membership. It can be contacted on 01480 493253 or at www.amed.org.uk.

Try to be aware of some of the newer techniques. For example, Neuro Linguistic Programming (NLP) is becoming a more popular tool – particularly in marketing and sales training, although it is useful in any situation where two or more people have to relate to each other (Bandler and Grinder, 1979, 1982; Knight, 1995).

Women's development training, while not a new technique, is still new to many organizations, primarily those that have not understood the implications of the demographic trends for the rest of this century and the changing nature of work. It is becoming increasingly important to retain and develop existing staff, and women are still under-represented in managerial positions (Willis and Daisley, 1992).

It is important, too, to consider other issues of diversity and training, for example for people with disabilities, those from ethnic minority groups and older people, although training for these groups is not as well developed as women's training. The need may not be to train these groups separately; it may be to work with everyone to ensure that diversity is managed to the benefit of all concerned. The HRD specialists should be able to offer advice. However, you need to be clear about what you expect them to deliver.

Attending specialist conferences is another source of information. Finding out how other managers in your particular industry are developing their staff may give you some ideas that would help you. For example, in IT the notion of the hybrid manager is posing new challenges and a requirement for new HRD skills for managers. The whole concept of knowledge management is becoming very important and will present opportunities for development. Conferences such as that of the Chartered Institute of Personnel and Development (CIPD) in Harrogate, where you can visit a wide variety of stands, and the Human Resource Development week in London will give you access to many professional managers, trainers and developers. If you are short of time, inviting a member of your staff to do this research or attend conferences and report back may be both a useful way of your gaining the information and a development opportunity for the member of staff. Part of the conference scene is the opportunity to 'network'; this is another way of finding out what other organizations are doing. AMED runs excellent conferences from time to time. It also has networks based in various locations. One of the things about networking is that it is quite amazing how many managers are happy to tell you all about their successes and failures in the area of HRD in a way that would not happen for another area!

ACTIVITY 11.7 KEEP UP TO DATE

What are the bright ideas being reported in your trade or professional journals? Are there any ideas you could modify and use?

What are the key issues being discussed in HRD journals, and are there any that would be of use to you?

Which conferences do you or should you attend? When was the last time you discussed HRD issues at a conference?

Who can you network with? Are there people you already network with who could help you with HRD?

What is there on the World Wide Web that is of interest for development?

MANAGING THE HRD PROFESSIONALS SO THEY WORK TO YOUR SPECIFICATION

Once the current organization strategy has been thought through and the part that HRD can play has been identified, the choice of up-to-date methods can be determined. The manager is now in a much stronger position to brief the HRD professional. To a certain extent, both parties will be speaking the same language. Many HRD professionals now think in terms of matching the organization's strategy and of contributing to return on investment, and they look for changes to the bottom line when evaluating the effectiveness of the HRD function.

Managers need to connect with the value system of the HRD professional. Speaking the same or at least an overlapping language is a good start to any conversation. However, for a true meeting of minds, more needs to happen. Both parties need to understand what drives the other. HRD professionals are often concerned about learning principles as discussed in Chapter 4, new government initiatives (see Chapter 1) and new ideas such as the learning company approach (see Chapter 8). Professional managers are usually concerned about getting the job done in the shortest amount of time and moving on to the next job. Managers who can spare some time to listen to the HRD professional will benefit. By listening to their ideas a manager will be able to understand their values and will be in a position to negotiate from a position of strength rather than ignorance. This should lead both parties away from the course directory approach and to a better, customized and consequently more effective approach.

ACTIVITY 11.8 KNOWING ABOUT THE HRD PROFESSIONAL

What are the values and leading ideas of the HRD professionals in your organization? What new issues are most important to them? When did you last talk to a HRD professional in your organization? Or in another organization? What did you learn?

HARNESSING THE HRD PROFESSIONALS' EXPERTISE TO ACHIEVE YOUR GOALS

HRD professionals are becoming increasingly more skilled and have a range of techniques and media to offer managers. They often want to move away from the course directory approach and to be able to use their skills to the full. Some companies have abandoned internal courses altogether. However, this all requires time, which both parties are probably short of. It can also require a change of culture within the organization. People become accustomed to one way of doing things and may feel vulnerable and disenfranchised if the usual directory does not appear. This can often be a very real concern when one's manager does not value HRD. There is even less chance of receiving the training or development required unless there is a prompt in the form of the directory. Abandoning the directory approach requires people to become more proactive and to liaise more directly with the HRD professionals than if they could choose off the peg.

While HRD will not hold the solution to all the problems, HRD professionals may often be able to contribute to the solution. They may have encountered similar problems elsewhere and be able to offer their expertise and advice on a variety of courses of action. They will also be able to administer some of the more complex solutions. For example, the move towards more competence-based developments is bringing with it a need for far better monitoring and control systems, as is the rise of self-managed learning. HRD professionals often have a system in place that can absorb some of the burden.

ACTIVITY 11.9 USING THE HRD PROFESSIONAL

What use have you recently made of the HRD professionals in your organization? What action did you take to ensure that you made the best use of their expertise?

RECOGNIZING THAT YOU ARE THE CLIENT

It is important for managers to adopt the role of client and to let the HRD professionals sell themselves and their services. Many organizations now use competitive tendering or outsourcing, and consequently, internal HRD professionals are having to compete with external providers. This can mean more work for managers. However, it also tends to mean that in-house HRD departments are becoming far more responsive to managers' needs and welcome the opportunity to use their expertise to the full. Andrew Leigh (1998) makes some germane comments on this subject when he suggests that those commissioning the work of consultants should be sensible in their dealings. He talks of the work put into drawing up a proposal that then appears to drop into a 'black hole', with the potential client never even bothering to acknowledge its arrival! While this is an important consideration when using external organizations, it is even more important when commissioning internal help. After all, you may need their help later!

ACTIVITY 11.10 BEING THE CLIENT

Does your organization use competitive tendering?
What services does your organization's HRD function have to offer you? How well do you treat the HRD staff?

WORKING TO CHANGE MINDSETS

In order for managers to achieve the biggest gains, they need to review their attitude towards HRD, which is often viewed as a cost in many organizations – something that keeps staff away from their jobs and from doing what is really important. If this is the case, then a change of attitude may be necessary. As work becomes more complex, as organization structures are slimmed down and as demographic changes impact, there will be an increasing need for HRD in order to retain and develop key members of staff.

Thinking of HRD as an investment rather than a cost can help to change mindsets. Managers often recognize the value of installing sophisticated computer systems that cost a fortune but give the capacity to work more effectively. There is a tendency to view this as an investment because of speculation on the benefits it will bring. However, spending time or money on developing an individual is often perceived as a cost. Perhaps when training was not custom designed for each individual this was a correct judgement. Nowadays, with the opportunity to hone HRD and provide specific events for each individual, it is no longer appropriate to see good, well-planned and well-executed HRD as anything other than an investment.

In this chapter we have alluded to training events. It is appropriate to mention here what some of these events might entail. Events can cover a very wide range: courses, job rotation, shadowing, projects, developing portfolios, attending meetings as a guest, conferences, visiting customers and suppliers (even competitors), think tanks, *kaizen*, becoming a trainer, coach, mentor, facilitator, organizing the Christmas party, and so on. . . So, while the events might be taking people away from their job in the narrowest sense, they should have been chosen in such a way that the new knowledge, skills or attitudes gained will be useful to them in their job, or developmental for the future.

Time away from the job has utility. It enables people to learn new knowledge, skills and attitudes or to reflect on old ones. If the events have been planned carefully and the participant is well briefed before going and is given the opportunity to discuss and apply what has been learned on their return, then the time will have been well spent.

ACTIVITY 11.11 ENABLING NATURAL LEARNING

What events have you or your staff been involved in recently? What part did the HRD professionals play in enabling them? What did you do to ensure that you were fully prepared for the event? What did you do to ensure that your staff were fully briefed before the event and what opportunities were made available for feedback and implementation after the event?

WAYS THAT ENABLE EVERYONE TO CONTINUE LEARNING

In the past it has been common for managers and staff to undervalue learning on the job. They have seen courses, with all their faults, as more important. Often, the more expensive the course, the more value it has been seen to have. In practice we have noticed that cost may have little to do with value in real terms.

Learning on the job can be designed in such a way that it is a very valuable experience, and not just for the learner. It can be a very useful revision method for existing staff, and becoming a trainer or mentor can provide a high level of motivation to an already skilled member of staff. With the move towards competences there is an increasing need for workplace trainers and assessors, and organizations are finding it beneficial to use existing members of staff in these roles.

CASE STUDY 11.1: YOUR OWN ORGANIZATION

Using the information contained within this chapter and the rest of the book, undertake a diagnosis and evaluation of the state of management development within your own organization. You can still do this if you are self-employed or a sole trader. Look for the strengths and weaknesses in the current provision.

If you could start with a blank sheet of paper and redesign the system from scratch, what would you do?

Share this diagnosis and evaluation of management development with a few trusted colleagues. What do they think should/could be done? Can you share this up the line?

Monitor the results. Let us know the results of your efforts.

SUMMARY

Managing the HRD function is becoming, increasingly, one of the key responsibilities of every manager. This chapter has shown some of the prime ideas that need to be considered. You may feel that there are other ideas for consideration. You may now wish to assess whether you are prepared for this challenging and developmental opportunity.

ACTIVITY 11.12 YOUR DEVELOPMENT

Write a development agreement and have your mentor work with you to complete it.

You might like to consider what you can do to increase your knowledge, what resources you don't currently use and could benefit from, and how you can work more closely with the training and development function in the future.

12

Learning for the future

INTRODUCTION

In this chapter we look at where development may be going in the future and bring in many voices that have something to say about development processes. Our contribution is to pull together and cluster what they say. In addition, we have inserted one or two quotes from published sources that add a particularly cogent vision of the future. The comments that we have assembled for this chapter are presented at some length so that you can make your own sense of them and see how they reinforce or challenge your view of how HRD should move forward in the future.

LEARNING OUTCOMES

By reading and reflecting upon this chapter, you will:

▌ identify how leading thinkers view the future contribution and direction of HRD;

▌ relate these views to your own perspective on HRD;

▌ develop an enriched sense of how HRD could be developed in your own sphere of influence.

PREDICTING THE FUTURE

Of course, predicting the future leaves hostages to fortune. However, we are fortunate to have obtained the considered views of a number of luminaries of the HRD world who are prepared to be specific about what it is that the future might hold.

ACTIVITY 12.1 DEVELOPING A STRATEGY FOR HRD

Look back to Figure 1.4, where there are a series of dichotomies or trichotomies listed, offering alternative perspectives on HRD and learning. For each item, do you have a preference for one end as opposed to the other? Or are both ends equally attractive and valuable? From your reading of this book, have you changed your opinion from when you first came across this figure? Bearing in mind your perspective, read this chapter and see how various business and academic leaders in the field agree with or challenge your view. Once you have settled on your final view, think through what this means for HRD in your sphere of influence. You may want to write a brief strategy paper outlining this view.

THE CONTRIBUTIONS

Holistic relevance

Jean Floodgate, who is a leading thinker within the development community in the Chartered Institute of Personnel and Development, emphasizes whole-systems thinking. Paul O'Donovan Rossa, a leading executive coach, envisages a future in which authenticity and responding to individual requirements become a central plank in suppliers' offerings:

> The HRD role will be an animator for all kinds of learning possibilities – with and between individuals and with and between groups/organizations. The stretch will be significant: from integrating learning into all kinds of business activity, through to earning true engagement and voice through participation. A 'whole-systems' thinker with a degree of independent positioning will make more holistic interventions and will work alongside

leaders and teams in the workplace. The words 'training', 'subject', 'provision', 'course', 'exercise' will be redundant. The key skills will be facilitative intervention, impactful consulting and strong relationship management/marketing of learning achievements. Learning will become a key business driver and goal, of interest to all stakeholders. The three conditions of successful learning in business will be Relevance, Relevance and Relevance. (Jean Floodgate, Insight Outreach and Chair of CIPD CPD Working Party)

By 2014:

1. Standard provision of learning services will be jolted into increasingly authentic and niche approaches.

2. Coaching and learning interventions will become more reflective of the diversity of individual learning requirements and approaches. An increasingly cogent question from suppliers will be 'Have the providers themselves embodied the work they are purveying?'

3. Meaning and balance will become more real for many (rather than a distant aspiration), particularly in view of the amount of choice now available, and with fewer societal rules to be steered by.

4. This concern for individual as well as corporate and societal meaning will increase pressures upon organizations and service deliverers to be purveyors of living solutions and insights rather than administrators of readily available or ungrounded techniques. Accepted wisdoms based on poor research or urban myths will be questioned.

5. The perception of the human energy required in corporate life will shift along the continuum from physical readiness and mental alertness to a mind astuteness and deep personal discernment of influences and outcomes.

6. Charisma will fall upon those who deliver development and sustainability more through a silent presence rather than by an invasion of a system.

7. Technological change will challenge us to consider the worth of human contact – should I travel 200 kilometres to my client or should I speak to them on my wall?

8. Measurable results will remain crucial, but complex forms of measurement involving human capital, aspiration and capability will evolve along with those encompassing business goals.

9. The assumption or wish that others should have the answers, and the dependency that this can bring, will increasingly be challenged – and the idea of providing further key and expansive questions rather than reducing an issue to answers will no longer sound like an escape from responsibility. (Paul O'Donovan Rossa, Executive Coach and presenter)

Business contribution

Paradoxically, we have two great ideas-generators who both see ideas as secondary to making a contribution to the business.

> There is a great need for 'managers of learning' to help all managers see how critical to success is the right capability at the right time. The majority of HRD practitioners are much more concerned with individual personal growth than with benefiting the organizations that pay for it. I do not denigrate personal growth at all; it's part of the psychological contract of most organizations that they 'help me to grow'. But it attracts to the profession more than its fair share of 'ID' people rather than 'OD' people. We need more numerate business-orientated people who can see how learning enhances effectiveness at every level! (Andrew Mayo, MLI Ltd, professor and author)

> As I see it, the push will be on HRD to play a greater role as a business partner with responsibility for revenue generation in its own right and as part of cross-disciplinary teams. It will also be expected to find more cost-effective ways to deal with what will inevitably prove to be growing demands to demonstrate that their employees are developed, 'rights-aware', and so on. They will need to find very good ways of doing this if they are not to become too weighed down by the bureaucratic load of compliance. (Bryan Gladstone, IdeaSmith)

Role model for success

A practitioner, Carol Whitaker, who is HR Director of the National Exhibition Centre in Birmingham, supports the business contribution theme and adds a point about being a role model:

> The future of HRD will depend on being able to demonstrate some quick wins but also flexibility of approach and real role models of behaviours required for success. (Carol Whitaker, HR Director NEC and member of the Membership and Education Committee, CIPD)

Researcher, not doer

Dean Royles, a senior manager in the National Health Service, sees the continuing growth in size of HR departments as a threat to their business contribution and he envisages a role for HR staff as researchers to identify bespoke solutions for their clients. So, having had researchers emphasizing business contribution, we now have a business leader emphasizing research:

> The recent 2003 CIPD survey on the future of HR is a welcome encouragement. It shows that HR is moving in the direction that most informed commentators would value. The HR function is becoming even more strategic, influencing board-level colleagues and focusing on the HR contribution to organizational performance. A surprising find, however, is that, despite predictions, the size of the function is growing rather than shrinking. Encouraging at first sight perhaps, but is this a desirable development for a function eager to promote its strategic credentials? Being bigger does not necessarily mean it will be better, in the same way that working harder is not the same as working smarter. In fact, larger departments are likely to maintain or inherit administrative functions to justify their size. It is becoming increasingly evident that HR practice and the concomitant organizational benefits cannot simply be imported from elsewhere in some dewy-eyed notion of best practice. The idea of transferable models of HR practice, particularly in the field of performance and reward, has long been at odds with the concept of human resource management. The essence of HRM is about managers creating an environment where *individual* talent can flourish. It is about the individual contributing to organizational performance *and* developing personally. This will often be in the context of working in teams, but personal motivations are as varied as the numbers of people working in the organization. To establish what works for these individuals will require a new HR role: the role of internal researcher. HR professionals will need to develop more advanced research skills, applied in organizations to develop bespoke, tested people-management practices that maximize local knowledge production and represent best organizational fit rather than a simple transfer of best practice. This role will speed up the devolution of people management to line managers who will have more ownership of bespoke practice that works for them and their team, rather than growing the HR department to manage ever more complex company-wide HR systems. (Dean Royles, Head of HR Capacity (England), Department of Health)

Individual insight and dialogue

In another nice paradox, we have an industrialist, Richard Field, advocating individual insight and understanding of others as the key contribution of development in the future. Mike Pedler and Ian Cunningham both support this individual orientation – Pedler emphasizing honesty, and Cunningham the need to attend to what is going on in schools as well as companies. These views stand in sharp contrast to those in the previous section, especially Andrew Mayo's. A quotation from Patricia Shaw (2002) adds to the arguments for dialogue, and a passage from Robert Greenleaf (1996), who has influenced many thinkers, including Peter Senge, emphasizes the need for leaders to be servants of those they lead.

> Rather than focusing on HRD, perhaps HRD needs to focus on what is happening in the world of organizational change. So what will be the focus during these next few years? My belief is that it will be the enhancing of individual effectiveness through better understanding of ourselves and others. By better understanding, I mean a better understanding of our thinking processes, our feelings and our behaviours. The harnessing of this energy towards a common cause can have, and is having, significant measurable positive results. These are chronicled in two books: *First, Break All the Rules*, a 25-year Gallup Poll study of over a million employees and 80,000 managers (Buckingham and Coffman, 1999); and *Good to Great*, five years of research into the attributes of great companies (Collins, 2001). The November 2003 issue of the *Harvard Business Review* records how business schools are also changing to take account of this phenomenon. The article is called 'The five minds of a manager' (Gosling and Mintzberg, 2003). Just one final point: we managers/directors need someone who can help us to understand ourselves and help us to understand others better. It's a fast-moving and frightening world and we need someone beside us who we trust – and, dare I say, who will care for us. (Richard Field, industrialist and top team coach)

Having just come from a day's meeting with senior HR people in a large company, here is a short download of their concerns:

▌ getting rid of people – slimming the organization down by 30% over the next 18 months;

▌ recruiting and developing other people for more ambiguous, flexible and changing roles;

▌ engaging everyone in making these changes;

■ persuading directors who think they have got it right that they haven't;

■ helping very senior people to work together well as teams and not just cooperative groups.

Unfortunately, this list does not capture the subtlety of these concerns. What's different from traditional HR practice? This work seems to mean being honest with people (a new idea!), and instead of selling visions, having conversations about futures, developing options, allowing choices and not handing down solutions. (Mike Pedler, professor, writer and consultant)

We need to move away from human resource development as a concept – people are not resources, and attempts to get credibility for development work via the HR model are not the best direction for the future. Trust, integrity, real care for people and organizations are more important than mechanistic competence development. If development professionals really care about the learning of others, this will automatically make them want to do a great job. And professional capability is at the core of making development work more effective.

We need to pay more attention to young people coming into organizations. Schooling as currently conceived does not equip most young people for the world of work – but there are examples of people trying to do better. Development professionals need to take a more active interest in this work. (Ian Cunningham, Strategic Developments International; professor, author and consultant)

There is a value in 'just talking'. . . I would pick out certain themes: The invisibility of everyday conversation. . . Acting into the unknown. . . Organizing the unorganizable. . . Wanting to capture knowledge. (Shaw, 2002: 12–19)

The servant-leader is a servant first. . . It begins with the natural feeling that one wants to serve, to serve *first*. Then conscious choice brings one to aspire to lead. The difference manifests itself in the care taken by the servant. . . Do those served grow as persons? Do they *while being served,* become healthier, wiser, freer, more autonomous, more likely themselves to become leaders? (Greenleaf, 1996: 3–4)

Addressing unpredictable change

Valerie Bayliss, from a career at the heart of government policy on education and skills, and from her recent experience authoring the second Royal Society of Arts report on redefining work, sees HRD as having a key role in responding to unpredictable change:

HRD has not only to live with the changing world of work but to get ahead of it, even though it can be difficult to see what change will look like. The knowledge economy, which everyone expected would change patterns of work, has developed in unexpected ways, for example by industrializing many jobs. Managers' behaviour, as opposed to their rhetoric, often remains rooted in old models of work; there is more bureaucracy, more micro-management. Alongside, individuals really have flexed up their attitudes to work, taking a much more instrumental line. Employers will have to live with all this and make it work. Have they the capacity and understanding to do so? HRD may turn out be the only function with the potential to face up to the reality of change and tell it like it is. In fact, its practitioners have got to gear themselves up to do this, because few others will. HRD is going to be more vital to successful business than ever before. (Valerie Bayliss, author of the RSA's reports on redefining work)

The role of the senior executive

Clayton Christensen and Michael Raynor advocate the value of disruptive growth. They suggest an agenda for those of our readers who lead organizations:

> First, they must actively coordinate action and decisions when no processes exist. . . Second, they must break the grip of established processes when a team is confronted with new tasks. . . Third, when recurrent activities and decisions emerge in an organization, executives must create processes to reliably guide and coordinate the work. . . And fourth. . . senior executives need to stand astride the interfaces of those organizations – to ensure that useful learning from the new growth businesses flows back into the mainstream. (Christensen and Raynor, 2003: 282)

ACTIVITY 12.2 LEADING IDEAS FOR THE FUTURE

What does your reading about leading ideas in Chapter 2 lead you towards in your view of the future of HRD? How do the extracts in this chapter add to or challenge this perspective?

How can you integrate these views and develop your perception of HRD further? Who can you engage with to propagate or test out these views?

SUMMARY

We are not in the business of predicting the future – rather, we are seeking to challenge your thinking in your own situation and with the resources and opportunities that you have. You know more about your situation than we do; in fact, you know more about this than anyone else in the world. We wish you well in your journey.

References

Ainley, P [accessed 9 March 1999] [Online] http://www.dur.ac.uk/~dps8zz2/Lave/PatAinley.html

Alvesson, M and Willmott, H (1992) *Critical Management Studies*, Sage, London

Anderson, J R, Reder, L M and Simon, H A (1996) Situated learning and education, *Educational Researcher*, **25** (4) (May), pp 5–11

Argyris, C (1991) Teaching smart people how to learn, *Harvard Business Review*, **69 (3)** (May–June), pp 99–109

Argyris, C and Schön, D A (1978) *Organizational Learning: A theory of action perspective,* Addison-Wesley, Reading, MA

Atherton, J (2000) [accessed 20 August 2001] *Legitimate Peripheral Participation* [Online] http://www.dmu.ac.uk/~jamesa/learning/situated.htm

Atkinson, J (1984) Manpower studies for flexible organisations, *Personnel Management*, **16** (8) (August)

Badger, B, Sadler-Smith, E and Michie, E (1997) Outdoor management development, *Journal of European Industrial Training*, **21** (9), pp 318–25

Bandler, R and Grinder, J (1979) *Frogs into Princes*, Real People Press, Moab, UT

Bandler, R and Grinder, J (1982) *Reframing*, Real People Press, Moab, UT

Banfield, P (1997) Learning to reassess the role of training, *People Management*.

Barham, K, Fraser, J and Heath, L (1988) *Management for the future*, Ashridge Management College and Foundation for Management Education, Berkhamsted

Bass, M and Vaughan, J A (1966) *Training in Industry: The management of learning*, Wadsworth, Belmont, CA

Bateson, G (1972) *Steps to an Ecology of Mind*, Paladin, London

Bateson, G (2000) The logical categories of learning and communication, in *Steps to an Ecology of Mind*, University of Chicago Press, Chicago

Baumbach, D, Brewer, S and Bird, M (1995) [accessed 9 April 1999] Using anchored instruction in inservice teacher education [Online] http://www.coe.uh.edu/insite/elec_pub/html1995/192.htm

Beard, C and Wilson, J (2002) *The Power of Experiential Learning*, Kogan Page, London

Bee, F (2000) How to evaluate training, *People Management*, **6** (6), pp 42–43

Binsted, D S (1980) Design for learning in management training and development: a view, *Journal of European Industrial Training*, **4** (8)

Bloom, B S *et al* (1956) *Taxonomy of Educational Objectives, Handbook 1: The Cognitive Domain*, Longmans Green, London

Boyatzis, R E (1982) *The Competent Manager: A model for effective performance*, Wiley, New York

Boydell, T and Leary, M (1996) *Identifying Training Needs*, Institute of Personnel and Development, London

Boydell, T *et al* (1991) *Developing the Developers*, AMED, London; Department for Employment, Sheffield

Braddick, B and Casey, D (1996) Developing the forgotten army: learning and the top manager, in *How Organizations Learn*, ed K Starkey, Thomson Business Press, London

Bramley, P (1996) *Evaluating Training*, Institute of Personnel and Development, London

Brown, J S, Collins, A and Duguid, P (1989) [accessed 31 July 2001] Situated cognition and the culture of earning [Online] http://www.ilt. columbia.edu/ilt/papers/JohnBrown.html

Buchanan, D and Boddy, D (1992) *The Expertise of the Change Agent: Public performance and back stage activity*, Prentice-Hall, London

Buckingham, M and Coffman, C (1999) *First, Break All the Rules*, Simon & Schuster, New York

Buckley, R and Caple, J (1990) *The Theory and Practice of Training*, Kogan Page, London

Burgoyne, J (1988) Management development for the individual and the organization, *Personnel Management*, **June** pp 40–44

Burgoyne, J G and Hodgson, V E (1983) Natural learning and managerial action: a phenomenological study in the field setting, *Journal of Management Studies*, **20** (3), pp 387–99

Calvin, W H (1996) *How Brains Think*, Weidenfeld and Nicolson, London

Carnall, C A (1995) Programmes of change, in *Managing Change in Organizations*, pp 170–83, Prentice-Hall, London

Cascio, W F (1998) *Managing Human Resources*, McGraw-Hill, New York

Chartered Institute of Personnel and Development (CIPD) (2001) *Performance through People*, Chartered Institute of Personnel and Development, London

Christensen, C M and Raynor, M E (2003) *The Innovator's Solution: Creating and sustaining successful growth*, HBS Press, Boston

Clarke, C (2003) *Towards a Unified e-Learning Strategy*, Consultation Document, The Stationery Office, London

Clutterbuck, D and Ragins, B R (2002) *Mentoring and Diversity: An international perspective*, Butterworth-Heinemann, Oxford

Collins, J (2001) *Good to Great: Why some companies make the leap. . . and others don't*, Random House Business Books, London

Confucius in *Pathfinder International* (2003) Tron Publishing, Glasgow

Constable and McCormick (1987) *The Making of British Managers*, British Institute of Managers, London

Cooper, C and Davidson, M (eds) (1983) *Women in Management*, Heinemann, London

Cooperrider, D *et al* (1995) *Appreciative Enquiry: An emerging direction for organization development*, Stipes, Champaign, IL

Coopey, J *et al* (1993) *Develop Your Management Potential*, 2nd edn, Kogan Page, London

Council for Excellence in Management and Leadership (CEML) (2002) *Final Report*, CEML

Csikszentmihalyi, M (2002) *Flow: The classic work on how to achieve happiness*, Rider, London

Cummings, G T and Worley, C G (1993) *Organizational Development and Change*, 5th edn, West, St Paul, MN

Cushner, K (1990) *Applied Cross-cultural Psychology*, Sage, Thousand Oaks, CA

Cushway, B (1994) *Human Resource Management: Planning – analysis – performance – reward*, Kogan Page, London

Daloz, L A (1986) *Effective Mentoring and Teaching*, Jossey-Bass, San Francisco

Darwin, J, Johnson, P and McAuley, J (2002) *Developing Strategies for Change*, Pearson Education, Harlow

de Bono, E (1970) *Lateral Thinking*, Penguin, Harmondsworth

de Geus, A P (1997) The living company, *Harvard Business Review*, **75**, pp 51–59

Deming, W E (1989) *Profound Knowledge*, British Deming Association, Salisbury

Department of Trade and Industry (DTI) (2002) *Productivity and Competitiveness Indicators 2002*, DTI, London

Dixon, N (1998) *Dialogue at Work*, Lemos & Crane, London

Dreyfus, H L, Dreyfus, S E and Athanasion, T (1986) *Mind over Machine: The power of human intuition and expertise in the era of the computer*, Free Press, New York

Duddridge, M (2003) The cut that's false economy, *The Grocer*, 28 June, p 66

Easterby-Smith, M (1994) *Evaluation of Management Development*, Gower, Aldershot

Egan, R (1995) A clear path to peak performance, *People Management*, **1** (10), p 34

Eisenhardt, K M, Kahwajy, J L and Bourgeois, L J III (1997) How management teams can have a good fight, *Harvard Business Review*, **75** (4), pp 77–85

Eitington, J E (2001) *The Winning Trainer*, 4th edn, Elsevier Science and Technology Books, Amsterdam

Erikson, E (1950) *Childhood and Society*, Norton, New York

European Human Resource Development (EHRD) (2000) [accessed 3 November 2003] [Online] http://www.b.shuttle.de/wifo/ehrd-per/wo01a.htm

Fitts, P M (1962) Factors in complex skills training, in *Training Research and Education*, ed R Glaser, Wiley, New York

Flavell, J H (1976) Metacognitive aspects of problem-solving, in *The Nature of Intelligence*, ed L B Resnick, pp 231–35, Erlbaum, Hillsdale, NJ

Fletcher, B *et al* (1992) *50 Activities for Managing Change*, Gower, Aldershot

French, J R P and Raven, B H (1959) The bases of social power, in *Studies in Social Power*, ed D Cartright and A Arbor, University of Michigan Press, Michigan

French, W L and Bell, C H (1990) *Organizational Development: Behavioural science interventions for organizational improvement*, Prentice-Hall, London

Gagné, R M (1970) *The Conditions of Learning*, Holt, Rinehart & Winston, New York

Gardner, H (1985) *Frames of Mind: The theory of multiple intelligences*, Paladin, London

Gardner, J W (1963) *The Individual and the Innovative Society*, Norton, New York

Garratt, R (1987) *The Learning Organization*, Fontana, London

Garvey, B and Williamson, B (2002) *Beyond Knowledge Management: Dialogue, creativity and the corporate curriculum*, Prentice-Hall, Harlow

Ghoshal, S and Bartlett, C (1998) *The Individualized Corporation*, Heinemann, Oxford

Gibb, S (2002) *Learning and Development: Processes, practices and perspectives at work*, Palgrave Macmillan, Basingstoke

Gill, J and Johnson, P (1991) *Research Methods for Managers*, Paul Chapman, London

Gill, J and Johnson, P (1997) *Research Methods for Managers*, 2nd edn, Paul Chapman, London

Gladstone, B (2000) *From Know-how to Knowledge*, Industrial Society, London

Goldberg, N (1991) *Wild Mind: Living the writer's life*, Rider, London.

Goleman, D (1996) *Emotional Intelligence*, Bantam Books, London

Gordon, J (2003) Games + Simulation = Learning, in *e.Learning Age*, pp 30–31, Bizmedia, Reading

Gosling, J and Mintzberg, H (2003) The five minds of a manager, *Harvard Business Review*, **81** (11), pp 54–63

Greenfield, S (1997) *The Human Brain: A guided tour*, Weidenfeld and Nicolson, London

Greenleaf, R K (1996) *On Becoming a Servant-leader*, Jossey-Bass, San Francisco

Guest, D *et al* (2000) *Employment Relations, HRM and Business Perform-ance: An analysis of the 1998 Workplace Employee Relations Survey*, Institute of Personnel and Development, London

Guile, D and Fonda, N (1998) Performance management through capa-bility issues, in *People Management*, issue **25,** Chartered Institute of Personnel and Development, London

Hamblin, A C (1974) *Evaluation and Control of Training*, McGraw-Hill, London

Hamel, G and Prahalad, C K (1994) *Competing for the Future*, Harvard Business School Press, Boston

Hamilton, B and Scandura, T (2002) Implications for organizational learning and development in a wired world, *Organizational Dynamics*, **31** (4), pp 388–402

Hammer, M and Champy, J (1993) *Re-engineering the Corporation: A manifesto for business revolution*, Nicholas Brealey, London

Handy, C (1988) *The Making of Managers*, National Economic Develop-ment Office, London

Handy, C (1994) *The Empty Raincoat: Making sense of the future*, Hutchinson, London

Handy, C (1995) Trust and the virtual organization, *Harvard Business Review*, **73** (3)

Hardingham, A (1997) *Designing Training*, Institute of Personnel and Development, London

Harrison, R (1963) Defences and the need to know, *Human Relations Training News*, **6** (4)

Harrison, R (1997) *Employee Development*, Institute of Personnel and Development, London

Harrison, R (2002) *Learning and Development*, Chartered Institute of Personnel and Development, London

Hart, L B (1991) *Training Methods That Work*, Kogan Page, London

Heaney, T (1995) [accessed 9 April 1999] Learning to control democratically: ethical questions in situated adult education [Online] http://nlu.nl.edu/ace/Resources/Documents/AERC95.html

Heron, J (1999) *The Complete Facilitator's Handbook*, Kogan Page, London

Hildreth, P (2000) [accessed 20 August 2001] Research details [Online] http://www-users.cs.york.ac.uk/~pmh/work.html

Hirsch, S K and Kise, J A G (2000) *Introduction to Type and Coaching*, Consulting Psychologists Press, Palo Alto, CA

Hirsh, W and Carter, A (2002) *New Directions in Management Development*, Report 387, Institute for Employment Studies, Brighton

Hmelo, C E (1999) [accessed 9 April 1999] Problem-based learning: development of knowledge and reasoning strategies [Online] http://www.cc.gatech.edu/cogsi/e...e/PostDocs/Pubs/Hmelo.cogsci.html

Hodgetts, R M (1991) *Organizational Behaviour: Theory and practice*, Prentice-Hall, Englewood Cliffs, NJ

Honey, P (1990) Confessions of a learner who is inclined to lapse, *Training and Development*, **June**

Honey, P and Mumford, A (1992) *The Manual of Learning Styles*, 3rd edn, Peter Honey, Maidenhead

Hunt, C (1999) Reflective practice, in *Human Resource Development*, ed J Wilson, pp 221–40, Kogan Page, London

Hunt, J W (1986) *Managing People at Work: A manager's guide to behaviour in organizations*, McGraw-Hill, Maidenhead

Hussey, J and Hussey, R (1997) *Business Research: A practical guide for undergraduate and postgraduate students*, Macmillan Business, London

Iacocca, L (1985) *Iacocca: An autobiography*, Sidgwick & Jackson, London

Industrial Relations Service (IRS) (1998) *Management Review: Learning strategies*, IRS, London

Institute for Employment Research (IER) (2003) *Skills in England 2002*, Learning and Skills Council report, London

Institute of Employment Studies (IES) (2002) *Modelling eWork in Europe*, Report 387, IES, Brighton

Jalali, F A (1989) A cross-cultural comparative analysis of the learning styles and field dependence/independence characteristics of selected fourth-, fifth-, and sixth-grade students of Afro, Chinese, Greek and Mexican-American heritage, unpublished doctoral thesis, St John's University, New York

Jaques, R (1996) *Manufacturing the Employee*, Sage, London

Jaworski, J (1996) *Synchronicity: The inner path of leadership*, Berrett-Koehler, San Francisco

Jolly, A (2003) *The Skills and Training Directory*, Kogan Page, London

Joy-Matthews, J (2003) The situatedness of learning: a phenomeno-graphical study of the personal and professional learning of post and under graduate students, Doctor of Education thesis, Sheffield University, Sheffield

Joy-Matthews, J, Andrews, I and Firth, R (1999) Marketing human resource development, in *Human Resource Development*, ed J P Wilson, pp 455–74, Kogan Page, London

Joy-Matthews, J and Gladstone, B (2000) Extending the group: a strategy for virtual team formation, *Industrial and Commercial Training*, **32** (1), pp 24–29

Kandola, D (1998) Is computer based training an effective training medium?, BA (Hons) Business Studies dissertation, Sheffield Business School, Sheffield Hallam University, Sheffield

Kanter, R M, Stein, B A and Dick, T D (1992) *The Challenge of Organizational Changes: How companies experience it and leaders guide it*, Simon & Schuster, New York

Katzenbach, J R (1997) The myth of the top management team, *Harvard Business Review*, **75** (6), pp 83–91

Kelly, G A (1955) *The Psychology of Personal Constructs*, 2 vols, Norton, New York

King, N and Anderson, N (1995) *Innovation and Change in Organizations*, Routledge, London

Kirkpatrick, D L (1967) Evaluation of training, in *Training and Development Handbook*, ed R L Craig and L R Bittel, McGraw-Hill, London

Knight, S (1995) *NLP at Work: The difference that makes the difference at work*, Nicholas Brealey, London

Knowles, M S (1980) *The Modern Practice of Adult Education: From pedagogy to andragogy*, Prentice-Hall, Englewood Cliffs, NJ

Kolb, D A (1984) *Experiential Learning: Experiences as the source of learning and development*, Prentice-Hall, Englewood Cliffs, NJ

Kolb, D A, Rubin, I M and MacIntyre, J M (1984) *Organizational Psychology: An experiential approach*, 4th edn, Prentice-Hall, New York

Krouwell, B and Goodwill, S (1994) *Management Development Outdoors*, Kogan Page, London

Kruse, K [accessed 7 May 2003] [Online] www.e-learningguru.com/articles/ezine/guru2_9.htm

Lave, J and Wenger, E (1991) *Situated Learning: Legitimate peripheral participation*, Cambridge University Press, New York

Lawler, E (2003) *Treat People Right!*, Jossey-Bass, San Francisco

Leavy, B (1998) The concept of learning in the strategy field: review and outlook, *Management Learning*, **29** (4), pp 447–66

Lee, G (2003) *Leadership Coaching: From personal insight to organisational performance*, Chartered Institute of Personnel and Development, London

Leigh, A (1998) Learning centre: into a pitch black hole, *People Management*, **July**

Lewin, K (1951) *Field Theory in Social Science*, Harper, New York

Lippitt, G L (1969) *Organization Renewal*, Appleton-Century-Crofts, New York

Locher, K and van der Brug, J (1997) *Workways: Seven stars to steer by*, Hawthorne Press, London

MacLachan, R (1998) Paper chase, *People Management*, **4** (6), pp 42–44

Malhotra, Y (2002) Information ecology and knowledge management: toward knowledge ecology for hyperturbulent organizational environments, in *UNESCO Encyclopedia of Life Support Systems (EOLSS)*, ed D L Kiel, EOLSS Publishers, Paris

Mantel, S J *et al* (2001) *Project Management in Practice*, John Wiley, New York

Matzdorf, F *et al* (1997) *Learning to Succeed: Organizational learning in the surveying profession*, Royal Institution of Chartered Surveyors, London

Megginson, D (1994) Planned and emergent learning: a framework and a method, *Executive Development*, **7** (6), pp 29–32

Megginson, D (1996) Planned and emergent learning: consequences for development, *Management Learning*, **27** (4), pp 411–28

Megginson, D and Clutterbuck, D (2003) Review of the conference, in *Proceedings of the 10th European Mentoring and Coaching Conference*, EMCC and Sheffield Hallam University, Sheffield

Megginson, D and Pedler, M (1992) *Self-development: A facilitator's guide*, McGraw-Hill, Maidenhead

Megginson, D, Stokes, P and Garrett-Harris, R (2003) *MentorsByNet: An e-mentoring programme for SME entrepreneurs/manager*, MCRG, Barlow, Dronfield

Megginson, D and Whitaker, V (1996) *Cultivating Self Development*, Institute of Personnel and Development, London

Megginson, D and Whitaker, V (2003) *Continuing Professional Development*, Chartered Institute of Personnel and Development, London

Mezirow, J (1977) Personal transformation, *Studies in Adult Education*, **9** (2), pp 153–64

Miles, M B and Huberman, A M (1994) *Qualitative Data Analysis*, Sage, London

Mintzberg, H (1983) *Structure in Fives: Designing effective organizations*, Prentice-Hall, Englewood Cliffs, NJ

Moorby, E (1991) Drawing the map: vision, mission, strategy, policy and plans, in *How to Succeed in Employee Development*, ed E Moorby, pp 30–45, McGraw-Hill, London

Morgan, G (1986) *Images of Organization*, Sage, London

Mumford, A (1988) Learning to learn and management self-development, in *Applying Self-development in Organizations*, ed M Pedler, J Burgoyne and T Boydell, pp 23–27, Prentice-Hall, Englewood Cliffs, NJ

Mumford, A (1989) *Management Development Strategies for Action*, IPM, London

Mumford, A (1997) *How to Choose the Right Development Method*, Peter Honey, Maidenhead

Myers, D (1996) *Social Psychology*, McGraw-Hill, New York

Neugarten, B L (1968) Adult personality: towards a psychology of the life cycle, in *Middle Age and Aging: A reader in social psychology*, ed B L Neugarten, pp 137–47, University of Chicago Press, Chicago

Nevis, E C (1987) *Organizational Consultancy: A gestalt approach*, Gardner Press, London

Organization for Economic Cooperation and Development (OECD) (2001) *Education at a Glance*, OECD indicators 2001, OECD, Paris

Pavlov, I (1927) *Conditioned Reflexes*, Oxford University Press, Oxford

Pedler, M (1988) Self-development and work organizations, in *Applying Self-development in Organizations*, ed M Pedler, J Burgoyne and T Boydell, pp 1–19, Prentice-Hall, London

Pedler, M (1996) *Action Learning for Managers*, Lemos & Crane, London

Pedler, M and Aspinwall, K (1996) *Perfect plc: The purpose and practice of organizational learning*, McGraw-Hill, Maidenhead

Pedler, M, Burgoyne, J and Boydell, T (1991) *The Learning Company*, McGraw-Hill, Maidenhead

Pedler, M, Burgoyne J and Boydell, T (1994) *A Manager's Guide to Self Development*, McGraw-Hill, Maidenhead

Pedler, M, Burgoyne, J and Boydell, T (1997) *The Learning Company*, 2nd edn, McGraw-Hill, Maidenhead

Perren, L and Megginson, D (1996) Resistance to change as a positive force: its dynamics and issues for management development, *Career Development International*, **1** (4), pp 24–28

Perry, W G (1968) *Forms of Intellectual and Ethical Development in the College Years: A scheme*, Holt, Rinehart & Winston, New York

Peters, T J and Waterman, R H (1982) *In Search of Excellence*, Harper & Row, New York

Pettigrew, A M, Jones, G R and Reason, P W (1982) *Training and Development Roles in Their Organisational Setting*, Manpower Services Commission, Sheffield

Pfeffer, J (1994) *Competitive Advantage through People*, Harvard Business School Press, Boston

Pfeffer, J (1998) *The Human Equation*, Harvard Business School Press, Boston

Piaget, L (1926) *The Language and Thought of the Child*, Harcourt Brace, London

Quirk, B (1996) *Communicating Corporate Change*, McGraw-Hill, Maidenhead

Rackham, N and Morgan, T (1986) *Behaviour Analysis in Training*, McGraw-Hill, Maidenhead

Rao, V T and Abraham, E (1990) *The 1990 Annual: Developing human resources*, University Associates, San Diego, CA

Reed, B D and Palmer, B W (1972) *An Introduction to Organizational Behaviour*, Grubb Institute of Behavioural Studies, London

Reid, M A and Barrington, H (1997) *Training Interventions: Managing employee development*, 5th edn, IPD, London

Revans, R (1965) *Science and the Manager*, MacDonald, London

Revans, R (1998) *The ABC of Action Learning*, Lemos & Crane, London

Reynolds, M (1998) Reflection and critical reflection in management learning, *Management Learning*, **29** (2), pp 183–200

Ribeaux, P and Poppleton, S E (1978) *Psychology and Work: An introduction*, Macmillan, London

Riso, D R and Hudson, R (1999) *The Wisdom of the Enneagram*, Bantam, New York

Rogers, C R (1969) *Freedom to Learn: A view of what education might become*, Charles E Merrill, Columbus, OH

Rosenberg, M J (2003) *E-learning Strategies for Delivering Knowledge in the Digital Age*, McGraw-Hill, London

Rosinski, P (2003) *Coaching across Cultures: New tools for leveraging national, corporate and professional differences*, Nicholas Brealey, London

Roth, W M (2000) [accessed 20 August 2001] Cultural re/production of science education: toward greater civility and solidarity, *NARST News*, **43** (3) 8/20/01 [Online] http://www.sci.sdsu.edu/CRMS/NARST_News/43_3p5.html

Rothwell, W J (1996) *Beyond Training and Development*, Amacom, New York

Sadler, P (2003) *Leadership*, Kogan Page, London

Scarborough, H and Carter, C (2000) *Investigating Knowledge Management*, Chartered Institute of Personnel and Development, London

Schroder, H (1989) *Managerial Competence: The key to excellence*, Kendal Hunt, Dubuque, IA

Sector Skills Development Agency (SSDA) (2003) *The Skills and Productivity Challenge*, Sector Skills Development Agency, London

Seebacher, U G (2003) *Management Development in Europe: German managers are made – not born*, USP Publishing, Munich

Senge, P (1990) *The Fifth Discipline: The art and practice of the learning organization*, Century, London

Senge, P et al (1994) *The Fifth Discipline Fieldbook*, Nicholas Brealey, London

Shaw, P (2002) *Changing Conversations in Organizations: A complexity approach to change*, Routledge, London

Skinner, B F (1953) *Science and Human Behaviour*, Macmillan, London

Snell, R (1992) Experiential learning at work: why can't it be painless?, *Personnel Review*, **21** (4)

Starkey, K (1996) *How Organizations Learn*, International Thompson, London

Stein, D (1998) [accessed 9 April 1999] Situated learning in adult education, *ERIC Digest* 195 [Online] http://ericacve.org/docs/situated195.htm

Stern, E. and Sommerland, E (1999) *Workplace Learning, Culture and Performance*, Institute of Personnel and Development, London

Straangard, F (1981) *NLP Made Visual*, Connector, Copenhagen

Summers, A (1994) Setting standards of competence for management training, *British Journal of Administrative Management*, **October–November**

Thorndike, E L (1932) *The Fundamentals of Learning*, Teachers College Press, New York

Thorne, K (2003) *Blended Learning: How to integrate online and traditional learning*, Kogan Page, London

Training Service Agency (TSA) (1977) *Glossary of Training Terms*, Manpower Services Commission, London

Trompenaars, F (1999) First class accommodation, *People Management*, **5** (8), pp 30–37

Tuckman, B and Jensen, N (1977) Stages of small group development revisited, *Group and Organizational Studies*, **2**, pp 419–27

Ulrich, D (1998) A new mandate for human resources, *Harvard Business Review*, **76** (1), pp 124–34

Warr, P B, Bird, M and Rackham, N (1970) *Evaluating Management Training*, Gower, London

Waterman, R H *et al* (1988) The 7-S framework, in *The Strategy Process: Concepts, contexts and cases*, ed J B Quinn, H Mintzberg and R M James, pp 271–76, Prentice-Hall, Englewood Cliffs, NJ

Wenger, E (1998) *Communities of Practice: The buzz and the buzzword*, Cambridge University Press, Cambridge

Wenger, E (2000) *Communities of Practice: Learning, meaning and identity (learning in doing)*, Cambridge University Press, Cambridge

Whitehead, A N (1929) *The Aims of Education*, Macmillan, New York

Whitelaw, M (1972) *The Evaluation of Management Training*, Institute of Personnel and Development, London

Willis, L and Daisley, J (1992) *Developing Women through Training*, McGraw-Hill, New York

Wilson, A (1993) The promise of situated cognition, in *An Update on Adult Learning*, ed S B Merriman, pp 71–79, Jossey-Bass, San Francisco

Wolfson, L and Willinsky, J (1999a) The relation of situated learning principles to service learning activities [Online] http://www.knowarch.com/index/front_office/evaluation/sit-table.html 04/09/99

Wolfson, L and Willinsky, J (1999b) [accessed 9 April 1999] What service learning can learn from situated learning: a proposal for a research framework [Online] http://www.knowarch.com/index/front_office/evaluation/situat.html

Woodall, J and Winstanley, D (1998) *Management Development Strategy and Practice*, Blackwell, Oxford

Zuboff, S (1988) *In the Age of the Smart Machine*, Heinemann, Oxford

Index

Also available in the MBA Masterclass series